D0017280

Fair Share
Divorce
For Women

Kathleen Miller, CFP, MBA
Certified Financial Planner

Library Resource Center
Renton Technical College
3000 NE 4th St.
Renton, WA 98056-4195

Miller, Bird Advisors, Inc.
Bellevue, Washington

346
.0166
MILLER
1995

Copyright 1995 by Kathleen Miller
All rights reserved
Printed in U.S.A.
Library of Congress Catalog 94-070322
ISBN 0-9644549-0-4

This book may not be reproduced in whole or in part, by mimeograph or
any other means, without permission. For information contact:

Miller, Bird Advisors, Inc.
1200 - 112th Avenue N.E., C-178
Bellevue, Washington 98004

CERTIFICATE OF VALUE

THIS FAIR SHARE DIVORCE BOOK IS FOR

A VERY IMPORTANT PERSON

Now this book and the knowledge in it is yours.
Please use it to help change your life.
Remember, this is the first day of the rest of your life.

DEDICATION

To my mother Eileen, sister Gina, and daughter Nicole

ACKNOWLEDGMENTS

I especially want to thank my family for encouraging me to write this book and for tolerating my passion for this project even when we were on vacations and I worked on my laptop computer for a few hours each day. My husband of more than 23 years has watched our "partnership" go through many changes as we have continually renegotiated our marriage contract. My teenage daughter Nicole has often traveled with me when I have presented at workshops and seminars across the country and has become a competent "assistant." My family has been patient, tolerant and encouraging.

I have several people who I would like to thank for their support in my writing this book. First of all, thanks to my partner, Kelly Bird, who has worked beside me for more than ten years developing the analytical models I have used in the pre- and post-divorce planning. Dave Bartosh has been invaluable in helping to edit and format this book and has helped to pioneer much of our work on the budgeting chapters. He has been on a fast track as a protégé for our work in the pre- and post-divorce area. Lisa Fitzmaurice has managed our office and worked as a securities assistant, helping the post-divorcing client to understand and implement her or his investments and has assisted in creating a monitoring and reporting system to keep the client informed.

Divorce is, first and foremost, a legal process which is managed by the attorney. I have been fortunate to work closely with many of the leading family law attorneys in our area. Together, we have been able to expand my area of expertise into all areas of the divorce process. There are many competent family law attorneys for you to choose from. If your attorney has not used a financial planner in the past, share this book with your attorney. Spread the word and the process.

Jan Reha, a career advisor, has worked with me over the past several years as a professional team member in developing workable career plans for the displaced homemaker. We have collaborated on several articles on such issues as the disparity of earnings and the use of experts in a divorce.

Patricia Minkove has been a friend and confidant through this writing process and has often provided me with a quiet setting to write this book. Her expertise in real estate, financing, and downsizing strategies has helped many women transition to a single life with knowledge and financial peace of mind. Her spiritual guidance and encouragement has made a difference.

I want to thank the women who have shared their divorce processes with me. Together we have pioneered a new way of looking at the divorce process.

TABLE OF CONTENTS

PREFACE

The wisest tips on how to develop a financial plan are of little use if they are not conveyed in an understandable manner, a manner which responds effectively to the time of stress, distraction, immobility, relief, fear, confusion, pain, self-renewal and fantasy, all condensed into a short period. This book was written to provide you, the reader, with practical information to help you organize your divorce process.

This is a "how-to-look-at-it" as well as a "how-to-do-it" book on divorce. I believe that a change in the way you view your divorce can profoundly influence the way you will live through it.

Although *Fair Share Divorce* was a three-year undertaking, this book was finished in two years. I have many people to thank; most important are the many women with whom I have worked, helping them to have a win-win divorce. I also have worked with many men in their divorce processes. Fair share does not mean equal; it means creating a strategy of equitable divorce for both the man and woman. Each divorce is different and the facts and circumstances require creativity when the property settlement and parenting plans are designed.

The ideas and organizational tools, as well as the models presented in the case studies, stem, for the most part, from my day-to-day work with women and men as they have struggled to take control of their divorce to create a winning strategy for themselves in the pre- and post-divorce process. Consequently, this book contains portions of many actual case histories. Confidentiality is essential to a financial planning practice, and all case descriptions have been altered in name and in other particulars to preserve the anonymity of my clients without distorting the essential reality of our experiences with each other.

Getting a divorce takes time — financially, emotionally and legally. Often in my presentation here, I have condensed the outcome to a shorter period of time than was actually the case in my planning practice. My clients come to me in various stages of divorce. It is never too late to take charge of your own divorce, no matter where you are in the process. Education means taking back your personal power.

I can tell you that there is Life After Divorce. I have been blessed to help many women and men get on with their post-divorce life with dignity and financial understanding. Some have remarried, others are content to be single. In either case, these people have been active rather than passive in their finances. The best part of my financial planning practice comes in the post-divorce phase where I have the opportunity to help women "get a life," one in which they can be successful and where there is happiness. Divorce is not a pleasant transition for most people — there is a lot of unpleasant endings and pain; but on the other side, there are new beginnings.

CHAPTER ONE

WHO SHOULD I SEE FIRST?

Fair share divorce does not always mean equal.
— *Kathleen Miller*

The answer to the question posed by the title of this chapter, Who Should I See First? goes back to my decision to write this book and aim it principally to women. Women urgently need divorce advice because they dislike confrontation, shy away from conflict, and traditionally have taken a back seat to men in the management of money. And money is what divorce is all about after the legal nasties have been exhausted and the husband and wife withdraw to lick their wounds and start to rediscover themselves.

We are all products of our childhood experiences and we bring what we've learned to our marriages. And that's the trouble for most women. Money issues are critical when you go through the divorce process. If you try to ignore them, you will suffer financially when the divorce is over and regrets won't be a solace for the financial assets you've lost.

You may be interested in learning how and why women come to me when divorce has become a certainty in their lives. Sean is a good example. She left an urgent message for me after learning my name from a client.

When Sean presented herself, her distress was obvious. She told me, biting her lip, that her husband had left over the weekend after informing her he wanted a divorce. He moved his personal belongings and clothing on Sunday. Sean had three children ages 15, 11, and 7. She and the children were trying to understand what was happening to them. Sean was calm with the children and attempted to keep them on their regular schedules at school and involved in things they would do on a normal day. Panicky, twisting a handkerchief with her fingers, Sean related the events of the weekend:

"Jim got up on Saturday earlier than usual after working late at the office on Friday and he told me he wanted to talk. We sat down and had a cup of coffee and he said he was leaving. Just like that. He had found an apartment and was going to move in on Sunday. He needed time away from me and the family. He was feeling overwhelmed at work and needed to be by himself. That's what he said.

"I asked if he was involved with someone else. He said that was not why he was leaving. He wouldn't answer my question directly. He said he would take care of me financially and continue to put his check in our account twice a month. We were only going to live apart for a few months. Other than that, he had no plans.

"I was stunned," she said. "I cried. John, our oldest child came into the room and we asked him to leave. We were having a private conversation. He could tell that we were both very upset and crying. John quietly went back to his room. Then Jim went upstairs and started packing his clothes. He was very methodical and organized and seemed to have a careful plan of what he was taking. He asked if he could take some of the furniture and gave me a list of the things he wanted from the various rooms in the house and garage. He would have a truck come by on Sunday to pick up his belongings and then he left. He came back on Sunday and moved out. The children and I sat at the kitchen table and watched him leave — it was so unreal. All of us were crying."

I listened to Sean carefully, sympathized and told her, truthfully, that I had empathy for what she was going through. Then, to get her mind on to practical matters, and because the files I wanted her to find would be important, I asked her to get a copy of her last three years' income tax returns, current year-end brokerage statements and a joint financial statement. I explained to her that a financial statement would have been required when she and her husband financed or refinanced their house. Also, I cautioned her that if she couldn't locate the information, we needed to find out why. Had Jim taken it with him? Was it in his office, on the computer? The importance of financial data early in a divorce can't be overemphasized. Later, you'll understand why.

I tell clients, like Sean, that they should see a financial planner who understands the divorce process as soon as possible when divorce looms. The qualified financial planner will help you to get your financial data organized for the attorney and the intimidating legal process ahead. The attorney's job is to get you through the legal process: who should file and when, how will you get money for yourself and the children, temporary restraining orders on various bank savings and checking accounts and other legal aspects of dissolving the marriage. In the case of Sean, no one had filed for divorce and Jim had told his wife that he hadn't planned to file at the point of their separation. That may or may not have been his intention. In my 14 years of experience dealing with divorce cases I have come to live by the motto: TRUST, BUT VERIFY.

My recommendation is that if divorce is in your plans, get organized as soon as possible, get the facts while the spirit of cooperation and guilt is on your side. Your life will never be the same. You cannot go back to the way it was, as if there never was an erosion of trust. Even if Sean and Jim eventually get back together, their lives together will be different.

I'll never forget the first woman who came to me about her divorce. Her name was Susan and she told me the divorce was going to be amicable. She and her husband had been married more than 25 years, had three grown children who had graduated from college. She was 45 years old; he had become involved with his secretary. The husband was president of a large and successful corporation. Their marriage had seemed like a happy and traditional one. She stayed home to raise the children, was his companion traveling on business around the world and had entertained business clients of his and associates from their gracious home. The children were now out of the nest and there was time for them to become a couple again. Or so she thought. In the years that followed Susan, I heard stories like hers time and time again.

Susan did not want a divorce but she couldn't live with the "other woman in the picture." Tom, she said, was torn. He did not want to lose his wife, but he was not willing to give up his girlfriend. These two people went to an attorney friend and attempted to negotiate their own property settlement. They did not want a long legal battle, big attorney fees, restraining orders, and the bitterness of a legal squabble. Over the next year they were able to negotiate a fair settlement. One of the issues for Susan was her earning ability. She had stayed home during the marriage and had been the primary parent raising the couple's three children. During the marriage Tom had done a great deal of traveling and she had spent a lot of time volunteering at school, driving the children to and from school activities, and helping them with homework. Both of the parents had placed a strong value on her activities during the child-rearing years. But now what? The children were out of the home. She was working 15 hours a week as a part-time marketing rep for a friend and she was earning $10,000 a year. Tom was president of his company, earned over $250,000 annually, had a generous profit-sharing plan, expense account, automobile, international travel allowance, etc. There was no doubt that Susan's life was going to change dramatically once she was divorced. She no longer would be a partner sharing in the corporate benefits with her husband. There would be no more expense accounts and stimulating journeys around the globe. If Susan was like most women I've interviewed, she would be plagued with fears, doubts and insecurities. Some women become almost paralyzed emotionally during this time. The last thing they can think about is what kind of a career should they pursue. They can barely force themselves out of bed in the morning and live through a day.

The man, on the other hand, is still reporting to work every day. He is occupied with a career that normally requires his full concentration.

Neither party escapes without some emotional and financial scars and pain.

Susan came to me after she had been separated for six months. Tom was physically out of the house. He still deposited half of his check into their joint account. However, she had been informed that next month he would be reducing her maintenance by 30 percent because he believed she didn't need as much as she had been getting. There had been no court order or a legal separation. The two of them had worked out the separation details together. In the meantime, Susan went to a career counselor to determine a career path for herself. Should she return to school? It was one option. She had earned an undergraduate degree in philosophy, but never worked in a real job outside the home since the first year of her marriage to Tom. Her major accomplishment was her mastery of being a corporate executive spouse, managing many business/social functions for her husband and for the business over the years.

Susan was really not interested in returning to school for another degree and was uncertain where she could apply her skills in the work place. Also, she lacked motivation and drive. After all, she had a full-time job as a wife, one she learned well; now the job had ended. She found it difficult to apply to herself the sobering statistics about the earnings of divorced couples: *a woman's standard of living drops 73 percent during the first year after a divorce and the average man's standard of living improves 42 percent during the same year.*

The career advisor to whom Susan was going was excited to learn that someone was working with Susan about finances. She now had an attorney, a friend of the family, but she still was not able to relate the property settlement numbers being discussed directly to her life. She needed to create a living financial plan for her post-divorce, but the reality of being on her own had not sunk in. She had married Tom at graduation and, other than living at her father's home and in a sorority, she had never really lived on her own as a single person. The financial wizardry of separating property was scary. Should she keep the 4,000 square foot home? It looked good on paper. She would get this asset and Tom would get some of the cash and most of the profit-sharing plan; she would get most of the furniture. Tom had purchased a town house and was living there with his girlfriend when he was not traveling for the company. Everyone seemed to have a plan but Susan.

I think it should be apparent to you if you are a woman considering divorce, or one being forced to think divorce by a husband who has declared his intention to separate from you, that the financial aspects of breaking the bonds can represent some of the most important decisions you will ever make during your lifetime. You have to protect yourself and that means, early in the divorce negotiating process, even while the shock is still sinking in, you have to make financial plans to preserve what you have contributed to the marriage. These are assets you have a right to share. Trusting that the legal process will take care of you is the worst assumption you can make. But you *can* emerge from divorce with your fair share. That's why I've written this book: to show you, by instruction and through the examples, good and bad, of other women, how important the first steps in a divorce can be to the final financial outcome.

CHAPTER TWO

WHAT CAN I EXPECT?

It always comes back to the same necessity:
Go deep enough and there is a bedrock of truth, however hard.
— Mary Sarton

Most women facing divorce do not know how much money their family has or even how much their husbands earn, according to a national survey of 208 leading divorce lawyers in 36 states. Fifty-two percent of the attorneys surveyed say that most of their women clients do not have a clear picture of family assets or income. This information comes from Lois Brenner, who conducted the study for her just-published book, *Getting Your Share: A Woman's Guide to Successful Divorce Strategies.*

Dozens of lawyers with whom I have worked in more than 1,200 divorces in 14 years report that at least some of the wives who consult them in divorce actions are fundamentally ignorant about money matters in the family. Many have never even examined the federal income tax form a husband places in front of them for signature. These spouses may know of a savings account and a couple of investments, but really have only the faintest idea about the overall finances of the family. This is even more true when there is a family business. Often the woman is actively involved in the business in the early stages, then moves away from any involvement in the later years to raise children and focus on the family.

The idea behind this chapter is to acquaint the woman who is thinking about divorce with the options she has as well as the process of legally disengaging herself from a partner. Common myths about getting a divorce are dispelled in this chapter. As a whole it is an important overview to the idea of divorce and it is an introduction to a legal process that can swallow a woman if she doesn't know the rules of the game.

The attitude a woman has about herself and the divorce process can affect the outcome and the economic benefits she can obtain for herself and her children. The right attitude can make a tremendous difference in the divorced woman's future.

Women by their very nature typically go into marriage with the view of entering a long-term partnership that involves sharing of the emotions, money, child-raising and retirement. Most women I meet are in emotional trauma over their divorces. They are deeply troubled. Many feel guilty and allow their feelings to affect their judgment. Often, they have been replaced by another woman, many times a younger one. The sense of betrayal, loss and anger can temporarily lower the woman's self esteem and throw her into deep depression and emotional stress. Financial decisions based on feelings of unworthiness can be disastrous. Meanwhile, hampered by her lowered image of herself, the woman is still fulfilling her role as the "super" mom, always in control and taking charge of the details of everyone's daily life. Mom's needs are not being met, and frankly, may not have been met in the marriage, but now she has been rejected, left to herself and what she can salvage.

In divorce you always have the leaver and the leftee. Both positions carry substantial emotional and financial baggage. I think it is very important to acknowledge the emotional stages of divorce. Women and men must realize that it is normal to go through identifiable stages. You are not alone, and you can pass through the stages to a safe and secure single life if you make yourself aware in advance of the difficulties you

Library Resource Center
Renton Technical College
3000 NE 4th St.
Renton, WA 98056-4195

will face. That's the object of this chapter and this book. Remember, when someone files for a divorce you are on the legal journey to dissolution. In Seattle, King County, Washington, once you file, a court date is established one year from the time of filing. The date is a beacon that shines day and night.

If you went into your marriage viewing it as a partnership, then you are going to assume that both spouses make substantially equal (although not necessarily identical) contributions to a marriage. If so, then you are going to assume that you should receive substantially equal financial benefits from the marriage and should not be left in a widely disparate position after the marriage ends. To achieve financial fairness, you need to be able to recognize the emotional stages in divorce. Janice is a good example.

She came into my office for an initial consultation, referred by a friend who had used our services. Less than six months before, Janice was secure, though naive, in a marriage to a high-income professional. Her lifestyle represented the ultimate in comfort typified by the American upper middle class — a home in the suburbs, new cars, extended annual vacations, annual company expense-paid trips, and an active social calendar. Today, however, the trauma and stress of the past few months is evident on her face. She has accumulated sizeable legal fees. She is dealing with a level of consumer debt she never has experienced before. She is attempting to establish a personal income stream, while struggling to maintain for herself and her children their previous financial lifestyle. And she is coping with decisions involving child custody, the division of property, and parenting issues. She is a woman in the throes of dealing with the classic contemporary divorce — unprepared, traumatized and without sufficient resources.

How does she get out of this maze and create a life for herself and the children when she feels so lousy, depressed, inadequate and out of control?

As I stated earlier, recognition of the emotional stages of divorce is important because it will give you the wisdom to see yourself through them without making financial decisions harmful to your future. There are five emotional stages of divorce and each one reflects the advancing process of disengagement. Understanding what you're going through gives you more control and a deeper appreciation of the changes you'll be making in your life.

PRE-DIVORCE PERIOD

This period is characterized by escalating marital dissatisfaction, often felt more acutely by one party than the other. Marital intimacy declines, and the couple may fight openly, see a marriage counselor or minister, visit an attorney, and physically separate into two households. This is a time of denial, uncertainty. You really don't want to acknowledge the possibility of divorce and are reluctant to see an attorney or a financial planner to address the economics of a divorce. You fear that seeing a professional might be the first step in actualizing the divorce. You are traumatized. Maybe you know consciously, or unconsciously, that your husband is having an affair — I believe most women know when this is going on intuitively. Should you see an attorney and financial planner during this stage? *Absolutely!* Protect yourself. If your husband is any kind of a business man and has any inkling of a divorce himself, you can be assured that he has looked at the business aspects of divorce.

It is important to see an attorney early to discuss your legal position, community and separate assets. You'll want to know answers to questions such as what you can expect in your state based on the length of marriage and your level of assets, what to expect if there is a divorce and how to protect yourself in the legal process of dissolution and the development of parenting plans.

The wife who sees divorce on the horizon must stabilize herself enough emotionally to gather the financial facts about her marriage. Too many times the financial information leaves the house with the husband and the wife spends hundreds and thousands of dollars with her attorney gathering this information. Know your finances, review the income tax return before you sign it, ask questions.

In many of my divorce cases, the woman has not taken an active role in the handling of the finances, other than the household budget. The husband has conducted the financial decisions and planning as the family provider. For the woman who knows little about the money situation, it becomes vital at this point that she gather information and take other important financial steps. These steps include copying and understanding income tax returns and investment reports, establishing a credit history in her own name, reviewing life and disability insurance policies, understanding employee benefits summaries, the mortgage terms on her home, vacation and rental properties, and clarifying the terms of pension and profit-sharing plans.

Take it slowly during the pre-divorce period. You are only organizing the facts. The role of a financial planner like myself is to give you the tools to get organized and a practical understanding of how your net worth and income would be affected in a divorce. I can help you to get focused. Women either get very energized and focused during this stage or go into a deep period of denial. If they go into the denial phase they could exemplify some of the behavior that Jane demonstrated:

Jane was 40 pounds overweight. She felt that losing her fat would cause her husband to become more interested in her. She lost the pounds through six months of exercise and a diet. But the marital situation didn't change much. Jane became depressed and, over the next few months, regained the weight and added 25 more pounds. She felt even worse about herself — a very low self-image. She and her husband did not seem to be connecting and neither of them spoke directly about making a change. This was the silent time. Jane did not want to find out about the finances and she withdrew and insulated herself from the family's money situation and from herself — denial.

Jennifer, on the other hand, became focused. She started photocopying important documents, took a computer course on budgeting and finances, reviewed the wills and other legal papers. She moved from a time of inertia into action. Her husband liked seeing her become involved. They have gone to marriage counseling and have started to take time for each other. Jennifer took a degenerating situation and, with action and persistence and her husband's cooperation, was able to turn the situation around.

Sarah became involved in the family finances and her husband became angry. Didn't she trust him, didn't she think he was doing a good job? Money management wasn't her role in the marriage; she should spend more time with the children. She had never been good with numbers and would only mess things up if she got involved.

He wanted control of the finances. So she backed off, went back into her cave and dreamed that every thing would be fine and they would live happily ever after. Six months later her husband filed for a divorce and took all the financial data with him. Sarah spent $7,000 with her attorney recreating their financial condition, gathering bank statements, tax returns, credit card receipts. When Sarah came back to me she told me what had happened, proving that no action can also be a decision. Getting organized benefits you at any time in life. Don't you feel better when you organize your closets during spring cleaning?

THE DECISION PERIOD

The decision period is a time when the woman with divorce on her mind is living in an emotional minefield. Marked by a mental state that is firmly focused on ending the marriage, the woman experiences a sense of relief, sadness, anger, or even exhilaration. This can be an extremely volatile time. Emotional swings include hope of reconciliation, denial, feelings of betrayal, immobilization from the fear of loneliness, anger and concern over finances. Compensatory behaviors may include overspending and running up credit card balances. Chronic depression capable of triggering suicidal tendencies may also appear.

If you have not seen a financial planner up to this time, do so. The planner can assist you in several ways, including preparing the financial affidavit you will need, or providing a record-keeping system to track all expenses and income. Too many times the attorney hands a woman a package of forms to fill out, bewildering questions to answer, and data to gather. Overwhelmed, she agrees for the attorney to do it and pays dearly for the service. A financial planner can help you organize this information in a methodical and meaningful way so that it can effectively be used by the attorney to establish historical spending patterns for the family to indicate the need for temporary spousal maintenance, and to determine your proposed budget post-divorce. See Chapter Six on creating a cash control system.

In my opinion, the decision period is one of the most important times in the divorce process for the woman to become involved and to take charge. Get your time of separation right from the beginning. Have your facts in order. Be organized. Judges have a hard time denying your motion for temporary support if you can provide them with detailed information about your income and particularly your expenses. It helps your credibility if you have an outside specialist like a financial planner work with you to organize and audit this information. Financial information is also valuable for your husband to have at the onset of the divorce. He probably has no idea how all the money he puts into the account each month is really spent. This is the time that you are honest about how the money was spent — for him, the children, and on yourself.

A financial planner knows about budgets and cash control systems. She can help you to get organized for the next phase of the data gathering on the valuation of assets, pension plans and tax issues. If you are constantly worrying about money, your decisions may be clouded. Your divorce could easily be the biggest financial decision of your life. You can do a lot of this work yourself and can actually save money for the later stages of your divorce process.

During the decision period, I encourage the woman to see a therapist. If she is a displaced homemaker, I recommend that she visit a career advisor. See my later chapter on this topic. You will be confronted with a lot of information and decision making during this time such as parenting plans, budgeting, schooling, career choices. It is easy to become overwhelmed and immobilized. If you can afford to hire a team of professionals to assist you in your divorce process, I can guarantee you that it will be easier to own your settlement and accept your compromises. If you cannot afford these services, go to the library and read. You can afford a book. Join a self-help group like Divorce Lifeline. And for goodness sake, don't call your attorney ten times a day for small things. Every time he consults with you on the phone, his clock is running and your divorce expenses go up. Instead, make a list of the questions you want to ask, and when he gives you an answer, feed it back to him with the statement, "Now, do I understand you to say ...?"

FINAL ACCEPTANCE

When you recognize the inevitability of the divorce, you have reached a milestone. A property settlement is about to be accepted, a counter offer is being considered, or a court date is near. Intense emotions are buffeting you again. You are being asked to make decisions, compromises that will permanently affect the nature of your new lifestyle. This is a time when you may find yourself changing your mind, vacillating with your decisions, getting angry, or going into hiding. What you need is your second wind to cross the finish line. If you have been doing your homework, working with your therapist, financial planner and attorney, the hard work and training will begin to pay off. This does not mean that this is an easy time for you. It's just that things are coming together, as they should. You'll be leaning on your financial planner, whose role it is to help you accept responsibility for the outcome of your divorce through your active involvement in understanding and selecting a settlement strategy. If you don't settle, your financial planner will provide expert witness testimony for you in court to be heard by the judge. This stage is a particularly active time in the divorce process and it represents the culmination of everyone's efforts. The goal is a negotiated settlement, which means compromise. If neither party can agree to settle, then everyone needs to prepare for court. Typically this adds up to more costs. Find out what these costs could be in your local area.

PERIOD OF MOURNING

Typified by a sense of failure, loneliness, depression, and low self-esteem, this is the period when you feel weary after having fought hard in the settlement negotiations, in child custody debates, and in finalizing parenting plans. The reality of the divorce has set in — emotionally and financially. I find my clients are particularly vulnerable during this stage. Up to this time we have talked about "what if" scenarios. Now we are talking about reality. It is as if this is the first day of the rest of your life. It is. You will have a new legal status, be filing your income tax return alone, creating your own individual financial statement, clearly having your own credit, becoming sole owner of investment and retirement assets.

A financial planner will help you to set up the post-divorce budget and a cash control monitoring system. You probably didn't get everything you asked for and on the terms you requested. You may be disappointed and disheartened and should continue seeing your therapist as you work on emotional rebuilding. We will be counseling with you to create a specific strategy to pay off the legal costs of your divorce, transfer assets, monitor career, education and job exploration activities, prepare preliminary income tax projections for quarterly payments to the Internal Revenue Service, recommend and review conservative investment decisions.

RE-EQUILIBRIUM

This last emotional stage in the divorce process occurs when you accept your new life as a single person and let go of the anger you have for your spouse. You find yourself working your plans, personal and financial, and accepting self-responsibility.

You cannot expect to arrive at this last stage overnight. For some of my clients, the stage is never fully reached. It takes time to heal at all levels, emotionally and financially. If there are children involved, I highly recommend post-divorce family counseling for the ex-spouses and children. Your legal documents don't begin to address the many questions and situations that are bound to arise in the post-divorce lifestyle. You can dramatically ease the tension and transfer period for your children by having a few joint sessions with a trained therapist who can work with all of you.

Give yourself time to heal and adjust.

TYPICAL DIVORCE QUESTIONS WOMEN ASK

Following are typical questions most women ask when they confront divorce. The answers you'll read will help you form your own questions about your divorce. I am certain that many of the considerations you'll find in this chapter may never have occurred to you. If you are like most women who have reluctantly decided to end their marriage, you hope to bring it to a conclusion with the least amount of dissension. You want to get your fair share and start over. But it's not that simple, as you will see ...

1. What about the attorney?

First, you should know that a divorce is a civil action to terminate marriage and the process is called a Dissolution of Marriage. Only one spouse needs to file or you can both file as co-petitioners. If you file, you are the Petitioner or the Plaintiff, and if you are served you are called the Respondent or Defendant.

You can get divorced without an attorney; however, this is not recommended unless the marriage is brief, you each have a career of your own, few assets to worry about and no children. Remember the divorcing couple who have a fierce battle in the movie *The War of the Roses?* Danny DeVito plays Oliver Rose's divorce attorney and he asked, "What's the moral? Maybe the moral is that a civilized divorce is a contradiction in terms." Is there really such a thing as a friendly divorce? A divorce in which lawyers are not needed? The answer is yes and no. But remember, divorce is probably the biggest financial decision you are going to face. Mediation is an alternative to the lawyer-managed process in the courts; I touch on it briefly in this chapter and at greater length in Chapter Three.

2. What if my spouse will not give me a divorce?

Don't you believe it. The judge grants a divorce, not your spouse. The divorce can be contested, and if so, you will have a hearing set with a judge in which each of you testify and then the judge can decide how to finalize the dissolution. If the divorce is not contested, you can be divorced in 90 days in most states.

3. Can I expect to get half of everything we own?

Remember, Danny DeVito in *The War of the Roses* when he makes the statement, "When trouble begins, it comes at you from directions you never expect." This is never truer than in a divorce case, and it certainly applies to the question of equal division of property.

One of the most common misconceptions held by women when they enter divorce proceedings is that justice will prevail. They think it will be simple to end the relationship and that money can make them whole. They think if they are divorcing a man with whom they have built up a comfortable net worth and there has been a growing income, it will naturally be divided equally and each party will go on his way to a new life.

This is not necessarily so. While we do have No-Fault divorce, this is not the same as No-Hassle divorce. When we got the No-Fault law it allowed couples to get a divorce for irreconcilable differences. The purpose of this law, which first came out of California, was to reduce the pain of divorce. In fact, I believe it has allowed the law to view marriage as an economic partnership. As such, the major contest centers on who gets what assets. We are now working under laws which adhere to equitable distribution of assets. Prior to No-Fault, women were getting support until remarriage or death. Today, support is provided for a stated number of years, and many women never collect it. The courts often do not help them, and if they do help, the financial cost to the woman may be greater.

Women are also losing their children. Suddenly, scores of men are seeking custody. Sometimes this is a clever ploy in the divorce process to use the offspring as a lever against the wife. Children are viewed as a weapon and become a financial asset in the negotiations with a threat of litigation. The child custody issue and the parenting plan is becoming the atom bomb of the '90s.

4. We disagree on some items, however, we do not want to go to court. How can we settle outside of court?

There are three primary ways to settle a divorce outside of court, and they are briefly: arbitration, negotiation, mediation.

Arbitration: This is the process in which you hire a private party who acts as a judge to hear your case. Your advantage here is that you can get a date much earlier than waiting for a court date. In many jurisdictions the waiting time for a court date is a year or more. The final agreement in arbitration is binding on both parties.

Negotiation: In this approach, as you may have seen on the television show, *L.A. Law,* each spouse and each of their attorneys are present and discuss requests, demands, claims and counterclaims until a settlement is reached. As a financial planner, I am often called in to these sessions to provide comprehensive illustrations showing the impact of various property settlement proposals for each of the parties.

Mediation: This is the process in which a neutral third party meets with both spouses to help them reach a legal agreement. The mediation team can include an attorney and/or counselor with other experts summoned to the mediation meetings as needed and agreed upon by both parties. The object is to reach a settlement plan both wife and husband can agree to amicably, if possible. The attorney does *not* give legal advice. Both spouses are encouraged to meet independently with their own attorneys, accountants and financial planners before signing a final agreement. The legal documents resulting from the mediation settlement are going to be entered in the court records. Mediation works if the spouses are not hostile toward each other. It can be an excellent alternative between doing the divorce yourself and going to court. It is particularly effective in the creation of the parenting plan where there are children involved.

BEWARE of mediation in the development of the property settlement. You must trust that each spouse is telling the truth about all assets, the existence of all accounts, community and separate property interests, retirement benefits, and tax consequences when receiving certain assets or liabilities. Use caution when dividing and arranging the property settlement. Trust but verify. People may think they are disclosing all the assets, but through ignorance or forgetfulness, may miss an asset. We are often brought into mediation sessions to help verify assets and to be sure they are accounted for in the settlement process.

5.   *We will just live apart for awhile — do we need a formal separation agreement?*

Beware of just living apart as a trial basis for divorce and not creating a separation agreement. The courts do look at how long the parties have lived apart and the scope of their reconciliation attempts when calculating spousal maintenance.

You should know that a separation agreement is a contract between a husband and a wife in which they agree to resolve such matters as property division, debts, custody and support when they separate from each other. It is best to have an attorney draw up this agreement. You can agree to the division of property and it can be binding on both parties in the event a divorce is the outcome of the separation. Income becomes separate property when two people are separated. If you are afraid that assets and income are disappearing and you don't trust your spouse, you would be better served to know that at the beginning. A separation agreement will protect you from too many surprises further down the road. You can work on the reconciliation, but that doesn't mean you should ignore your portion of the economic partnership.

We do see cases of two parties living apart and sharing the income for months or even years with no major debts incurred. Each divorce is unique and needs to have its own financial plan. What works for one situation may or may not work in the next. Often clients do separate and share income equally as I described. Then the person who is providing the money usually starts to decrease the amount being passed over to the other party. This can play havoc with a budget. You need to be able to depend on payments which have been based on a budget the two of you worked out when you decided to separate. If the income stream is changed dramatically, you must be prepared to see an attorney and make a claim for more temporary spousal maintenance. There is no guarantee that you will ever get all that you request. The chapter devoted to the budget process will help you anticipate your needs realistically. In it you'll find information on determining historical spending, getting the funds requested for temporary spousal maintenance, and the post-divorce budget.

I definitely recommend the budget process whether your separation is formal or informal. Be prepared. You may not have enough time to respond if the other party suddenly decides to file. Also, historical personal spending in the marriage, whether it is more or less than what should be allowed in the separation, is fair game for either side to use as the standard that should be applied during separation and post-divorce.

6. We agreed that I would give up my career while the children were in school. My role was first as a wife and mother. My husband's role was to earn the money for our family. What now?

This statement expresses the marital philosophy that has dominated our culture for decades. For many couples this statement represents the basic foundation of the family partnership that was set up by the couple at the time of their marriage and for the planning of their family. Unfortunately, this arrangement is not supported in our society — either with the payment of maintenance or alimony to the non-earning spouse or in the collection of child support.

Maintenance is viewed as "temporary support" in most parts of the country and is used to "rehabilitate" the non-working spouse so she can enter the job market and earn a living. Unless there is a long-term marriage — 30+ years, and the woman is in her late fifties or has health problems — the chances of long-term maintenance through the court system are slim. A three- to five-year maintenance schedule is much more likely. It will terminate at death or remarriage of the receiving spouse, it is likely to be modified if the financial circumstances change for the paying party, and the amount often decreases over the span of the short maintenance period. Creating a win-win settlement with the couple which has a disparity of earnings is one of the most difficult dissolution cases of all.

Let me give you another example. John and Jane have been married for 18 years and have three children ages 8, 14 and 17. John is a successful physician earning upwards of $350,000 per year. Jane was a nurse when she met John; he was in medical school. She worked as a nurse for the first three years of their marriage and helped John through medical school by earning the family income. Then they decided to have a family. Both John and Jane were raised by parents who felt the mother should stay home with the children. Following in her mother's footsteps, Jane did volunteer work at the school and church and maintained the home for the family. This was what John and Jane wanted.

But now John, firmly established in his medical practice, has grown apart from Jane. He wants a divorce, but is committed to staying involved with his children.

John is 47 years old and Jane is 45. He has worked long hours and has been a partner in the clinic and an owner in an office building for the past eight years. The couple has built a substantial retirement fund of $350,000, owns a home valued at $500,000, and has investment assets of $60,000. Their $375,000 mortgage is their primary liability. Their house payments are $2,800 per month. John wants Jane to go back to work and earn money to support herself.

She is devastated and is trying to deal with the emotional and financial realities of her divorce while continuing to be the primary caretaker of the children. In the next few months, she sees a career counselor and decides that she would like to pursue a career as a medical librarian. This will mean another three years of schooling. With no experience, Jane can expect a starting salary in the $25,000 to $30,000 range. She is concerned about attending school full-time at her age while keeping the home going and raising their children. A live-in nanny to help with the childcare and housekeeping responsibilities is a good idea, but will cost her $1,500 per month.

Who will pay for all of these expenses? John, reluctantly. And then there is college funding for their oldest child. He is planning to attend an eastern school where the tuition and dormitory costs are estimated to be $25,000 per year. Currently $15,000 has been put aside toward college expenses for the boy in a special fund.

By now, you should be getting the picture. We have two adults and three children who were consumers, with the surplus after family expenses going to pay for the purchase of the office building, an expensive mortgage, and a "spendy" lifestyle for everybody. Two households will not be able to live in the same style as the single unit. Both John and Jane want continued expensive vacations and clothing. There is only so much money to go around. Jane will need to have a detailed budget demonstrating the family's historical spending, a concise budget for the temporary maintenance period. In Washington the separation period lasts up to one year after filing, before a scheduled court date arrives for the final divorce decree. There will be many motions along the way. A post-divorce budget takes into account some of the following: college funding for Jane and the couple's son, a monthly salary and benefits for the nanny. Meanwhile, John has rented a three-bedroom condominium so that he will have a home for the children when they visit him. He is considering asking for at least one of the children to live with with him, making his home the child's primary residence.

In a landmark study, *The Divorce Revolution,* Lenore J. Weitzman, a sociology professor at Harvard University, found that in the first year after divorce a man's standard of living increases by an average of 42 percent; a woman's falls by 73 percent. This demonstrates the skewed arithmetic of the typical divorce: unfair property division. Undoubtedly, it will happen with John and Jane.

The intent of new laws enacted during the past 25 years has been to make divorce fairer for women. The No-Fault laws, now on the books in every state except South Dakota, were designed to allow either spouse to sue for divorce without showing cause, such as adultery, abuse, or mental cruelty. They were meant to take the public shame and blame out of splitting up and to provide a safe escape from an unhappy marriage. For many women, No-Fault filing has been expensive. It has done away with the concept of the "injured party." Historically, if the injured person was the wife, she would be compensated with property or money. No-Fault also removed an important bargaining chip for the woman — the basis upon which she would agree to give the husband a divorce in exchange for a fair settlement.

We are now in the era of "equitable distribution laws." This means, as I said earlier, that marriage is viewed as an economic partnership. The idea is that contributions have been made to the partnership inside and outside the marriage and that assets should be divided "equitably" to account for these contributions, no matter whose name is on a deed or investment account.

The experts will tell you that the concept of "equitable" is indeed a slippery one which leaves too much to interpretation by judges and attorneys. The way property is registered legally can be crucial to a partner in a marriage. Washington, for example, is a community property state. If you commingle your assets in this state, they are deemed to be community property and can be divided equitably. Even if you have kept the registration separate, the property can be shared or your community assets can be allocated disproportionately so that there is an equitable distribution of property. Judges have wide discretion in dividing assets and setting maintenance or alimony schedules.

The sooner the non-earning spouse gathers the financial data and creates a financial plan, the sooner she can assume control of her life. Too many times we see women who put their heads in the sand. They think justice will prevail and that they can count on maintenance because, after all, it is only fair.

7. *What about keeping the family residence?*

I devote a major section of Chapter Eight to this decision-making process. There are income tax issues, home maintenance costs to think about, and a soft real estate market can affect resale values. There are many factors to consider before either partner decides to keep the house. It may prove to be better if two homes are purchased instead of the one.

8. *Won't I automatically get custody of the children, since I have devoted much of my adult life to being mom?*

So you say to yourself, I will get the kids. There are never any guarantees that this will happen. More and more, I am seeing cases where fathers are asking for joint custody, often hiring a nanny to help them caretake the children when they are with him. This means less money to the ex-spouse for child support. Often the replacement nanny could be earning more than the ex-spouse in her first job. The courts are getting more involved in determining what arrangements are in the best interests of the children as they relate to child custody, support and visitation arrangements. In Washington, the divorcing parties are required to file a parenting plan with the divorce papers as well as an order for child support. Washington has standard guidelines to use in determining the amount of child support required from each parent to maintain the care of dependent children.

9. *How can I create a win/win divorce?*

I see clients all the time who tell me they want a friendly divorce, no attorneys. They will do their own divorce with a "do-it-yourself kit," or they will seek a mediator. Beware of trying to handle the entire divorce by yourself. The laws are ever changing and are complicated when it comes to getting a divorce. Divorce could be the most important financial transaction of your lifetime. Don't trust the process to someone lacking the knowledge to give good advice, including yourself. Even when using a mediator, take your non-binding agreement to an outside attorney before signing the document and having it filed.

10. How can I make sure I get the crystal and china which we received at our wedding as a gift? It is mine, mine, mine.

Thousands of dollars can be spent on dividing up the personal belongings. Some people get all of the items in the house appraised, or they draw numbers and each alternate choosing an item, keeping track of the cost. In some cases, one will go out and buy new furniture to set up a new home, justifying the cost from community assets and leaving you with the old. Try and be reasonable. Remember *War of the Roses* and the fights over the "stuff?" This an area of contention involving sentiment and practicality and people often torture and harass each other. Paying an attorney $200 an hour to divide up your "stuff" can become very expensive. Tell your grievances to your psychiatrist, not your attorney. Give the attorney your list of requests, but not expensive hours of explanations.

11. I married for life. What about our marriage contract?

"I have fulfilled my role as a wife and mother. He was supposed to take care of me financially." I hear statements like this all of the time. "At least 50 percent of the assets and half of his income should be mine for life. We made a commitment. He wants out — but financially, I deserve half of his income for my life." Well, it doesn't work like that. Several factors are taken into account when dividing the assets and the income; the size of the estate, the duration of the marriage, separate and community assets, and the age and health of the parties, among others. You can eliminate the word "should" from your vocabulary when divorce starts. The whole question of distribution of assets is taken up in subsequent chapters. Look at the one on Surviving After Your Spouse's Earnings Have Been Withdrawn.

The sooner the family is realistic about finances and the new lifestyle, the better life will become. Sit down with your children, discuss budgets, work responsibilities, visitation with the other spouse, etc. Try and be proactive instead of reactive.

12. I don't want a major court battle and conflict. Can't we be reasonable?

Statistically, only about three percent of divorces are actually settled in the courtroom by a judge. Most are settled in negotiations prior to a court battle. That doesn't mean that you won't be in front of the judge for various motions along the way, such as setting a child support and maintenance schedule, interpreting areas of dispute, etc. Many women dislike conflict and will do whatever they can to avoid it. They may hire an attorney to do their dirty work or just become passive, expecting the "right" thing to happen in their case. Many men, on the other hand, look at divorce as a business transaction. They want to get to the bottom line quickly and get the divorce over with. If they do get emotional, they still want the divorce over quickly and inexpensively. They are resistant to high legal fees and get angry if the wife can't trust them about the finances and the final settlement. As you can see, this is a dangerous combination and there is a delicate balance to be maintained between the parties.

Divorce does not need to be a totally negative experience. While it generally is not a positive act, people who are divorcing are hopeful of a future. At least the person who starts the divorce action usually feels this way. It makes a big difference if you are negative or positive about your future when it comes to dealing with the emotional aspects of divorce. Often, a psychologist can be of tremendous value to help you go through the various stages of mourning for the hopes the marriage represented. You are separating yourself from your spouse, legally. But I must make this warning to women: if you believe your husband will be generous because he is feeling GUILT, forget it. Guilt, or the "G" word, will only take you so far. Then you are in a business transaction and men can and do separate business from their emotions. That is what the business world requires, whether you are male or female.

This chapter has been designed to make you aware of what you are facing — some of the questions, decisions, considerations, strategies, self protections, safeguards and personal planning you have to undertake to emerge from a divorce, if not a big winner, at least with a fair share of the assets you and your spouse have accumulated during your marriage.

This book is structured to give you all the information you will need to prepare for divorce. If it accomplishes nothing else but to serve as a warning that you — the woman, the person who avoids conflict, the one who believes in fairness — must remove your rose-colored glasses and fend for yourself if you are going to get what you deserve, then I will have accomplished my objective. Remember, the system does not protect you. Your own sharpened sense of survival and your diligence will.

CHAPTER THREE

HOW DO I CHOOSE THE DIVORCE PROCESS THAT BEST SUITS ME?

The meeting of two personalities is like the contact of two chemical substances;
if there is any reaction, both are transformed.
— *C. G. Jung*

Women typically go into marriage with the view of entering a long term partnership of sharing emotions, money, child raising and retirement. Most women I get to know are beset by emotional trauma over their divorces. Often, they have been replaced by another woman, frequently a younger one. It is a bitter pill for them to swallow. The woman's sense of betrayal, loss and anger can temporarily lower her self-esteem and throw her into a deep depression. While she is fighting to regain a solid perspective of herself, the discarded wife is probably still performing her role as the "super" mom — always in control, taking charge of the details of everyone's daily life. Mom feels like she's sliding on ice, helpless to change the direction to disaster; and she is trapped with kids to take care of and a missing husband who's suddenly become hostile.

In divorce there is always the one who leaves and one who stays behind. Probably, the woman who stays behind is the most disoriented in a divorce. She's the one who must be reminded by her familiar physical surroundings of the failure of her marriage. Every picture on the wall, candid photo, discarded pair of male golf shoes, the basketball hoop over the garage door that somehow never got straightened, or the ragged sweater he insisted on wearing, are endearing reminders of ruined hopes and broken promises for an enduring future. Permanency, forestalled by divorce!

I've already described the emotional stages of divorce in Chapter Two. It is important for each of the partners in a divorce to acknowledge the stages, for you will be able to manage your new life better if you know what you're passing through.

If you viewed your marriage as a partnership, then you are going to assume that both spouses made substantially equal (although not necessarily identical) contributions to the marriage. With this perspective, it is natural that you should think that you should receive substantially equal financial benefits from the marriage and should not be left in a disadvantaged position after your marriage ends. This area of concern is specifically addressed in Chapter Eleven which explores equitable distribution and how it works.

Let's look at Janice, who I introduced in Chapter Two, who now has to decide which method of the divorcing process — mediation, litigation, or arbitration — is best for her.

How did she finally get out of her maze and create a life for herself and the children when she felt so lousy, depressed, inadequate and out of control? The answer to that question involves the information presented in the balance of this chapter. Janice had to go through the financial process of learning the steps and making choices. You can read about her personal outcome at the end of this chapter.

I had to explain to Janice some divorce terminology: equitable distribution (to which I've already referred), separate and community property, mediation, arbitration and litigation. I pointed out to her that the state in which a divorcing person lives may make a difference in divorce strategy. She needed to know the laws and statutes in her state as well as those in other states where she may have lived with her husband.

I also pointed out to Janice that she could have her divorce handled in one of three primary methods: mediation, arbitration or litigation. What are the advantages and disadvantages? For an exact answer to that question, you — as I advised Janice to do — should go to the library or bookstore and get a good book on getting a divorce in the state where you are living. We have one called *Divorce In Washington.* You can learn the terminology, the process, the time frame, and what to expect from the court system. You will have a how-to book to use as an overall framework for your process. By studying the book describing your state's laws, you can become your attorney's most important paralegal. You can save hundreds of dollars and you can be more informed about the choices you have. I am not trying to dodge the responsibility I have to the reader to inform about mediation, arbitration and litigation. That comes in this chapter. What I am suggesting is that you don't stop with my brief explanation. Get more information in broad terms on the subtleties of the divorce process in your state.

It is probably worthwhile for me to comment generally on the states which seem to have a better climate, or more favorable ones, for divorce. To do this I call on a portion of a *Fortune Magazine* article by Trisha Welsh:

"Each [state] has different rules for splitting up property, awarding alimony, and deciding who takes care of the kids — and thus could be better or worse for you, depending on whether you're a breadwinning husband or a 20-year homemaker with children in school.

"Though many states will now allow you to be single again in as little as three months, business is still booming in Nevada, the quickie divorce capital. The state's six-week residency requirement is almost unparalleled. (Most states demand that you live there at least six months and sometimes up to a year year before you can file for divorce. One exception: Alaska, where you can file the day you arrive, though it will take at least a month to get unhitched.) Once Nevada's residency rules are satisfied, an uncontested divorce can be completed in as little as 48 hours.

"More important, the grounds for divorce may be easier to deal with there than in your current home state. New York, South Carolina and Virginia, for example, don't accept incompatibility as a reason to split. If that's your problem, one solution is to fly to the Dominican

Republic, where you can get divorced in 24 hours provided your spouse consents.

"In most divorces, the main issue isn't how quickly you exit but how you divide up the pot. A wealthy spouse looking to keep all his or her toys should steer clear of the nine community-property states — Arizona, California, Idaho, Louisiana, Nevada, New Mexico, Texas, Washington and Wisconsin — and head for states that divide property by the equitable-distribution method. Even here, however, it pays to be picky. 'Judges have a lot of leeway with equitable-distribution rules,' says Lester Wallman, a New York City attorney. He advises wealthy clients with multiple residences in New York and Connecticut or New Jersey to seek divorces in New York because 'judges there seem to favor the breadwinners.'

"Gifts and inheritances generally aren't up for grabs, though at least 12 states, including Connecticut, Georgia and Hawaii throw them in the kitty with everything else. Finally, though fault isn't a factor in getting divorced these days, nearly half of all states still consider it when divvying up the goods.

"To avoid paying alimony, the best state is Texas — it simply doesn't exist there. If your spouse cheated on you, you'll get the last laugh in Georgia, Louisiana, North Carolina, or Virginia: These states won't award a cent of alimony to anyone guilty of adultery. And if you supported the louse or lousette through a medical degree and then got dumped, take heart! Fifteen states, with New York leading the way, have ruled that professional degrees and licenses are marital property whose value can be considered when dividing up property and determining support.

"Worried about your children? It's increasingly likely that Congress will mandate a national uniform child support standard, requiring that a certain percentage of your income be paid for each child. This would leave unaddressed the biggest problem: collecting. Right now, many states will garnish your spouse's wages to ensure that support is paid. If money is tight and Junior is ready for higher eduction, get your divorce in New Jersey. Though most such payments end when a child reaches 18 or finishes high school, in the Garden State the supporting spouse is obliged to ante up for college too."

MEDIATION, ARBITRATION, LITIGATION — WHICH PROCESS IS BEST FOR YOUR DIVORCE?

Mediation, as I explained to Janice, is a voluntary and confidential process in which an impartial third party (trained mediator) helps disputing parties reach a mutually agreeable settlement. Arbitration leaves the final decision in the dispute up to the arbitrator. You agree beforehand to binding arbitration. The arbitrator's decision is binding and it's public. Mediators suggest solutions and their suggestions are confidential. In mediation, the power is reserved to the parties. In a litigated divorce, the marriage partners have a judge hear the case in court and his decision is binding.

I explained to Janice that one mediator in our area compares a family conflict to a wound. Using that definition to build on, then the court process could be compared to surgery and the third party (the judge) is the surgeon called in to "cure" the situation with a legal knife. In a successful divorce mediation, both of the wounded parties go through a mutual healing process. Mediation acts through a hearing process in which both husband and wife get to present their sides of the story.

Mediation can be conducted by one professional acting in the guiding role. The mediator may be an attorney, financial planner, CPA, psychologist and/or social worker. In a divorce mediation, there are usually two professionals acting as co-mediators. Since the divorce deals with both emotional issues and financial assets, you will often see a counselor working with an attorney to help the parties negotiate and bargain their property settlement as well as the parenting plan. If you elect mediation, make sure, as I advised Janice, that you are working with a trained mediator. I've drawn up a list of questions at the end of this chapter which cover the concerns you should voice when you interview the mediators in your area.

It is important that you have a trained and skilled mediator who has the skills and tools to get stalled negotiations back on track. The mediation setting often turns into a forum for both parties to vent their anger, frustration, guilt, fear and sadness, sense of loss, and many other emotions. These feelings need to be acknowledged. The skilled mediator, however, will help the husband and wife focus on an effective resolution and channel their energies towards a negotiated and comprehensive settlement. For women especially, the job of the mediator is to address their fears and help them to understand the financial aspects of their pending single lifestyle. Knowledge brings power. A skilled mediator will re-focus the parties on the ultimate conclusion of the mediated settlement, rather than on divisive issues that delay cooperation.

I explained to Janice that mediation is an intense time of negotiation between the divorcing parties. One of the major advantages of mediation is that there are no witnesses, evidence, or a public trial. The husband and wife are in complete control of their process. For some women, this can be very frightening since they may have acted the role of caretaker in the family and the husband handled the finances. If this is the case, the mediator needs to be certain that the less knowledgeable spouse seeks outside professional legal and financial help to aid her in understanding the economic implications of the proposed settlement.

As a financial planner, this is the point in which I would enter the negotiations. Typically, the attorney or one of the parties will be meeting with me to determine the economic impact of the future settlement. We will guide that party to understand and focus on her new lifestyle. We will look at short- and long-term cash flow, the expectation of income after schooling, if applicable. We'll also evaluate housing options, constructing the post-divorce budget, analyzing the income tax consequences of maintenance, and we'll look closely at employment and investment income. Mediation is commonly used in child custody disputes. I believe it can also be used effectively in settling financial issues.

If mediation is the choice you make to dissolve your marriage, it is important that you bring to the negotiating table all of the "lost assets" that need to be weighed for reimbursement to you in the settlement. One of these is the "lost opportunity" cost of your marriage.

This concept was explained in an article in *New Woman Magazine:* "Many married women put their husband's career ahead of their own. They may switch jobs so he can relocate, or reduce overtime to help him with business entertaining — and still more drop out of the work force or take less demanding jobs so they can raise children. There's a *cost* to doing this, and it's one that can't ever be quite made up, according to recent research."

Arbitration is a binding process for both parties. You and your attorney present your case and the arbitrator determines the financial outcome. Typically, the divorcing parties predetermine the financial issues to be settled in arbitration.

You have probably watched *Divorce Court* on television at least once. The courtroom and litigation processes take place in a formal setting where the divorcing parties — most often represented by their respective attorneys — present their position to a judge. Each attorney presents the facts, brings in expert witnesses to support his position, and the judge determines the final impact by interpreting the laws and statutes of the state. Expert witnesses can come in many forms, such as business evaluators, financial planners, psychologists, doctors, economists, actuaries, career advisors, and accountants.

I have found the courtroom procedure to be cold and impersonal. You speak when spoken to, and give answers to specific questions when required. You pay to have your day in court: preparation by your attorney, including depositions of the divorcing parties and their experts. Going to trial can be a costly process. Maybe that is why over 95 percent of divorces are settled out of court. No matter which process you choose — get good sound, comprehensive financial and tax advice before signing your final agreement.

WHAT ABOUT THE LAW? DO I NEED AN ATTORNEY?

A do-it-yourself-divorce is as dangerous as walking through a red light at a busy traffic intersection and hoping you can dodge the cars and trucks that come hurtling at you!

If you have any property, children (who are assets), and a desire to emerge from divorce with something more than an empty pocketbook, hire an attorney.

The following questions are ones I have developed on the basis of consulting with hundreds of women facing divorce. They represent information I also passed on to Janice. As a result, she was able to select the facts that helped her make a choice of attorneys.

WHAT KIND OF AN ATTORNEY DO I WANT TO HIRE?

First of all, you want an experienced domestic relations lawyer. Look around and find a good personality fit and one you can afford. Don't draw back about asking the cost of legal fees. Be wary of paying below the norm and finding the best fee bargain in the matrimonial field. Often, "deals" come from inexperienced lawyers who try to make up in determination and persuasion what they lack in experience.

If your case is likely to involve lengthy negotiations and a complicated property settlement, or may go to trial, you should never take a chance on someone who is not recognized in the family law area. Look at who your spouse has hired as his attorney. Make sure you have someone who can work with him. If there are issues of abuse or child custody, be sure your attorney has experience in this type of case. Many established attorneys will not take this type of case. You are going to be spending a lot of time with your attorney. Make sure that your working styles are compatible.

WHERE DO I LOOK FOR THE ATTORNEY?

Ask your friends who have gone through a divorce if they have a recommendation. A good divorce is often described as one in which neither spouse is happy. Divorce means compromise. If you are active in your church, ask your clergyman. Contact the bar association in your state. Ask for a listing of those attorneys in the state bar association who live in your area and are members of the Family Law Section.

Call the local bar association listed in the white pages of your phone book and ask if there is a lawyer referral service for domestic relations lawyers.

Go to the library and look through a volume called *Martindale-Hubble*. This huge book has listings of lawyers by city throughout the United States. There is a listing of attorneys, and what the specialty of the firm is. Make sure to read the biographies. Also, make sure the attorney you pick is active in organizations for lawyers. By far, your best bet is an attorney who has been recommended by a woman who has gone through the divorce process with him or her and at the end still is happy enough with him to pass him or her on to you.

WHAT ARE SOME TIPS, WHEN LOOKING FOR AN ATTORNEY?

Do not use an attorney who is a family friend or business associate of your spouse. Don't set yourself up for a problem that might arise with divided loyalties. This third party could be brought in at the end of the negotiations to give perspective, but be very cautious. You could lose a friend and be unduly influenced in an emotionally unstable time of your life.

Do interview several attorneys (at least three) before making your final decision. You will be looking for a good personality fit, evaluating costs, and discussing the payment of a retainer fee. The retainer fee a lawyer initially charges is for taking on your case and rarely represents the entire fee. Typically, the attorney will work on an hourly basis, billing against the retainer on a monthly basis. The retainer fee "reserves" his or her time to pursue your case.

Do make a commitment between the two of you. Make sure you have an attorney who will work with you rather than for you. This is the team concept in which you cooperate to do your own paralegal work.

WHAT KIND OF QUESTIONS SHOULD I ASK MY ATTORNEY IN THE INITIAL INTERVIEW?

The following are the ones I handed to Janice on a typed sheet:
- Will you charge me on a retainer, hourly basis, or will you sign a contract for a set fee?
- What kind of expenses should I anticipate and who will pay for them?
- What is a realistic time frame for our working relationship and for this divorce to be final?
- How can I get money out of out joint accounts to pay for some of these costs?
- Have you ever worked with the opposing attorney?
- How many divorce cases did you handle last year?
- How many of your cases went to trial? How long did the trials last?
- What portion of your law practice is devoted to Family Law?
- How much of the work do you do and how much is handled by your assistant?

- What is the billing rate for your assistant and staff time?
- Do you use experts often and if so, in what capacity? Who pays for these services?
- Do you work with financial planners as part of your professional team?
- Do you work in mediation or arbitration cases?
- Can I expect any attorney fees or expert witness fees to be paid by my spouse?
- What kind of temporary maintenance do you think I can get with our income levels?
- How detailed is your request for temporary maintenance? Do you usually get what you request?
- What can I expect in child support?
- Can you give me the names of some books I should read regarding getting a divorce?
- Do you have any articles or information that can be helpful in my case?
- Do you recommend a therapist whom I might see? How do you work with the therapist?
- What are the strengths and weaknesses of my case at this time?
- How do I protect myself and children during this time?
- Should I try and get a job now or change jobs?
- My spouse has taken all the financial information. What do I do? How can we get it from him?
- When do you have your next trial or hearing scheduled? I would like to see how you work in the courtroom.
- Where do you think I can go to get money to pay your fees based on what I have shown you about our situation?

Remember, when you hire an attorney to represent you in your divorce, you are depending upon him or her to get the most for you he or she can out of the divorce process. The attorney you want must be smart and have your ultimate benefit as his or her primary goal, rather than the dollars you represent.

CHECKLIST — *INITIAL MEETING WITH YOUR ATTORNEY*

Be organized when you go on your initial interview. Here is a list of information you might have ready. I gave the same list to Janice for her to use when she first saw her attorney.

- Date of marriage, name and ages and date of birth of you, your spouse and children.
- When and where you were married. Where have you lived your married life.
- History of each of your employments.
- A recent income tax return.
- A summary balance sheet including assets and liabilities; even if this is incomplete, it will be helpful.
- A preliminary budget.
- Identify separate and community assets if you can.
- Why are you getting a divorce? Describe your reasons briefly.
- Separate, pre-nuptial or community property agreements.

As to Janice, once she understood that she had to rely on herself for good advice, she read the book, *Divorce In Washington,* hired an attorney, authorized him to find a professional mediator and with her husband's reluctant cooperation, managed to legally end her marriage with a fair settlement. Both Janice and her husband had separate legal representation apart from the mediator. Janice also worked with a financial planner, career advisor, accountant and therapist during and after her divorce.

CHAPTER FOUR

LIVING WITH CHANGE DOES NOT MEAN DEALING WITH AN ENEMY

Trust, but verify.
— *Kathleen Miller*

NO FRATERNIZATION!

You have decided to file for divorce. You have been living apart from your husband for the past three months trying to determine your next step. He has taken an apartment and you have stayed in the home with your two teenage children. You and your children are trying to get on with your lives under an emotional cloud. You and your husband share the money that comes into the house from a joint account upon which both of you write checks. Now he has informed you that he wants a divorce — he wants out and says he is going to start the filing process. What do you do next? Do you stop seeing each other, hire an attorney, wait for the papers to be served, cry, talk to your friends, go to church, what?

I am sure there are numerous thoughts going through your head at this start of the dissolution process. The truth is that the ending of your marriage probably has been coming for quite some time and you chose not to see the signs or believed you could change the events. After all, as a woman, you subconsciously believed the Fairy Godmother when she said you would live happily ever after.

The period right after the shock of his announcement of divorce is a good time to have a "cooling off" and not to see each other for a while. I've learned that women need time to gather their wits emotionally, while men typically want to divide the estate and determine the business aspects of their married life quickly. Both of these requirements will take place in the divorce process.

You have to immediately get used to the idea that divorce means separation, emotionally, physically, and financially. It does not mean that you are no longer going to be parents to your children. However, because feelings of hurt and injustice run high, it is important for you to find a method of communication with your estranged partner which will not require you to meet face-to-face or have voice-to-voice contact. You can choose to exchange messages on answering machines or exchange notes. But don't make your children the delivery service. That puts them in the middle, a place that is not safe or fair for them.

Get some distance during this time of divorce preliminaries. Spend it getting yourself organized as I have described in the first three chapters of this book and will describe at greater length in the coming chapters. The "Don't fraternize" rule may be difficult to put into motion because it's human to want to justify yourself with the person who has offended you. If you need to let off steam, do it with a friend, not your ex-partner to-be.

DON'T TALK TO HIM ABOUT THE DIVORCE CASE

Many women I've met let divorce overwhelm them. Don't! In particular, don't abdicate your participation in financial fact gathering, so important in this first phase of divorce. Take the time to get comfortable with the financial issues of your marriage and don't allow yourself to be badgered by your ex-to-be. Many of the men whom I see in a divorce case are dividing the income and assets as they leave the house. They have been planning the divorce and their exit for some time. Your strategy should be to listen, and gather the facts, figures, documents you will need. Encourage your husband to provide this information without a struggle arising between your attorneys. Point out to him in a note that cooperation will save both of you money.

The initial petition for divorce often has such inflammatory clauses written into the boiler plate as "freezing of assets in a joint account," "comprehensive and all inclusive restraining orders." These orders are there to protect you. Your husband is probably going to be upset if your attorney puts this type of wording into your legal response to his petition. He may think your attorney is encouraging you to be adversarial. Your husband wants you to be cooperative, to TRUST him. The byword for you to memorize is: TRUST, BUT VERIFY. Believe his actions and not his words. Trust your intuition. Listen to your inner voice and protect yourself legally.

As an aid to your intuition, review in your mind how your husband handled himself in business transactions in the past. Did he act like a controller? Was he detail-minded? Did he like to win, play hard ball in negotiations, win through the art of intimidation? Did he use religion on you to keep you subservient? Did he treat you as an equal partner in your financial affairs, or have you sign the income tax return at the very last minute without explanation? Or did he ask you to sign the return only after you thoroughly understood the facts and figures? Did he work with you on a written budget for the family? Did he encourage you to work outside the home? Think about the answers to these questions, then ask yourself is he suddenly going to change and be cooperative now when there is a lot at stake?

Make up a list of your husband's strengths — emotionally and financially. How does he deal with people in business and in friendships?

Make the same list for yourself.

Next, write down how you think your spouse viewed you during your marriage. For example, did he think you were a spendthrift, a time waster, a good mother, a good listener, a companion, physically fit, a good money manager? Is his opinion of you going to change suddenly? Is he going to try to use some of your weaknesses against you?

This is the time to keep a journal. Write your feelings down rather than keeping them pent up inside. Eventually, you will begin to see some behavior patterns unfolding. You will have an opportunity to change and refine habits during this time of self examination.

If you are going to talk about the divorce with your husband — have an agenda. If you can't talk or communicate effectively about financial matters — most divorcing couples need help in this area — suggest to him that you meet with a financial planner who can help you to understand all of the issues you are facing. Your husband is no longer the trusted advisor and partner. You need to equalize the power. Suggest a settlement conference with your attorneys and financial planners if you believe it will facilitate a timely and fair property settlement

Too many times I see the woman attempting to negotiate with her husband, or she may allow him to provide countless proposals, or may have countless telephone conversations when she doesn't understand the full economic impact of what is being discussed. The divorcing woman needs an attorney to handle the legal aspects of her case and to quarterback her professional team. That team will need players with different areas of expertise. I urge you to get help where you need it. If your husband argues against this help, pause and take a hard look at what is going on in your case.

DON'T ALLOW HIM TO DRIVE A WEDGE BETWEEN YOU AND YOUR LAWYER

If you have hired an attorney with whom you are comfortable after interviewing and rejecting those who were unsatisfactory, I am assuming that you are using him or her to help you take control of organizing your financial information. Also, I assume that you are following the guidelines outlined in this book. If you are not, it is never too late to get started, no matter where you are on the path to the big DIVORCE. If you have an attorney who is not responsive to you and your calls, and with whom you are not communicating, then write a letter explaining your frustrations. If this doesn't work and he or she continues to ignore your requirements, then you may need to fire him or her. If your husband is a controller, he is not going to like the divorce process and the legal requirements for supplying information to you and your attorney. Your entire financial life is going to come under scrutiny as an overall strategy is determined for the division of assets, the sharing of income, retirement benefits, personal belongings, a parenting plan and custody of the children. These financial concerns are just the beginning. You can share information cooperatively or forcibly, with subpoenas. The latter is far more expensive and adversarial in nature. Some attorneys are confrontative and adversarial. I would choose an attorney who compliments your style rather than one who is "like you." You and your attorney are going to be working very closely together and you need to have mutual respect and trust.

I clearly remember a case I worked on two years ago. The couple was in their early forties. He was a physician and she had been a nurse until their children were born ten years before. This couple had built up a large amount of savings through a careful savings program practiced by both of them. They had sixty percent equity in their home, and over $200,000 in retirement assets. She wanted out of the marriage for reasons of emotional incompatibility and because of his long working hours, with little family time. She decided she did not want the house and moved into a rental home a few blocks from the family residence so the children could be close to both parents and stay in the same school district. I cautioned her about leaving her home at this point, but it was what she wanted. She thought she and her husband had reached a joint financial decision about dividing the furniture, purchasing new furniture and handling the costs of her moving from their savings. They had agreed on a base amount for her living expenses for the first month and then they were supposed to sit down and revise the numbers. She did all of this in "good faith." Her husband then filed a petition with the aid of a well-known adversarial attorney.

There were restraining orders, a bid for custody of the children, a claim that she was an unfit mother. He hired a part-time housekeeper to compete with her being home with the children after school. His strategy was that the cost of his "hired wife" would reduce the amount he had to pay her for maintenance and child support. Court evaluators were appointed to make recommendation on the parenting plan. She had to hire separate financial experts to have his medical practice evaluated for the assets and goodwill. Originally, they had agreed to hire the same business valuation firm.

Now, he did not want to sell the house so funds would be available for each of them to purchase two new residences. He hired a detective to follow her, even though the action was a "no fault" divorce. His actions through his attorney were hostile and aimed at preserving the lion's share of the property for himself.

In the end, she received custody of the children and a flexible parenting plan. She moved to another area of the city and purchased a new home after he refinanced their residence to provide her with a down payment. He was required to pay maintenance for four years on a declining scale while she upgraded her nursing skills to become a nurse practitioner. His retirement assets were divided, and he signed a promissory note secured by the house to buy out her interest in the medical practice over the next five years. She will receive 22 percent of his average earnings for the next four years. If his earnings are above this historical average, these dollars will be shared as follows: 15 percent of the gross to the wife and 10 percent of the net to the children for the maintenance period.

This wife worked her way through an ambuscade of letters from his attorney harassing her every move, such as unnecessary requests to review how she spent her temporary maintenance and child support, and other frustrating requests.

Of course, her husband was furious with her attorney and his actions to systematically checkmate the husband and his attorney. Often, the controlling husband will hire an attorney who he can control, even down to the letters and information submitted to his wife and her attorney.

If you are in this type of divorce you have no choice but to checkmate your husband's actions, systematically and methodically. It will cost you money, but, remember, men have controlled women with money historically and the strategy often developed is designed to wear you down, reduce your self-esteem and heighten your sense of guilt and failure, so that you will settle for less. Strategies such as these are why it is critical for you to do your own homework and to save yourself money if you can perform some of the necessary paralegal work.

To keep your costs under control, ask questions, have an agenda when you meet with your attorney and experts, and ask what you can do to conserve your money. Ask for a monthly bill and call your attorney only when you have something important to say. Remember, you are being billed for your phone calls. Look carefully at the attorney your spouse has hired. Find out what you can about him or her. Ask your own attorney about his or her adversary; ask your other experts. You might want to view your husband's attorney in action in the court room on another case. Do your research. Be prepared. Prepare a defense and do not allow yourself to be bullied. Always seek good, comprehensive financial advice from your financial planner, accountant and attorney. Be sure your experts talk and share information by fax, phone calls or copying letters to each other as appropriate. Divorce is a time of highly charged emotions. Many times you will feel like the process is "crazy making" time.

WATCH OUT FOR HIS LATE NIGHT TELEPHONE CALLS

Keep a diary of all your husband's phone calls, and if they are harassing in nature tell him that you are recording the conversations. If he writes notes to you offering helpful hints on how you should live your life, organize your time, how to look, what to say, who to trust, or where to go to church, keep them filed chronologically. When the divorce is final and you are ready for your paper cleaning, you'll have something to burn.

The late night phone calls from your husband can be tearful, angry, sad, or an attempt to reconcile. They may be humorous, guilt-ridden — or all of the above. Remember, both of you will go through the emotional states of divorce described earlier. You can keep moving through these emotional phases or get stuck. Refresh yourself on the emotional stages, so that you can identify the changes that are happening to you and mark your progress by them. Consider hiring a therapist to help you in this time of transition.

WHAT NOT TO TALK ABOUT WHEN YOU SEE YOUR HUSBAND

When you and your husband meet, it's important that you don't give away information which may allow him to take advantage of you. Here are some "Don'ts" to remember: Don't talk about what you don't understand, what you have heard through the grapevine or rumor mill, your proposed financial settlement, your plans to move away from the area, your health problems, your sex life, how you spend your free time, how much money you are saving or spending, your detailed vacation plans, or your career plan until it is firmed up in your mind. Women often talk too much and give away their position on a financial strategy, child custody issues and other aspects of the divorce.

I suggest that you rent the video movie *Kramer vs. Kramer* with Dustin Hoffman and Meryl Streep, also, *War of the Roses* with Michael Douglas, Kathleen Turner and Danny DeVito. As you will see, good intentions are often changed in the divorce process to bitter enmity. I've mentioned one of these movies before, because I was impressed by its similarity to divorce cases I've been involved in.

NEVER ACT AS YOUR OWN ATTORNEY

Obtaining a divorce means going through the legal process. I should remind you to buy a book on getting a divorce in your state as a complement to this book. Look at the forms you will be required to complete and the deadlines you must meet. Become your own paralegal, but don't try to become your own attorney. This is particularly true if you have any assets. You may have property which you don't consider assets and it could easily be left out of your property settlement documents. The laws surrounding investments, real estate, taxes, retirement plans, insurance policies, and debt obligations are complicated with many layers to understand. You need to know the cost to get in and out of your legal agreements.

If you have concerns about your divorce agreement, get a second opinion. I definitely suggest that you obtain an outside attorney if you are going through mediation. A qualified mediator will be sure to recommend this step. If this step is not recommended, get out quickly.

DEALING WITH YOUR HUSBAND

For many people death is easier to deal with than divorce. When you divorce someone or he divorces you, you will still see each other occasionally. If there are children and common friendships, I encourage you to try and work out some way of dealing with each other if you must share the same geographical situation. To help you deal with your ex or ex-to-be, I've compiled a list of things to do and not to do.

Things to do:
- Stick to the facts and details; don't wander or invite commentary on "what was."
- Take a deep breath before you speak.
- Have a joint mediation session to handle the dispute.
- Don't look at your husband during the deposition, or in the trial if you feel intimidated by his aggressiveness. Or, the reverse strategy, if you feel strong, is to look him in the eye when you talk and stare him down.
- Call 911 if you feel threatened.

Things not to do:
- Don't argue with your husband or threaten. Keep to the facts. If you don't want to talk, leave the situation until you feel you can deal with him.
- Don't get into what he has or has not done. Listen to your inner voice and say what is the truth for you. Stay with your own truth.
- Keep your children out of the middle; if you don't, they will be angry with both of you.
- Don't quiz the kids about his actions, his new girlfriend, how he spends his money, and don't try to turn your children into spies when you can't communicate with him.
- If your husband won't communicate with you, he won't communicate with you. But just remember, he can't avoid you forever; he'll be forced under the legal system to deal with you through your attorney.

One woman who came to see me a few months ago was quite proud that she had no relationship with her soon to be ex-husband. She had decided what she wanted and didn't want from her divorce. She had written a property settlement proposal, she had her children not speaking to their father, she told everyone at their church about his departure and his infidelity. She insisted on referring to his new girl-friend as his "floozy."

This client was in total denial of the reality of her situation. Her expectations for the property settlement and her maintenance request were very unrealistic. She was smug, controlling, inflexible and unwilling to consider any point of view other than her own. I listened to her for an hour and a half and then sent her on her way. I was unable to break through her untested, iron-clad position. She had no attorney and intended to handle her own settlement. I asked her to do some reading about the emotional and financial aspects of settling a divorce after a long-term marriage, 38 years in her case.

She came back to see me one year later after going to court finally to get her settlement. It was quite different than what she had proposed. She was bitter and angry with the legal system, with society, with her ex-husband, with her children for living with their father, and with anyone else who had crossed her path. I politely told her that she should see another advisor for her post-divorce planning as I did not work with victims. Recovering victims, I'm delighted to see and help with their new life.

In summary, I want you to know that I do not recommend a "her against him" mentality. Instead, I suggest one that creates a win/win settlement, emotionally, psychologically, and financially. This will take time and it takes two people working together. I do not think it is realistic for most divorcing couples to remain trusted friends after a divorce. It just seldom happens. The best you can hope for is mutual respect from a distance. It also is a lot to ask that you like each other. If you have been through a court battle, child custody conflict or have been the recipient of many "nasty" letters, the best you can hope for are controlled conversations and contact where you deal with the facts and leave the emotions out. This is not easy and will take time. If there are no children there may be no need to see each other ever again.

Most divorcing couples have common friends, common hobbies, churches, or children which they have shared and which will bring them into contact. When there are offspring, I recommend that the parents attend post-divorce counseling sessions with the children. Create a safe haven for them. They need to understand the parenting agreement and all the things that are not written in to it. How do you share information about school, social activities; what do you do in a crisis or emergency? These are things that should be settled by agreement. Create a safe haven for the children to talk; let them know how you care for them in a mediated session with a qualified therapist. Plan on four sessions over a three month period. If there are new step-parents, get them involved. We know that more than sixty percent of the second marriages end in divorce. See if you can prevent your children from becoming a number in these statistics.

Chapter Five

WHAT DETERMINES THE COST OF THE DIVORCE?

The cost of a thing is the amount of what I call life
Which is required to be exchanged for it,
Immediately or in the long run.
— *Henry David Thoreau*

One of the questions I am often asked is what determines the cost of a divorce? My answer is — you do. That may sound like a cryptic reply, but it is not intended to be one. You will find a more complete answer in the checklists you'll discover at the end of this chapter.

Most attorneys and qualified experts charge by the hour for their services. You have to pay a retainer to each of them. Depending on the complexity of your divorce, the list of experts you'll need varies. Experts can include an attorney, family or business accountant, a financial planner, business valuation expert, an appraiser for both personal property and real estate, a career specialist if there is a displaced homemaker or other potential career issues involved in the divorce, a psychologist, medical doctor, employee benefits specialist, or actuary if there are pension plans to be valued. Adding to the list of persons are stock brokers, trust officers, social workers if there is a child custody dispute, and school teachers and administrators. The list can go on and on. The more experts, the more money you can expect to spend. Each divorce case is unique and requires an individualized strategy. The more organized you are gathering the financial data, the less money you will have to spend with experts and attorneys to do this job.

Let me give you an example. Several of the experts listed above are going to need copies of your income tax returns. You can make these copies at a discount copy center and place them in organized folders for your experts or you can have your attorney copy them and have them sent to the expert. In the first case it will cost you $5 at the most and in the other case $150 or more. Keep track of the date delivered and who has received what paperwork in writing.

Or what about the budgeting area? Are you going to code and organize your checks and deposits or are you going to have an expert's staff person do this laborious work? You can do a lot of the delivery work between your experts. A fax machine is also a good investment in a divorce case, and so is a recorder on your telephone so two-way communication can occur. You also will have the ability to record any "nasty-grams" or threats that may be coming from the estranged spouse.

Learn the buzz words and procedures for what is ahead of you. Then you can ask intelligent questions and have a better understanding of what to expect. Have you ever read a divorce decree, property settlement agreement, financial affidavit, or a parenting plan? Do you know what to expect at a deposition hearing? Are you really aware of what a restraining order can and cannot do? Do you have any idea what legal rights you have during separation? What would happen if either you or your spouse should die during the divorce process? The divorce process could easily represent the biggest financial transaction of your life. Become prepared. After all, it is your money. Otherwise you could become a legal annuity.

The good attorneys want you to be educated, helpful and not naive. Handling divorce can be stressful for all parties concerned, including the professionals. Even if you are organized and do all of the things I outline in this book, there are many instances in which our legal system creates a money-spending monster that gobbles up your capital.

Let me give you an example: My client is 53 and her husband is 58. He is an attorney in the real estate mortgage business, living abroad, and she is a university professor. They have one child who is a junior in college and his two older stepsons by his prior marriage. The couple has been married for 25 years. He has lived out of the country for much of the past ten years. They own a beach house, a major estate house ($1.5 million in assets) some antiques, less than $200,000 in retirement funds and autos. The total estate is about $2 million. The husband is a wheeler-dealer and decides to represent himself in the courts. He knows real estate law, but not family law. The woman hires one of the foremost attorneys in town to represent her. Because of his attitude and style, the husband is found in contempt of court several times over the year of their divorce process.

The husband definitely wants his day in court. He loves drama and sees the courtroom as a stage for a Columbo-like performance. He can be very convincing and wins more times than not in front of judges. Judges are also somewhat intimidated by him. They are cautious because he is a lawyer representing himself and they could easily make mistakes that could extend the case on appeal for years.

Time and time again my client, his wife, goes into court trying to enforce a ruling which has been made by the court and which he ignores. In such instances, the judge awards her $300 for court costs and she owes her attorney $1,000 or more just to get what was already agreed to in an earlier session. The husband ignores subpoenas, cancels depositions, doesn't get his experts listed on time, and so on.

Finally the court date is set. After five days in court, the property settlement is one of the most convoluted decisions I have seen in years. No maintenance is awarded. A 55/45 split of the assets is ordered and a small allowance given for the wife's court costs. This happens even though it is acknowledged that she has provided all of the information and did all of the data gathering, and patiently waded through an uphill battle of deplorable legal antics by her husband. They are divorced, but now will need to sell the house and small rental and then split the proceeds.

He must pay the mortgage and she must pay the utilities until the property sells. It is agreed the house should be put up for sale immediately. They must agree on the realtor and fixing-up expenses. The house has been up for sale for over 10 months now. They have been back in court five times for clarification of issues, such as who the property should be listed with, how to determine the sales price and what constitutes fix-up costs. Finally the husband won the decision to have his inexperienced son, who has a real estate license, list the house. The next time they appear in court, the ex-husband is arguing that only the son can show the house and no other realtor can represent the house unless through him. There goes the benefit of a multiple listing of the house.

Next, the ex-husband is working on a deal with the Norwegians and is attempting to cut out all of the real estate people from the transaction. The wife, meanwhile, is paying all of the utilities costs for the properties. The rental proceeds from the houses are placed in a trust fund out of which real estate taxes and insurance are paid. An intricate formula for recovery of the expenses of husband and wife is probably unfair to her because she has paid more than $4,000 out of pocket, money which we believe should be coming out of the joint rental account.

Do we go into court at $200 per hour, plus preparation time to clarify what should have been clarified by the judge at the beginning of the process? You are probably getting the picture. A combative, quarrelsome husband, and the next hurdle for legal courtroom drama will come with the house sale and who is to pay the closing costs.

You may be interested to know how this case ended. Well, the divorce has been final for two years. The husband finally did purchase the house from his wife. His new live-in loaned him the money and my client received a cash settlement for her interest in the home. One would think this would end the on-going nightmare. Not so. Now the husband is appealing the divorce settlement and the purchase of the residence from his spouse. He is arguing that the sale should be a normal sale between a buyer and seller and not incident to divorce. If this viewpoint were accepted, it would cause my client to have a substantial gain on the sale of the residence and she would have a significant income tax liability. She would not be able to defer part of the gain into the purchase of a new residence. She received the vacation home in the property settlement and is not interested in having another home. She negotiated this final, final, final sale in good faith. Her husband is a real estate attorney and is certainly an expert in the tax area. He continues to represent himself in the appeal of the case, while my client continues her "legal annuity" with a new set of attorneys to handle her response in the long appeal process.

Will it ever end? This is a question my client keeps asking. The answer: Probably not for another year or so. Stay tuned!

Another example of the legal annuity I have described comes when there is a dispute over child custody. There is a definite trend in the divorce market for fathers being more involved in the raising of the children. Joint custody is becoming more popular and is working for many couples. I wholeheartedly support cooperative efforts in the raising of children. However, I think the plan has to be practical and must also take into account the children's emotional well-being. Some of the parenting plans I have seen require the children to be transported back and forth between parents two times a week while attempting to attend school and keep up with school activities. The family might consider a joint nanny or housekeeper. Instead, what often happens is that the spouse with the higher earning power hires a nanny, the wife attempts to go to school and still raise the children and possibly even work part-time. Yet child-support is based on the amount of time you have the children. Because she works part-time, money that would have gone to the wife in the past is now going to the nanny. If one of the spouses is on a business trip, should the other parent have the children instead of the nanny? How do you resolve these conflicts after divorce? Is it mediation or back to court for enforcement?

I encourage families to have post-divorce counseling by a family therapist. The parents and children attend these sessions and work together to come up with some practical solutions to everyday family happenings. Parents do get in traffic jams, miss appointments, and don't always have time to make the perfect dinner each evening. The parents have divorced each other and not the children. Too many times the children become the pawns in the unfinished business between the parents.

If you are dealing with someone who is unreasonable, and we all are at some time or another, it is very difficult to get on with your life. There are legal and financial issues at every turn with which you must deal. As one wife said to me when I attempted to have her give up her battle for custody, "I couldn't live with myself if I put a price on my children." Sometimes, however, you need to know when to back off — for your own well being and for that of the children.

I mentioned that children were becoming more of a financial asset and an integral part of the legal annuity system. Let me elaborate. If you want to intimidate the other party, cause him to become somewhat unhinged emotionally, and get into a nightmare marathon with the courts, just question his suitability to be a parent, or even worse, accuse him of sexual abuse. In the past three years I have seen many such accusations. The court becomes involved, a variety of court-appointed guardians, psychologists and social workers are called, the divorce process is slowed down, child custody becomes an issue, the children are only allowed to be with the accused parent in the company of a therapist. It goes on and on. The financial costs are astronomical, the emotional costs are beyond calculation.

One client of mine has spent more than $50,000 trying to resolve visitation rights with his daughter over the past four years. The wife lives out of state and has made it her career to keep him away from his child. He is an heir to a sizable fortune and she has consistently demanded part of this inherited money. She has been receiving child support in excess of $5,000 a month for several years, plus private school costs. This woman was ten years his senior and he married her when he was 20. They stayed together for 10 years. He has totally financed college education for his two step-daughters by her prior marriage. We talked recently and he told me that he had been unable to see his daughter over the Christmas holidays. The trip had been arranged for two months, airline and hotel reservations had been made. But the wife decided the ten-year-old daughter did not want to see him. He has decided to withdraw from trying to see his daughter in an attempt to stop the drama his former wife insists on playing. Visitations will now be set up by his attorney in her state of residence.

This chapter is about getting organized, about becoming your own paralegal. To do this, you must become informed about the divorce process and what to expect, to know what financial stages you will be going through.

In Chapter Six you will learn about how to create the budget, both historically, for the temporary spousal maintenance period, and post-divorce according to the format provided by the courts through the financial affidavit or declaration you will be required to complete.

Earlier in this chapter, I gave you examples of people who have struggled during their divorce as well as the client who finally gave up the struggle years after his divorce was final. These people were at very different stages in the divorce process. As you will see, there are essentially five phases through which every divorcing person must pass. In each of the phases, there are both emotional and financial transitions which occur. The chart on the following page attempts to summarize these phases.

PRE-DIVORCE PLANNING — PREPARATION
This is the phase in which neither of you have filed for divorce. However, one of you is thinking about it. This is the time that you gather the information on the document roundup list provided in Chapter Three. You may also want to speak to an attorney about how to protect yourself legally during this time. You may never hire an attorney or get divorced.

I had an interesting case a few months ago when a client came to see me at the pre-divorce stage. I will call her Cynthia. She had been married for more than 15 years. It was a second marriage for her and her husband. Cynthia was 56 years old and her husband, Sam, was 58. Sam had four children by a prior marriage, all of whom worked in the family business. Cynthia lived in a lovely home out in the country and Sam was generous in providing her with a comfortable monthly budget for the household. They traveled together and generally were happy.

Cynthia felt insecure, however. Sam did not talk about the finances with her. She was concerned about his gambling. She had receipts showing that his gambling losses were more than $150,000 in the previous five years. Sam kept detailed receipts at home and had

THE INTEGRATED DIVORCE PROCESS
A Team Approach to Divorce Settlement: How to Use Your Experts

Pre-Divorce Planning:	**Phase I:**	**Phase II:**	**Phase III:**	**Post-Divorce Planning:**
PREPARATION	**DIVORCE INITIATION**	**ANALYSIS AND PLANNING**	**SETTLEMENT/ NEGOTIATION**	**IMPLEMENTATION**
Steps:	**Steps:**	**Steps:**	**Steps:**	**Steps:**
(1) Evaluate Client Needs	(1) Hire Attorney & Select Experts	(1) Valuation of Assets	(1) Negotiate Property Settlement	(1) Post-Divorce Planning
(2) Stabilize Client Situation - Financial - Psychological - Physical Aspects	(2) Research & Data Collection	(2) Identify Liabilities	(2) Allocate Income (Child Support/ Maintenance/ Wages)	(2) Income Tax Planning
(3) Plan: What Experts Will Be Needed?	(3) Prepare Financial Affidavit w/ Expert	(3) Determine Community& Separate Assets	(3) Rebuttal of Opposing Expert Report	(3) QDRO - Retirement Asset Transfers
	(4) File for divorce	(4) Begin Career Assessment & Educational Plans	(4) Finalize Parenting Plan	(4) Cash Flow Management
	(5) Request for Maintenance	(5) Create Post-Divorce Budget	(5) Court Testimony	(5) Implement & Monitor Investment Asset Allocation
	(6) Request for Child Support			(6) Career Implementation & Followup Plans on an On-going Basis
	(7) Formulate Parenting Plan			

Phases Encountered by Expert Witnesses:

DISCOVERY → **DEPOSITION** → **SETTLEMENT CONFERENCE** → **COURT TESTIMONY** → **DIVORCE SETTLEMENT**

been audited once by the IRS. She was concerned for her financial security. She wanted to know what their personal finances were like and how she would be protected if Sam died before she did.

I helped Cynthia gather documentation on their personal finances and I also prepared a budget establishing how the household funds had been spent and what it would take for her to live if she was divorced. She found the data gathering very empowering. She was finding out more and more about their finances and finally was able to get a copy of their most recent income tax return. The fact that Cynthia was asked to sign the tax return each year on April 15th, at the last minute, never having time to review the return is not unusual in many families.

I also recommended to Cynthia that she see a therapist. After six months of therapy, working with our office and an attorney, she decided not to go forward with the divorce. We did recommend, and the couple agreed, that they see an estate planning attorney.

Cynthia showed interest in her family's personal finances and is learning about her financial security as it is today and what Sam has planned if he pre-deceases Cynthia. Cynthia certainly does not have all of the answers, but has a better understanding of her legal rights if there is a divorce or death.

PHASE I

I believe there are three primary phases in the divorce process when it comes to dividing the property. I do not believe there are any shortcuts. Typically, division of property is the biggest financial decision many people will be part of in their entire lives. Always remember, it is your money. You need to have a strong, fundamental interest in the process. Work with someone who specializes in this area. Check his or her credentials, ask questions. In another chapter I've provided tips to help you choose advisors and experts in the divorce process. Read it carefully, be prepared.

Following, I'm going to discuss the first analysis phase of the divorce process. This is the point at which I prepared Cynthia's budget. In Chapter Six, I will discuss this phase in greater detail.

Step 1: Prepare an historical budget for your family.

From this information prepare your budget request for temporary spousal maintenance and child support.

Step 2: Create a temporary parenting plan.

Preparation of the financial affidavit is often the first formal budgeting process and cash flow management process the divorcing client faces. Preparation of the financial declaration is usually the first step after filing for the divorce. For many people this becomes an overwhelming task. You are asked to enumerate your income and expenses in great detail. To derive total income, wages and all other sources of income are listed. Next, you are asked to list your anticipated expenses in several categories provided by the standard financial declaration form. This data gathering and organizing of the financial information for the divorce takes time.

A financial planner can provide special expertise at this phase. The numbers which the client is about to provide for temporary spousal maintenance will be those upon which she must rely for income for a long time, often up to a year until the divorce is settled, or until there is a court decision. I believe this first phase of the divorce process is critical for the client's financial and emotional well being. This year prior to the final divorce decree will be filled with compromises about the parenting plan, custody of the children, valuation and division of assets, payment of legal and expert fees. All of these compromises and decisions will have a money counterpart. Money is always a major issue in a divorce. No one understands the numbers about living expenses better than the person living her life. It is your money, and there will be a strong need to protect it. The spending habits of each of the divorcing spouses will be under microscope. There will be accusations and comments about each party's spending habits during the marriage. Men, women, money and relationships are a topic for another article or book. However, in most relationships one person is perceived to be the dominant spender and the other party less active, but only as a question of degree. Two lifestyles typically cost more in separately maintained households.

Financial planners are used by the attorneys to track the inflow and outflow of money into bank checking and savings accounts. I work with clients to gather the information and organize the data so that the attorney can use the information in his or her negotiations as it relates to the sharing of income or the misuse of community funds in preparation for a divorce. Once all the data has been entered, I am able to produce many different reports. For example, the attorney may want to segregate children's expenses by child, as one child may be attending college in a few months and his expenses need to be separated from the ongoing budget for the family. An historical budget also will have expenses for both of the spouses. These expenses can be segregated by individual and by category, such as clothing, travel, entertainment. If there has been movement of funds in preparation for the divorce these transfers are readily apparent. But the most important outcome of this step in the divorce process is that the client and attorney receive an accurate, comprehensive summary of how the couple spent their money. Both attorneys can use this information for future budgeting for their clients. Men often are not aware of how the money is spent inside the home, particularly when it comes to the children's expenses. They see their salary being deposited to the account and then everyone starts spending. The detailed budget report can be very enlightening for both of the people who are divorcing. One observation I can make as a result of specializing in the divorce planning arena is that the person who has the income usually wants to keep as much of it as possible.

The two most common mistakes I see in the historical budget analysis are that the client provides an incomplete summary of the expenses and the information is disorganized. The client leaves expenses out and later on in the divorce process complains that she does not have enough money. If the client is called in for a deposition by her spouse's attorney, she may be unable to explain where her numbers have come from. Judges are very busy. As a result, the more detailed and accurate the information you provide in a hearing, the better results you can expect. Clients who have adequate cash flow tend to be much easier to work with than the client who is always worrying about the next dollar she must spend and where it is coming from.

An increasing number of clients use the financial planner in the construction of the historical budget. Since many women are too passive during this pre-divorce stage and regret their lack of organization later in the divorce process, you can see it is essential to do it comprehensively from the beginning. Also, the process gives the client control, understanding and a sense of organization about her past and her anticipated future.

Then, I review the historical spending patterns, and calculate the net monthly income available for child support or maintenance. There are always issues when the chief breadwinner is one who takes a draw or minimum salary from his business and takes bonuses for a substantial portion of the annual income. Another problem arises with the business owner who has the business paying for expenses used to supplement the family lifestyle. Normally, the spouses agree to share the income derived partially from the business in some acceptable manner. Any new bonuses earned post-separation are generally considered to be the separate property of the person earning the money.

I recently worked with a client whose husband moved to a new job in another state over a weekend, notifying her of his plans as he was packing to leave. He thought everything would remain the same at home: she would wait for his "indefinite" return. She filed for divorce one month later when he returned home for a visit. In his absence she was able to review their finances in great detail. More than $30,000 had disappeared from the sale of their residence and the purchase of a new house in the previous year.

She found other irregularities in the spending and deposits in their personal checking accounts during the previous few months. She would never have discovered the missing money if she hadn't inspected the bank statements, checking and savings, cash withdrawals and the brokerage statements. Up to her investigation, the wife had only handled the household budget.

She also had commingled her inheritance and separate funds over the past year with her husband and his name was on the brokerage account where her separate funds were held. When she tried to remove her husband's name, she found she couldn't without his signature and he refused. Immediately she had a restraining order placed on this account and several others. Money is often in motion before one party files for divorce from the other.

PHASE II

The various states differ somewhat on marital property laws, however, the three concepts discussed will help you with some background information.

Equitable Distribution: Most states have adopted this system, whereby courts are given the discretionary power to divide marital property in a fair and equitable manner. Decisions are based on the ages of the spouses, their employment, length of marriage and income. There can be wide variation in the law's interpretation. This concept draws from both common law and community property law. Property acquired during a marriage is regarded as marital property regardless of which spouse holds the title and the court may divide such marital property proportionately.

Common Law: This concept is based on the old English legal system in which a wife's real property (land plus its buildings, crops, rents, etc.) is transferred in total to the husband at the moment of marriage. Present day interpretation of common law recognizes property held in both spouses names as owned jointly. Property with title in one name can be sold or given away without the other spouse's consent. A problem arises if a wife does not work outside the home and all the property is held in the husband's name. The court can regard the husband as the sole owner. Only three states, Mississippi, South Carolina, and West Virginia, retain vestiges of common law.

Community Property: Property acquired during the marriage is owned 50/50 by spouses, even if the title is in one name only. The basic premise is that the labors of both parties are recognized as contributing to acquiring marriage assets. To keep a specific property item in separate ownership it must be kept separate (not commingled with the community [marital] property). Nine states: Texas, Louisiana, New Mexico, Arizona, California, Nevada, Idaho, Wisconsin and Washington use some form of this law.

WHAT ARE THE FOUR BASIC WAYS OF OWNING PROPERTY?

Joint tenancy: You both own half, but you cannot will your half to anyone other than your partner who automatically inherits your portion when you die.

Tenancy in common: You own half, and you can will your portion to whomever you like.

Tenancy by entirety: In separate property states only, this form of ownership works like a joint tenancy, but is reserved for married people exclusively.

Community property: A special form of ownership for married persons in community property states.

This stage of the divorce is when you should do research on how you own your property in the state in which you reside. There may be a difference between how you think you own property and how it is actually registered. You may think you have separate property which you received in an inheritance — however, if you have registered this inheritance in a joint account at a brokerage house you may have some difficulty holding to the separate property notion. I have a case currently in process where this is an issue. There is a restraining order on this account requiring that both husband and wife need to agree and sign for any cash withdrawals. The wife continues to manage the investments as she has done in the past. The husband is arguing that she gifted her inheritance of some $200,000 into the community when she put his name on the account. The attorneys will give their arguments before the judge to determine the ultimate division of this property in the divorce property settlement.

In another case two years ago the woman had received an inheritance of $100,000. Initially, she kept the funds separate. Then the husband and wife saw an estate planning attorney who had them sign a community property agreement as part of their estate plan. This document renamed everything they owned presently, in the past, and in the future to be community property. This case went to trial and I will never forget the tough questioning my client faced from the husband's attorney in the courtroom.

My client had opened a joint brokerage and credit union account with her husband several months after receiving her inheritance. She told the judge that her husband had encouraged her to do this, as his credit union had a better interest rate than hers. She could not open an account without his name on the account. This was the Boeing Credit Union. The judge ruled that the inheritance had been commingled and would be divided with the remainder of the marital assets. My client was very bitter about this result.

She felt betrayed by the system, by her estate planning attorney for recommending the community property agreement, and by the credit union and brokerage house for not sufficiently explaining to her the new account form she had signed and the implications if there was divorce or death. Most of all, this professional woman blamed herself for not doing her own research. Her husband earned eight times her income as a physician. During this marriage, her pattern with him was to give in to his requests for the sake of the children and to maintain her married status in the community … "economic bondage."

Financially, he had made some poor investments in limited partnerships over the prior ten years — one investment cost them more than $100,000 in back taxes, and they had to mortgage their home to pay off the debt.

WHAT KIND OF PROPERTY DO I DIVIDE IN A PROPERTY SETTLEMENT?

There are three kinds of property to be divided: *real property which consists of land and the buildings (improvements) on it, tangible property* such as cars, jewelry, furniture and antiques, and *intangible personal property* such as bank accounts, stock and bonds, vested pensions, life insurance, annuities, money market accounts, and retirement accounts.

Before you agree to keep one asset over the other you should keep a record of the date and amount the asset was acquired, the tax basis of the asset, potential for sale, current market value and the value at date of separation. Know what your state laws say about property.

For example, do you live or have you lived in a community property state? Have you ever signed a separate property or community property agreement?

Separate property is:
- What you bring into the marriage.
- What you inherit during the marriage.
- What you receive during the marriage as a gift.

To keep it separate you must not commingle the separate assets into a joint account or sign a community property agreement which specifies that everything you have now and in the future is joint property — ours. Assuming you have not signed a community property agreement or commingled the assets, the following are examples of separate property:

Assume your aunt died and left you $50,000. If you put the money into an account with your name only and do not commingle the funds, then they can continue to be viewed as your separate property. On your income tax return where you list interest and dividend income or capital gains, put your initials beside listed separate property income.

Another example might be a gift you received from your grandmother of $10,000 and the check was made out to you and not to you and your spouse. If you put the funds into a separate account, these funds remain separate. Beware if you are buying a house with your separate assets and then funding the payments with joint income. You will need to trace the contribution of separate funds with written documentation and records. You may be converting part of your separate assets to marital property. See an attorney for an opinion on these matters.

Marital property is any property acquired during the marriage no matter whose name is on it, and in many states the increase in value of separate property can be deemed to be a marital asset. Again, this should be discussed with your attorney. A financial planner can work with you to trace assets over a long-term marriage and create a spreadsheet with documentation to support your claim. It is up to the person who has the claim of separate property to prove that it is in fact separate property.

CAREERS AS A FINANCIAL ASSET

Career assets can be very important in a traditional marriage where the wife has stayed home and raised the children or worked part-time helping the spouse to receive an education. The spouse, or wife in this instance, is oftentimes called a "displaced homemaker." There are courses at community colleges and career experts who work to counsel women in this situation. If you are in this category, seek help as soon as possible to determine your rights and a course of action. Long-term maintenance is almost impossible to receive out of a mid-term (10-25 year) marriage in most states.

Career assets can include education or training, the license or degree you have, job experience, seniority, life insurance, health insurance, disability insurance, unemployment, social security, paid sick leave, vacation time, present value of defined benefit pension plans, retirement plans, and a network of professional contacts and goodwill in a business.

PHASE III

This is the phase that requires a budget for the client in his or her post-divorce lifestyle. The income components will be made up of wages, investment income, spousal maintenance, child support, income from separate property, and a property settlement note if applicable. The expenses will be projected based on this future lifestyle. Many times clients will be selling a residence and purchasing a more cost-effective home. The monthly costs of maintaining a home, real estate taxes, mortgage costs and the need for a smaller space to maintain are usually factors that go into this change in lifestyle. The post-divorce budget reflects the changes in house and utility expenses. Likewise, depending on the parenting plan and the amount of time each parent has the children, the expenses for them are shared so that one party does not pay more than her share of child support to the custodial parent. In the case of a displaced homemaker, there could be a need for increased child care expenses while the parent is attending school and preparing to re-enter the job market. You may be pre-qualifying for a mortgage, looking at an alternative piece of real estate to buy as a residence, and/or fixing up your current residence for resale.

Phase III is the time in which the property settlement is negotiated, mediated, arbitrated or litigated, or subjected to a combination of these settlement procedures. The outcome from this phase is the final divorce decree, property settlement agreement, and permanent parenting plan. The child support is set and, if applicable, the spousal maintenance terms are set. At the end of this phase you are divorced and starting the *first day of the rest of your life* as a single person. I am seeing more and more settlements where the divorcing spouses are making compromises regarding the sharing of assets, income and the payment of expenses. Rather than going into court, they are going into settlement conferences or mediation.

An increasingly popular dispute resolution choice for negotiations in our local area is JAMS (Judicial Arbitration and Mediation Services). It is a private forum for the resolution of civil disputes offering its services through a panel of retired trial and appellate court judges and justices. The firm was founded in 1979. You can have a retired judge work with you and your spouse and your attorneys to reach a dispute resolution to your divorce. You have to agree that the property settlement, if agreed upon, will be binding. You and your attorney can select the judge and select a mutually convenient time to settle the dispute. This is typically in time for you to go to trial if you do not come to some agreement. You will do the preparation for a trial and can have your experts come to the mediation session. Typically, each attorney and client meet in a separate room and the judge goes back and forth between the parties attempting to negotiate and mediate a settlement. This process is expensive. However, compared to the costs of going to trial it is often cost effective.

There are several alternative dispute resolution methods which allow you to own your own compromises. The setting for these compromises is much more pleasant than in a courtroom. Check for qualified mediators in your area using many of the same questions outlined on page 37. You can cry, scream and negotiate in a private setting. The facilities afford the clients privacy and confidentiality.

I work very closely with the attorney and client during these negotiations. I do short- and long-term cash flow projections to determine the economic impact of various property settlement proposals. I help the client and attorney structure the property settlement proposal presented to the mediator. I have done the work on the future budget and the expenses in the new lifestyle. A career and education plan has been proposed with the costs and time frame determined by the career counselor. I know what current sources of income are available to be shared by the divorcing clients and have a proposal as to how the income and assets can be divided.

Using computer models, I have the ability to show the client and attorney how the property settlement proposals provided by each side financially impact my client. I am able to help all the parties involved in the divorce see the economic impact today and in the future of various property settlement proposals. I am able to provide an integrated and comprehensive analysis of this new lifestyle, a tax and cash flow analysis that incorporates income from all sources. These include wages, bonuses, investment income, maintenance, child support, settlement notes, pension, social security and IRA distributions, less expenses to include living expenses, college education costs for the spouse and/or children, private school education, and income taxes.

From this cash flow analysis I am able to show where both parties are likely to be after five to ten years with respect to their net worth as well as a yearly estimates of taxes and net cash flow. This analysis plots where there are shortages or a requirement for additional maintenance. It may show that there is not sufficient income to provide the maintenance requested, and the sale of an asset may be necessary as well as reduction in the standard of living for both parties. The cash flow spreadsheet can be your guide as to exactly what you are giving up or getting. It is important that this work be done for both spouses. I don't believe a property settlement proposal should be exclusively analyzed for just one of the parties. However, this philosophy is not shared by all attorneys or financial planners. Many of them prefer not to get into this part of the analysis because it is necessary to deal with projections and assumptions. It is my belief that this work is essential to understanding and accepting your property settlement.

In each of my financial models I will show you what your short-
and long-term cash flow, income tax and net worth will look like with
alternative property settlement proposals. You will have decision-
making models to apply to your new life. After you are divorced, we
then go into the post-divorce planning. I have devoted an entire chapter
in the book to this phase of your divorce process.

A trend I have been experiencing working with attorneys is a
request that I attend the settlement meetings or be available to revise
spreadsheets during the settlement conference. More judges and mediation attorneys are calling now to discuss how one of their recommendations would change the financial situation for one of the parties. I am also
being called to discuss the income tax impact of various settlements as
they relate to not just one, but both of the parties divorcing. Samples of
the models are provided in the case studies in subsequent chapters.
Below is an example of a couple with some special circumstances in
which I was able to directly assist in the negotiated property settlement.

Charles and Marian have been married 22 years. He is a successful physician earning $450,000 per year. Marian taught school for
the first two years of their marriage after Charles was out of medical
school and starting his practice. They have three children, ages 6, 12,
and 16. The practice has been valued at $550,000; they own a residence
valued at $600,000 with a $300,000 current mortgage balance. The
retirement assets consist of $325,000 held in Charles's profit-sharing
plan, and $12,000 in IRAs in Marian's name. They own two 1991 auto-
mobiles free and clear and of equal value. Their personal property is
valued at $125,000 including antiques, shop tools, jewelry and furs.
They have $50,000 in a brokerage account of stocks and municipal
bonds, and $25,000 in savings accounts. Their children attend private
schools and the annual cost is $18,000 per year for their education. Both
parents would like to continue to send the children to a private school.

Marian has gone through career counseling and has decided
she would like to return to school to update her teaching credentials
and complete her masters degree. This would take two years to complete
and then she would look for a job. She anticipates her starting salary will
be $32,000 per year. Charles and Marian are each 46 years old. Both
parents are interested in being involved with the raising of the children.

Charles has hired a nanny for the children when they are with him, about 40 percent of the time presently. Marian wants to attend school part-time and teach part-time until the youngest child is in middle school, about six years. Marian would like to be the custodial parent and is concerned that the children need to have one home base.

Charles is concerned about national health care proposals being considered by the Congress and is predicting a 20 percent reduction in his income. Both parties would like to have the primary residence. Charles has a net income of $18,000 per month after he pays his taxes, his payment to buy into the medical practice, the children's private school tuition and his $30,000 annual pension contribution. Before the separation, Charles and Marian were spending $15,000 per month on their living expenses. They have a 15-year mortgage and their principal and interest payments are $3,900 per month.

This separation finds both of them feeling strapped for cash. Arguments have already begun as to how the net income should be shared. I have been asked to come up with the historical spending pattern and determine Marian's expenses during the separation. I will help Marian create a realistic budget and cash control system for the upcoming year. Both Charles and Marian face a lifestyle change. Marian is very emotional and frightened about her financial security. Charles believes Marian does not manage money wisely and is sending Marian $3,000 per month after paying the mortgage and children's tuition. Marian is struggling to make ends meet. She is preparing to make a motion for temporary support and child support. There are attorney fees, expert witness fees and other professional fees to pay, including money for the financial planner, accountant, business valuator, career counselor, and the psychologist she and the children are seeing. Custody of the children is becoming an issue and a court evaluator has also been hired to provide a recommendation for primary custody of the children. We have a financial and emotional minefield. Getting through this minefield is much easier when both parties can see the reality of their former spending habits, the new financial shape of things during separation, and the financial portents for the future based on cash flow. Providing this information is what makes pre-divorce planning so effective, aiding in the difficult emotional transition.

POST-DIVORCE PLANNING

Post-divorce planning is the phase in which a financial planner applies your property settlement to your life. I create a personal and realistic cash control system for the client. I develop a strategy to pay off the legal expenses of the divorce, taking into account cash flow and income tax considerations.

If assets are being transferred between the divorcing spouses I help to get these assets re-registered. Typically, I give the client form letters to send out for the change of ownership and tell her about the procedures. The client can take care of many of these transfers and save herself money. If a Qualified Domestic Relations Order (QDRO) needs to be administered, I help the client select the new custodian for the retirement assets and arrange for the transfer of the assets. These assets need to be transferred with no check being sent to the client, thereby preventing an immediate income tax liability. Specific planning ideas will be shared in another chapter. Post-divorce planning is a critical and vulnerable time for the woman. She will need a financial plan to get her under way properly as a single person. Post-divorce is also the time to systematically address each of the elements of the financial plan.

I wish I could tell women that their financial worries are over in the post-divorce phase. Too often this is not the case. If your property settlement has been achieved with stress, volatility, lack of cooperation, and costly legal maneuvers it probably will continue in this vein and enforcement will be your next hurdle. By now both you and your attorney are ready to have your case over and done with. As a matter of fact, after the divorce many attorneys all but drop out of the process. There are no trial dates facing them. But sometimes you will have to go back to court for interpretation or enforcement — more time and money. The struggles in Phase I, II and III are usually strong indicators of what is ahead. That is why in Phase III you want to be sure that your final property settlement agreement is as detailed as possible leaving little for interpretation and protest.

By following the recommendations listed you can significantly reduce the cost of your divorce.

CHECKLIST FOR REDUCING THE COST OF YOUR OWN DIVORCE

1. Read about divorce and the divorce process in your state. Go to the library or bookstore and gather information.
2. Interview at least three attorneys to represent you.
3. Have an asset and liability as well as income and loss statement available when you visit the attorney. Have questions ready to ask your attorney. Tell the attorney your story first. See if there is a comfortable and trusting relationship possible. Trust your instincts.
4. Gather your documents and be organized. See Document Roundup on page 77.
5. Have date of marriage, history of where you have lived, birth dates for everyone in the family, and a brief history of the marriage, your moves, employment history, etc.
6. What are your major concerns about the divorce process? List them for yourself.
7. Do you want the divorce? Why or why not? Be prepared to answer this question.

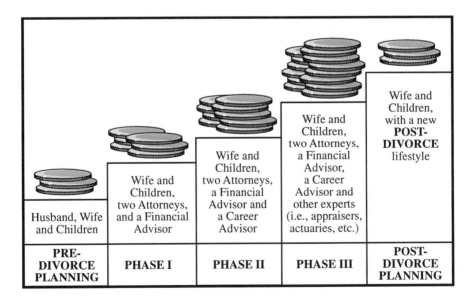

PRE-DIVORCE PLANNING	PHASE I	PHASE II	PHASE III	POST-DIVORCE PLANNING
Husband, Wife and Children	Wife and Children, two Attorneys, and a Financial Advisor	Wife and Children, two Attorneys, a Financial Advisor and a Career Advisor	Wife and Children, two Attorneys, a Financial Advisor, a Career Advisor and other experts (i.e., appraisers, actuaries, etc.)	Wife and Children, with a new POST-DIVORCE lifestyle

Getting a divorce is like going up an escalator. If one party wants it, you can bet you will eventually be divorced. An escalator has a series of steps. You can walk up the steps or stand still. Either way, you will have to get off of the escalator in a limited amount of time, willingly or unwillingly.

My role is to provide tools to help you understand and take control of each step in your divorce process so that when you go off the escalator it is under your own control. It is essential that you understand the financial aspects of the divorce and can make your own compromises. If you can't negotiate, the courts will settle it for you. But this is certainly better than living under the Napoleonic Code in which women had few civil rights. Still, court is not the best place to be.

If a client comes to me before either she or her spouse has filed, but is contemplating divorce, I recommend that she gather the information displayed on the document round up list at the end of this chapter. Frankly, anyone who is in a marriage which she regards as a partnership would be well served to know the location of this information and to understand it. Get informed, whichever way you can. Some women I've known photocopy records long before they file for a divorce, or at the first sign of trouble.

It is not unusual to see clients separate and come back together before filing for a divorce. Often, they are attempting to reconcile. This is an excellent time to get more knowledge of your finances. If your spouse doesn't want to share, you should put yourself on notice to learn everything you can about your joint assets.

I should point out something that seems obvious, but is often overlooked by divorcing women — how money was acquired in your marriage and your expectation of financial support after the marriage.

Remember, there have always been three primary ways to achieve wealth in our society. You can work for your money, marry and participate in jointly creating wealth, or inherit wealth. All three of these methods of achieving wealth become significant when you are getting a divorce and attempting to win a fair and equitable division of assets, liabilities and income. Our courts do not support long-term maintenance for women. Let me repeat that: Our courts have not, do not, and probably will not support long-term maintenance for spouses who are getting a divorce. The only bright light is a trend toward longer terms of maintenance if an economic need can be demonstrated. In Washington, maintenance can be awarded to rehabilitate, or can be deemed compensatory. Whenever possible, however, I recommend obtaining cash or assets up front as an offset against maintenance — a sure thing versus a promise to pay which could be defaulted.

I mentioned trends above. We really have three classes of marriage and I will be discussing financial strategies for each group throughout the book. These classes are short-term marriages, under 10 years; mid-term marriages, 10 to 25 years; and long-term marriages, over 25 years. One of the toughest cases to work with is the mid-term marriage. Typically, the clients are in their forties, the children are five to fifteen years old, the woman has stayed home with the children and the husband earns the majority, if not all, of the family income. The house and a pension or profit-sharing plan are the major assets. These marriages represent the success of the consumer years, so the couples have not created a lot of savings. Accumulation usually starts happening in the late forties and fifties. I'll be demonstrating the problems in mid-term marriage divorces later in the book.

Whatever term your marriage is when divorce comes up, the document roundup is very important for you.

DOCUMENT ROUNDUP

Following is the list I promised. Do yourself (and your attorney) an enormous favor and save yourself money by assembling the following for your first data gathering appointment: (Besides copying account numbers, make copies of the actual statements; it makes tracking and verification easier.)

Document Roundup List
1. Federal income tax returns for the last three to five years.
2. Copies of W-2 statements for each tax return.
3. Last three pay stubs for both spouses that show deductions from gross pay.

4. Your current check register and bank statements for the past year.
5. The most recent annual statement of pension or retirement benefits furnished for each spouse. Three years would be better.
6. Savings passbooks, now and for the prior year.
7. Stock brokerage account statements. The current statement and the prior year-end statement for the past two years.
8. Money market fund statements, current and past two years' endings statements.
9. Certificates of deposit, treasury bills and the like.
10. A list of the contents in your safety deposit box.
11. A copy of your current will.
12. A copy of any community, separate property or pre-nuptial agreements.
13. Financial statements given to a banking institution in connection with a recent loan application (within the last two years).
14. Monthly or quarterly bank statements for all checking and savings accounts.
15. Credit card statements for the last two years. American Express and many gold cards now offer an annual recap of spending for members.
16. The history of the purchase of your current home; closing documents, a list of improvements, current mortgage information, Form 2119 from your income tax return if you deferred the gain from a prior home into the current home. This Form 2119 (sale of the primary residence) would have been filed with your income tax return in the year you sold the prior home and purchased your current home.
17. Warranty deeds, contracts, title insurance and other documents establishing ownership to real estate and your residence.
18. Title certificates and registration statements for boats, cars, recreational vehicles, trucks.
19. Property and casualty insurance premiums for all of your homeowner and auto insurance broken out by the item being insured. Also get information on any personal umbrella liability insurance you might have. Get the name and the phone number of your insurance agent.

20. Get copies of any life or disability insurance policies on each member of the family. What are the premiums by policy? When are they due, and how are they paid? Do the same for health insurance policies.

21. If a business or businesses are owned, the most recent income tax return, annual profit and loss statement, and most current monthly and quarterly profit and loss statements. Go back at least three years if possible.

22. List all current debts, monthly payments, interest rate and reason for the debt.

23. Current property tax statements on any real estate owned.

24. Each employer's annual statement describing the corporate benefits package including medical/life insurance benefits, balances and loans on 401(k) plans, pension summaries, deferred compensation balances and terms, stock options exercised and non-exercised (find out what restrictions there are on any of these stock options as far as ownership, exercising, taxation).

25. Do you think either of you will have an inheritance coming to you? Is there one in process? Are there any side loans with family members? Provide information.

26. Do your children have funds set aside in trusts for college education? Provide statements, if so. Who provided these funds, where are they located, who is the trustee or custodian on these accounts?

27. Has there been any unusual spending or movement of funds which you have noticed in the past two years? If so, list what you know and the history surrounding any transactions.

28. Is there another person involved in the divorce, a boyfriend or girlfriend? Have community finances been diverted to this account? Provide as much of a history as you can.

29. Has there been a history of drug, alcohol or sexual abuse? Do you have documentation and dates of treatment?

30. Are you receiving money from other family members to help you financially? If so, please describe.

31. How long have you been separated? Are you separated? Do you want to stay in the house for now? Has anyone filed at this time? Does the other party have an attorney?

32. What are the current financial arrangements with your children or any relatives? Please describe.
33. Are either of you in school? Did either of you get a degree during your marriage? Did you live together before marrying? What separate financial assets did either of you bring into the marriage? Please describe.
34. Provide complete K-1 reports on any limited partnerships you may own. The complete K-1 is not filed with your annual income tax return. Also gather any depreciation schedules which are being used on your current income tax returns.

Make more than one copy of this information. Make a notebook for yourself, your attorney and ultimately for your financial planner. As you meet with experts, you can copy the documents each will require. There will be some duplication.

One client I had effectively kept this information on notecards. As she gathered additional information, she added it to her summary on separate notecards. She and her husband owned several pieces of real estate, had loans, boats, and other assets, and this method of record-keeping kept everything organized and vital information readily accessible.

Be organized. You will pay for your own disorganization. You also want your attorney and experts to be organized and efficient with the massive amount of paperwork which is heading their way. You are attempting to unwind the family "marriage" business relationship, and you are doing it during a time of intense emotion. This organization will help you take control. Remember when I described the divorce process being like a ride up an escalator? You will go off the divorce escalator eventually. You can walk up the steps methodically, or you can stand still and wait to be "dumped off." I believe if you can take control of your divorce process easily, one step at a time, you will be better prepared for that final step: the actual divorce. In our area you are usually given a court date one year from your filing date. Your attorney can provide you with a list of important dates for each of you to be aware of during the year ahead. Be sure you also have this list of dates and give a copy to your experts. After all, you are creating a professional team of experts to help you through the divorce process.

No one says you have to rush into getting the divorce. You may want a legal separation. Know what this entails legally. Or maybe you don't want to do anything at all for the time being, only gather information. People do reconcile, sometimes for good. Often reconciliation is not successful and divorce is the final outcome. The objective for you to keep in mind is to survive the divorce with as much of your financial world intact as you can preserve, so that you can construct a solid new financial future for yourself.

CHAPTER SIX

THE BUDGET PROCESS

Never ask of money spent
Where the spender thinks it went.
Nobody was ever meant
To remember or invent
What he did with every cent.
— *Robert Frost*

The budget process — and how to prepare the following:
   A. Historical family budget
   B. Temporary family budget

In this chapter I'm going to present a case history of a divorced woman and how I helped her create an historical, temporary and post-divorce budget. This information is a how-to approach for every woman in divorce who wishes to conserve her assets and create a financial recovery.

Judith Jessup is a 43-year-old divorcing mother with two children. We have met three times, and each time I hear about how her dwindling savings account is down to nearly nothing in order to meet the family's current living expenses. When she presented her proposed temporary budget to the court three months ago on the financial declaration, she admitted she "estimated" her projected expenses. Each day she finds expenses she had not anticipated in her budget. Now she realizes the importance of detailed information.

Her attorney told her to make preliminary estimates and they would make adjustments later. Later has arrived for Judith. She has paid a retainer to her career specialist, additional attorney fees and now she is seeing me. She feels a lot of financial pressure and does not want to charge more to her credit cards to finance her divorce. She did not want the divorce, but her estranged husband, Jake, became emotionally involved with another woman and wants his freedom.

Judith went to an attorney only after she had been served divorce papers. She had a limited amount of time to respond and Jake had assured her that he would take care of her and the children. It is apparent now that neither of them truly understood what this meant in the short and long term. Based on the financial declaration which Judith was required to submit to the courts, she required $3,000 per month in maintenance and $1,500 in child support. On the surface these amounts seemed to be sufficient, however, when she started reviewing the numbers more carefully and began actually paying out, she discovered there was inadequate cash flow.

Judith arrived in my office feeling stressed, out of control financially and in a panic mode. She has borrowed money from her parents to make ends meet the past month, but she doesn't want to ask them for more. Her parents live comfortably but can't support her and the children. Jake doesn't want to talk with her. He feels she is being too emotional and won't listen to any of her financial concerns. He thinks she should tighten her belt and get on with her life. Meanwhile, her attorney has asked her to gather financial information for a preliminary settlement conference. The children are seeing a therapist and are not handling the divorce very easily. Their grades have dropped in school and they do not want to visit their father with his new girlfriend.

Judith's plight is not unusual. In an ideal situation, the client comes to see me pre-divorce and we complete the document roundup and gather all the financial records. We complete the budget documentation and the accompanying reports, and we have everything ready for the first hearing on temporary maintenance and child support. We go into this first court session well organized. I admit that most of my divorcing clients underestimate their true expenses.

It is still nine months before Judith has a trial date. She has 270 days and nights of daily living before the absolute finalization of her divorce. My goal is to help her regain her power in the divorce proceeding. We will start with the budgeting process and help her prepare a motion for reconsideration. When we started, Jake was keeping 53 percent of the family's discretionary income. He was taking care of himself, while she was managing the house and children, a household of three receiving less than half of the net family income.

I like to use an ascending staircase as a comparison to help clients understand the process of going through a divorce. With a staircase in mind, be ready to rise to the challenge of each step as it occurs. I am going to show you, step by step, how to create a more detailed comprehensive budget you can use from the beginning to the end of your divorce process. This budget plan will be the foundation of your cash control system and will take you through the period of temporary spousal   maintenance and into your post-divorce budget, which will probably include a maintenance award into the future transitional years until your career goals are realized. I have found that if you thoroughly understand your own budget numbers it is much easier to make the appropriate financial compromises when you need to. This basic information will give you the control you need to be an active participant in your own settlement negotiations.

With the tools I'll give you, you'll be able to argue for a fair and equitable divorce settlement with the legal guidance of your attorney, rather than responding emotionally. Remember, the court system in not interested in how you feel, only in facts. This is one area where documentation and good record-keeping skills can work in your favor. You will probably be surprised by what you find out about yourself and your marriage partner. This is especially true in the discovery of expenses involving a husband's girlfriend. You will be able to trace any "unusual" transactions in the pervious year. Be prepared to become your own "Sherlock" about your family finances.

This is the time to step up and admit if you have spent discretionary funds freely for clothes or personal expenses in the past. You were married and it is assumed that you were partners and equally responsible for your lifestyle. Don't hide expenses. Honesty is the best defense. What you can do, however, is identify those areas in which you are suggesting changes in your temporary and post-divorce budgets based on your change in circumstances. This is where you want to appear reasonable and realistic about your finances.

The system works both ways. Usually men come into these budget hearings with even less documentation and detail for their living expenses. It can be very effective for you to have your expenses and income placed side by side with his showing what both of you anticipate spending during the period of separation and in your post-divorce lifestyle. Let's get started with Judith so you can see how this budget process works in a real life situation.

In this chapter, we will discuss the how and why of the budget process as it applies to the temporary maintenance order. In a subsequent chapter, I will focus on Judith's case using my sample report as the basis for discussion. The preparation of the temporary budget is typically the first step in planning a fair and equitable settlement.

Time period: two weeks to one month depending on your involvement and organization.

BUDGETING SESSION 1

The first time I meet with someone, I like to get to know her or him. With Judith, I spent nearly a half hour talking about her feelings and about her current situation. More often than not, however, this dialogue provides me with some valuable insights about the spending patterns of the household. Judith is at the point of having a temporary maintenance order in place which is severely inadequate based on her true financial needs, especially in the short term. It is not indicative of anything other than a gross misrepresentation of her married lifestyle. Even in the short term it is important to be conscious of goals, so we discuss hers, both short and long-term.

After the meeting, she immediately begins to gather as many financial documents as she can — bank and credit card statements, money market accounts, and anything else which shows how she spent money in maintaining the household. It is time for Judith and Jake to see how much was really spent.

I look at the historical spending for a least one year prior to separation. I then, from the available data, select one or more years as my baseline for establishing the historical spending pattern for the family unit. All bank checking and savings account statements, money market accounts, and credit card statements are entered into a budgeting computer program. I have found the Microsoft Money program provides the maximum flexibility for the type of reports that I need to generate. When I look at the bank statements I am establishing the source of all funds deposited into the checking or savings account. Then I categorize and code all of the checks written out of the account into the expense categories provided on the financial declaration form. The list on the following page summarizes these codes as they are listed on the financial declaration.

In Chapter Five, I reviewed the steps in the preparation of the historical budget so that the benefits to both parties, and to both attorneys were apparent. Judith could certainly see the benefit of having more detailed information in both preparing the budget and in justifying proposed expenses. The process begins with Judith providing me with data, usually beginning with checking account statements. An associate inputs each of the checking transactions (deposits, checks, fees, interest earned) as they appear on the statements. While this occurs, Judith assigns the budget codes (below) to each transaction on her credit card statements. Where possible, she determines to whom each transaction applies. For instance, was a clothing purchase for the children applicable to Judith or Jake?

BUDGETING SESSION 2

By the time Judith completes her credit card statements, the majority of the checking statements will have been data entered. The checking information, however, is still incomplete, since the payees and budget codes for each check are still unknown. A little honesty will certainly make the next step easier. Judith had been pretty good about maintaining her check register, but she occasionally neglected to write

INCOME CATEGORIES

3.1   GROSS MONTHLY INCOME
   a.   Wages & Salaries
   b.   Interest & Dividend Income
   c.   Business Income
   d.   Maintenance, Other Rel.
   e.   Other Income (Specify)
3.2   MONTHLY DEDUCTIONS
   a.   Income Taxes
   b.   FICA/Self-Employ. Taxes
   c.   State Industrial Ins. Ded.
   d.   Mandatory Union/Prof. Dues
   e.   Pension Plan Payments
   f.   Spousal Maintenance Paid
   g.   Normal Business Expenses

3.3   MISCELLANEOUS INCOME
   a.   Child Support, Other Rel.
   b.   Cash Value ofLife Insurance
   c.   Other (Specify)

EXPENSE CATEGORIES

5.1   HOUSING
   1.   Mortgage/Rent
   2.   Improvements
   3.   Furniture/Appliances
   4.   Taxes & Insurance
   5.   Yard Care & House Repair
5.2   UTILITIES
   1.   Heat (Gas & Oil)
   2.   Electricity
   3.   Water, Sewer, Garbage
   4.   Telephone
   5.   Cable
   6.   Other (Specify)
5.3   FOOD & SUPPLIES
   1.   Food for "X" Persons
   2.   Supplies
   3.   Meals Eaten Out
   4.   Other (Specify)
5.4   CHILDREN
   1.   Day-Care/Babysitting
   2.   Clothing
   3.   Tuition (if any)
   4.   Other Child Related Exp.

5.5   TRANSPORTATION
   1.   Vehicle Payments or Lease
   2.   Vehicle Insurance &
        License
   3.   Vehicle Gas, Oil, Maint.
   4.   Parking
   5.   Other (Specify)
5.6   HEALTH CARE
   1.   Insurance
   2.   Unins. Dental, Ortho., Med.
   3.   Other (Specify)
   4.   Prescriptive Drugs
5.7   PERSONAL EXPENSES
   1.   Clothing
   2.   Hair Care/Pers. Care Exp.
   3.   Clubs & Recreation
   4.   Education
   5.   Books, Newspapers, Mag.
   6.   Gifts
   7.   Other (Specify)
5.8   MISCELLANEOUS
   1.   Life Insurance
   2.   Other (Specify)
   3.   Other: Federal Taxes

down the whole payee, substituting neat little acronyms like "M.J.Sit.," which, 11 months later, even she couldn't place as "Michelle J---, Babysitting." Therefore, session two typically involves meeting to decide the best method of handling the checking accounts and determining which statements, if any, are missing.

In Judith's case, a report is quickly printed out which shows the check number, date cleared and amount for each transaction. She is asked to take the report home to fill in the payees and to determine the appropriate code, which only she can decide. She is also told that there are two pages missing from two separate bank statements which she is to obtain from her bank. Judith also indicates that she didn't know what to do with several expenses, so she made up some categories for them, a strategy which works as long as you're consistent. It is quite easy to consolidate the information at any time by reassigning the expenses to the appropriate category on the financial declaration.

Regardless, session two is typically the shortest meeting, with only a few questions and less detailed information to cover. Between session two and three, Judith will be filling in the blanks on our report, locating copies of any missing or unrecorded checks, and gathering whatever other information needs to be assembled in preparing the historical budget report, including missing bank and credit card statements.

BUDGETING SESSION 3

The number of sessions and the information discussed really depends on how organized you are. Most people can have a complete, detailed budget prepared in four or five relatively short meetings while others come in six or more times in attempting to resolve all the details. Judith is a fairly organized person and her records are mostly complete, so when she comes in for our third meeting, we are able to resolve most of our major questions. She presents us with the report of the data on their checking account and we plan to meet next time to prepare the budget report. This is the report which will be used as a baseline for our maintenance request.

BUDGETING SESSION 4

When Judith comes in this time, we are ready. With typically only a few quickly unresolved matters, Judith and I are ready to prepare the temporary budget proposal. In her case we are providing this information to be taken before the judge for *reconsideration* of the current temporary maintenance award. Therefore, a revised financial declaration is prepared, along with a series of detailed footnotes which support my assumptions for the budget proposal and explain any significant variances from historical spending patterns. For instance, a change in residence might mean higher mortgage/rent expenses, increased utilities, and possible payments on replacement furniture and appliances.

In addition the budget will account for projected costs of experts, such as a financial planner, career advisor, business appraisals, therapists for both Judith and the children, any immediate educational expenditures, and an estimate of the income tax liability which Judith will incur on her maintenance income. Since she already has a court order, the maintenance income received after the temporary order is in place is taxable, and waiting to make an estimated payment to the IRS could result in additional penalties and interest.

The budget on the following pages is submitted by the attorney with the motion for reconsideration of the original temporary maintenance order: The historical budget period included in the report is all of 1993. The proposed temporary budget covers the months of separation prior to the final property settlement and divorce being finalized. These are the months that Judith and her family contemplate the financial impact of the divorce on the family's lifestyle and create a new budget for the post-divorce lifestyle, including housing alternatives, schooling and career goals, etc.

PROPOSED TEMPORARY BUDGET FOR JUDITH JESSUP

1/1/93 Through 12/31/93

PREPARED BY KATHLEEN A. MILLER, CFP, MBA

MILLER, BIRD ADVISORS, INC.

INCOME

	Historical Total Expenses	Historical Monthly Budget	Jake Proposed Temporary Budget	Judith Proposed Temporary Budget
3.1 WAGES & SALARY				
a. Wages & Salary	$8,500	$708	$ -	$479
b. Interest & Dividend Income	412	34	17	17
c. Business Income	140,000	11,667	12,500	-
d. Other Income - Jake's Bonus	10,000	833	1,250	-
Total 3.1 WAGES & SALARY	158,912	13,243	13,767	496
3.2 MONTHLY DEDUCTIONS FROM INCOME				
a. Income Taxes ($5,500/qtr. + Judith's withhold.)	23,275	1,940	1,964	-
b. (1). FICA/Medicare (Judith)	633	53	-	36
b. (2). FICA (incl. Self-Emp.)/Medicare (Jake)	11,057	921	494	-
c. State Industrial Insurance	2,030	169	-	7
d. Mandatory Union/Professional Dues	-	-	-	-
e. Pension Plan Payments	-	-	-	-
f. Spousal Maintenance Paid	-	-	-	-
g. Normal Business Expenses	-	-	-	-
Total 3.2 MONTHLY DEDUCTIONS	36,996	3,083	2,459	43

PROPOSED TEMPORARY BUDGET FOR JUDITH JESSUP

1/1/93 Through 12/31/93

PREPARED BY KATHLEEN A. MILLER, CFP, MBA   MILLER, BIRD ADVISORS, INC.

	Historical Total Expenses	Historical Monthly Budget	Jake Proposed Temporary Budget	Judith Proposed Temporary Budget
INCOME, continued				
3.4 MISCELLANEOUS INCOME				
a. Child Support, Other Relationshipss	–	–	–	–
b. Cash Value of Life Insurance	–	–	–	–
c. Other: (Specify)	–	–	–	–
Total 3.4 MISCELLANEOUS INCOME	–	–	–	–
TOTAL INCOME	**$121,917**	**$10,160**	**$11,308**	**$453**
EXPENSES				
5.1 HOUSING				
1. Mortgage/Rent	$34,552	$2,879	$1,100	$2,879
2. Improvements/Repairs	1,277	106	–	–
3. Installment Payments for Furniture	1,725	144	75	50
4. Taxes & Insurance	4,868	406	237	428
5. Yard Care & House Repair	1,630	136	30	125
Total 5.1 HOUSING	44,052	3,671	1,442	3,482

EXPENSES, continued

5.2 UTILITIES

1. Heat/Gas	1,137	95	90	90
2. Electricity	948	79	75	80
3. Water, Sewer, Garbage	621	52	50	50
4. Telephone	1,826	152	125	100
5. Cable	566	47	35	25
6. Other: Specify	-	-	-	-
Total 5.2 UTILITIES	5,099	425	375	345

5.3 FOOD & SUPPLIES

1. Food for 4 Persons	6,746	562	300	400
2. Supplies	819	68	50	40
3. Meals Eaten Out	1,847	154	250	150
4. Other: Pet Care	688	57	-	60
Total 5.3 FOOD & SUPPLIES	10,100	842	600	650

5.4 CHILDREN

1. Child Care	418	35	-	-
2. Clothing	4,624	385	-	350
3. Tuition	-	-	-	-
4. Other Child Related Expenses	12,667	1,056	500	1,000
Total 5.4 CHILDREN	17,709	1,476	500	1,350

PROPOSED TEMPORARY BUDGET FOR JUDITH JESSUP

1/1/93 Through 12/31/93

PREPARED BY KATHLEEN A. MILLER, CFP, MBA   MILLER, BIRD ADVISORS, INC.

	Historical Total Expenses	Historical Monthly Budget	Jake Proposed Temporary Budget	Judith Proposed Temporary Budget
EXPENSES, continued				
5.5 TRANSPORTATION				
1. Vehicle Payments or Leases	-	-		
2. Vehicle Insurance & License	1,379	115	115	106
3. Vehicle Gas, Oil, Maintenance	2,134	178	150	125
4. Parking	117	10	35	-
5. Other: Repairs	732	61	50	25
Total 5.5 TRANSPORTATION	4,362	364	350	256
5.6 HEALTH CARE				
1. Insurance	-	-	-	-
2. Unins. Ortho, Dent., Med.	363	30	20	35
3. Other: Counseling	1,589	132	-	240
4. Prescription Medications	1,160	97	30	56
Total 5.6 HEALTH CARE	3,112	259	50	331

EXPENSES, continued

5.7 PERSONAL EXPENSES

1. Clothing	5,619	468	200	250
2. Hair Care/Personal Care	1,535	128	50	100
3. Clubs & Recreation	1,432	119	100	115
4. Education	-	-	-	-
5. Books, Newspapers, Magazines	386	32	30	25
6. Gifts	1,760	147	50	75
7. Other: Vacations, Entertainment, Dry Cleaner	867	72	100	70
Total 5.7 PERSONAL EXPENSES	11,599	967	530	635

5.8 MISCELLANEOUS

1. Life & Disability Insurance	-	-	60	-
2. Other: Bank & Credit Card Fees	298	25	-	10
3. Other: Federal Taxes on Maintenance	-	-	-	537
4. Other: Donations	638	53	-	25
5. Other: Professional Fees	5,213	434	150	125
Total 5.8 MISCELLANEOUS	6,150	512	210	697

TOTAL HOUSEHOLD EXPENSES	$102,183	$8,515	$4,057	$7,746

PROPOSED TEMPORARY BUDGET FOR JUDITH JESSUP
1/1/93 Through 12/31/93

PREPARED BY KATHLEEN A. MILLER, CFP, MBA   MILLER, BIRD ADVISORS, INC.

	Historical Total Expenses	Historical Monthly Budget	Jake Proposed Temporary Budget	Judith Proposed Temporary Budget
ADJUSTMENTS TO 1993 EXPENSES				
JAKE'S SEPARATE EXPENSES	$7,419	$618		
5.8 MISCELLANEOUS				
6. Other: Capital Expenditures	-	-		
Total 5.8 MISCELLANEOUS	-	-		
TOTAL ADJUSTMENTS	7,419	618		
TOTAL EXPENSES	$109,602	$9,134	$4,057	$7,746
INCOME LESS EXPENSES	$12,315	$1,026	$7,251	($7,293)

SUMMARY OF HISTORICAL INCOME

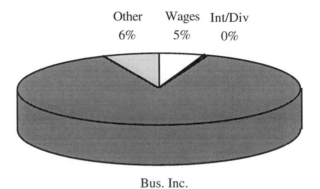

Other
6%

Wages
5%

Int/Div
0%

Bus. Inc.
89%

SUMMARY OF HISTORICAL EXPENDITURES

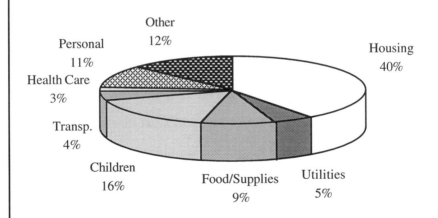

Other
12%

Personal
11%

Health Care
3%

Housing
40%

Transp.
4%

Children
16%

Food/Supplies
9%

Utilities
5%

FOOTNOTES TO PROPOSED TEMPORARY BUDGET
FOR
JUDITH JESSUP

GENERAL NOTES

All information contained herein has been provided to Miller, Bird Advisors, Inc. by the client, Judith Jessup. The data has been entered into our accounting software from the account statements. We have used a full year as the baseline for our analysis, showing household expenditures from all sources. Transactions entered into by Jake Jessup which pertained only to him (i.e. - business travel, his clothing, etc.) were removed from the historical household budget and included in the analysis as an adjustment to the expenses. Capital expenditures are assumed to occur only once and were also listed as an adjustment.

The expenses listed under Jake's Proposed Temporary Budget were taken from his financial declaration. The budget proposal does not include a detailed analysis of historical income. There are complete records of monthly deposits into the various household accounts, but they do not indicate the income of either party since it is at the discretion of the individual as to what portion of income is actually deposited. We will use our Income Tax and Cash Flow models in determining our income projections when we have adequate information regarding the assets and liabilities of both parties. Please note that budgeted expense requirements cannot be met assuming that Jake receives the agreed upon (first mediation session) 1994 business income of $150,000, with an expected and also agreed upon $15,000 "bonus" (extra payments to Jake should the business generate adequate revenues). Judith's expected gross wages are $8,500 in 1994. Based on the information available, we believe that the net income available to both parties in 1994 will be approximately $141,132 or approximately $11,761 per month. Combined budgeted expenses are $11,803, resulting in a deficit of approximately $42 per month.

The section of the report entitled "Adjustments to Expenses" applies only to the historical budget as a means of reconciling the historical expenditures with the account information compiled by Miller, Bird Advisors, Inc. The line for "Jake's Expenses" attempts to segregate expenses belonging to Jake which do not pertain to the household in any way. As such, no allocation is made in the budget proposal. These expenses are assumed to be included in Jake's budgeted expenses.

Cash Expenditures:

Unless otherwise noted, checks written for cash were allocated among the following estimated percentages:

ALLOCATION OF CASH EXPENDITURES

CATEGORY	Subcategory	JUDITH'S ESTIMATE	% OF TOTAL
5.5 TRANSPORTATION	3 Gas	$100	17.7%
5.3 FOOD & SUPPLIES	3 Meals Out	150	26.5%
5.3 FOOD & SUPPLIES	1 Groceries	70	12.4%
5.7 PERSONAL EXPENSES	7 Personal Entertainment	35	6.2%
5.4 CHILDREN	4 Other Child Rel. Exp. – Personal, Sam	15	2.7%
5.4 CHILDREN	4 Other Child Rel. Exp. – Personal, Frances	15	2.7%
5.4 CHILDREN	4 Other Child Rel. Exp. – Personal, Jacob	15	2.7%
5.4 CHILDREN	2 Clothing – Sam	25	4.4%
5.4 CHILDREN	2 Clothing – Frances	25	4.4%
5.4 CHILDREN	2 Clothing – Jacob	25	4.4%
5.4 CHILDREN	4 Other Child Rel. Exp. – Piano, Sam	10	1.8%
5.4 CHILDREN	4 Other Child Rel. Exp. – Personal, Sam	30	5.3%
5.4 CHILDREN	4 Other Child Rel. Exp. – Personal, Frances	25	4.4%
5.4 CHILDREN	4 Other Child Rel. Exp. – Personal, Jacob	25	4.4%
TOTAL ESTIMATED CASH EXPENDITURES		**$565**	**100%**

NOTE: Judith has indicated that she believes that the above amounts accurately reflect her monthly expenditures from cash machine withdrawals. Total withdrawals were $8,930 from June 1, 1992 through May 31, 1993, which is $744.16 per month. Her estimates resulted in a total of $730 which is 2% below the actual monthly average. We applied the percentages listed under "% of Total" to every cash machine withdrawal transacted by Judith (as indicated in their joint check registers). Cash machine transactions recorded as belonging to Jake totalled $6,200 and were included in the budget under JAKE'S SEPARATE EXPENSES.

NOTES TO SUBCATEGORIES

5.1 HOUSING
4. Taxes & Insurance
Judith will pay the property taxes on the residence from her combined wages and maintenance. Property taxes are approximately $4,750 on the family residence, for a monthly average expense of $395.83. Judith will be paying homeowner's insurance premiums of $32 per month until the residence sells. Total expenses for this category are budgeted at **$427.83 per month.**

5.3 FOOD & SUPPLIES
General
The historical budget for food and supplies did not differentiate between groceries and supplies on some of the larger checks written to a local discount shopping organization. They were allocated 50% to each subcategory, resulting in food expenses which were too low and supplies which were too high. We have adjusted the budget figures accordingly.

5.4 CHILDREN
4. Other Child Related Expenses
Judith pays in cash each month child related expenditures totaling $210, as noted above in the "Allocation of Cash Expenditures." In addition, she spends approximately $800 additional dollars on various check and charge card purchases, including school supplies, sports fees sports equipment, movie theater and video rental expenses, travel/vacation expenses, personal expenses, etc.

5.5 TRANSPORTATION
2. Vehicle Insurance & License
Judith will continue to drive the van since it is paid for. We estimate her monthly cost for insurance and licenses to be $410.64 twice per year for auto insurance plus $450 in license fees. The total annual expense is expected to be $1,271.28 for a monthly average expense of **$105.94.**

3. Vehicle Gas, Oil, Maint.
The monthly average expense for gas, oil and maintenance is $177.80. However, this total includes several small charges made by Jake on the family gas card. Most (approximately 90%) of Jake's gas and maintenance costs are paid by the company. We estimate that Judith's portion of gas, oil and maintenance to be **$125 per month.**

5.6 HEALTH CARE
1. Insurance
Judith will continue to be covered under Jake's plan until the divorce is final.

2. Unins. Dental, Ortho, Med.
Judith will be paying her costs only for health insurance in the temporary period. We assume that Jake will pay for the children since they will be covered under his plan. This reduces potential problems with filing claims and handling of insurance reimbursements. If it is determined that this is the best method of handling medical expenses, an adjustment will need to be made to Jake's budget. The historical total does not incorporate Jessica's recent need for orthodontia and the current payments of $115 per month. We assume that Jake will pay this cost. We recommend that Jake's budget for uninsured medical expenses be approximately $175 per month (Note: projected and agreed upon income levels will support this figure).

3. Other: Counseling
Judith has been seeing a counselor and would like to continue to do so. The weekly cost for each visit is $60, or $240 per month.

5.7 PERSONAL EXPENSES
6. Gifts
During the budget period, all gifts which were assumed to be from both Judith and Jake were allocated to Judith in attempting to isolate Jake's separate gift purchases. For the proposed budget, we allocate approximately half of the historical average expense.

5.8 MISCELLANEOUS
3. Federal Taxes
We estimate Judith's income tax liability to be $537 per month on maintenance income of $54,000, wages of $8,500, bank interest of $200 and a $2,000 deductible IRA contribution. There is a Federal Income Tax savings of over $3,000 if both parties file separately in 1993. She will be filing as head of household with two exemptions, one for her and one for Tiffany, as agreed upon in their second mediation session. Jake will file as Single with three exemptions.

The budget, as shown with accompanying footnotes, is the foundation for the post-divorce budget. While the final budget amounts for the temporary and post-divorce reports may differ, the objective is to be accurate the first time through so that costly adjustments will be unnecessary in the future.

BUDGETING SESSION 5

"Session" does not really describe what follows the preparation of the temporary budget; it is not just a meeting. It encompasses all the work done from the time the temporary order is in place through the final decree and may take several meetings and several months to accomplish. This step goes outside the realm of simple budget preparation and becomes more subjective.

I will continue to keep Judith's budget current until she goes to trial or is in the position of making or receiving a property settlement from her husband and his attorney. Judith will periodically drop off the coded budget information for data input.

A fairly solid understanding of the cash flow requirements of the household prior to the dissolution should have been established by now. If it hasn't in your case, start asking questions. The responsibility of maintaining the financial balance is in your hands, and the less you understand about your financial future, the harder it will be to keep it from toppling. Always keep in mind your goals, your financial future and your career. During the preparation of the post-divorce budget, we work toward establishing the best course of action in achieving the financial goals you identified way back at the beginning of the budget process.

You may recall that the temporary budget usually differs from the historical spending patterns of the household. The same is true of the temporary budget and the proposed post-divorce budget. Your perception of how things have changed since the temporary budget was prepared, along with incorporating the long-term financial goals, may result in yet another "compromised" financial plan. Having established a temporary budget, it becomes more relevant to consider the effects of such things as inflation, increased income taxes, salary changes, and other economic conditions which affect the long-term needs of the household. Until now, these factors have been considered only on a short-term basis and have really not affected the budgeted amounts. This is where the use of financial planning models can provide a simplified means of showing what the most likely outcomes are for both parties for the various settlement proposals which are presented.

I meet with Judith about the other financial and tax issues in her case, and for the purpose of helping the attorney with the data gathering, financial and tax analysis, and property settlement proposal. Judith and her attorney, with my help, will be doing "what if" projections creating various decision-making models for Judith to look at to prepare her for her settlement negotiations or trial. Remember, over 95 percent of all divorce cases never go to trial.

During this time Judith will evaluate her future financial needs and try to answer some of the following questions: *[Judith is doing her own guided research to determine what her post-divorce lifestyle will look like — she wants to be in the position of speaking about the details of her new life rather than taking what is left over — this is an important concept to get across. This is not Jake's plan for Judith, but Judith's plan for Judith and her family.]*

Housing
- Will she keep or sell the family residence?
- Will she refinance the family residence?
- What kind of a loan is best for Judith, a fixed or variable mortgage?
- What are the current mortgage rates available and what are the points on these loans?
- What income is required for Judith to qualify for a mortgage? Judith needs to meet with a mortgage broker and take notes and bring these back to our meeting.
- Will the current lender refinance the mortgage and on what terms, fee?
- Since Judith and Jake have sold their house, Judith needs to look at new housing. She should bring in the listings on three houses that could work for her and the children. Judith needs to have three real estate firms provide her and Jake with a market analysis on their current home.
- What does Judith estimate the utilities, heat and electricity, water, sewer and garbage expenses at this new home to be? She can call the

power company and, given the address, they will provide her with information regarding the average expenses.
• What will the real estate taxes be in this new home?
• Will Judith need to replace furniture, appliances or make improvements to this new home?
• What is the cost of the homeowner's coverage for this new house?
[Note: If Judith decides to rent for the long-term, the above questions will need to be answered for that scenario instead of her owning a home.]

Children
• How will these expenses change post-divorce?
• Does Judith need day-care for the children while pursuing her career?
• What are the after school and summer day-care costs?
• What sports activities and hobbies do the children participate in currently and those they will have in the future? Be very detailed about these anticipated costs.
• Will the children see a therapist in the future, how often, cost, duration?

Transportation
• What is the automobile insurance for Judith's coverage on only her car, the van?
• Will Judith have parking fees while attending school and during any internship?

Health Care
• What is the estimated cost for comparable health insurance for Judith? Under COBRA and under a new plan? Judith needs to get at least two comprehensive bids for her sole health insurance coverage.
• How will Judith be reimbursed for uninsured medical costs paid by her for herself and the children even though the children are under Jake's health insurance policy?
• What are Judith's costs with visits to her therapist? How long does she plan to continue these sessions, how often will they meet?

Personal expenses

Put yourself in Judith's shoes and ask yourself the questions below that she had to answer:

- Specifically, how will your clothing expenses change from the time you are in school to the time of full-time employment?
- What are your education costs listed in the career plan prepared by your vocational expert?
- What vacation budget do you have for one trip for yourself and a major trip with the children annually? (Be detailed.)
- How have you adjusted your purchases of gifts for family and friends? Detail your costs by holiday and person receiving the gift.
- Are you taking up any new sports with your children or have you joined a health club as a family or are you planing to maintain the current club membership?

Miscellaneous

- You will be maintaining a life insurance policy on your husband's life securing death benefit coverage for you and the children for the time period during which he has an obligation for child support and maintenance. What is your estimated monthly premium cost?
- Is your husband insurable and with limited health problems?
- Will you continue with the current insurance coverage or have you looked into new coverage?
- What are the costs of these policies, term or whole life insurance?
- What do you estimate your annual tax preparation fee to be in the future?
- Will you need on-going financial planning services? What are the fees for these services?
- What is the cost to have your new will prepared by an attorney?
- What is the cost to have a durable power of attorney and directive to physicians documents prepared?
- Are you paying your legal bills as you go through this dissolution process? What does your attorney estimate these costs to be before your first settlement conference, to prepare for trial, going to trial, writing the divorce documents and/or reviewing these documents,

coordinating the transfers for your retirement and non-retirement assets, court filing of your decree?

• What are your current credit card balances by card? What is your minimum payment and interest rate charged on each card?

• What have you paid in attorney fees to date and what do you currently owe to the attorney and any experts who are working on your case?

This chapter will be an important one for you to get started. I assume you have an attorney and are in the process of gathering data. If not, you should begin assembling the information listed at the end of Chapter Five so that your budget can be prepared in conjunction with the other tax/cash flow and asset allocation models.

Once the divorce becomes final, it would seem that the budget process ought to be complete. However, for all the time and effort spent in creating this budget to be worthwhile, four things must occur: 1) bills must be paid and money spent with the budget in mind, 2) time needs to pass, 3) a comparison needs to be made between what you thought you would spend and what you did spend, and 4) the budget needs to be evaluated for necessary changes. This is where you follow through with your hard work and establish your financial freedom.

If these steps sound familiar, they should. We've already discussed them in greater detail as the budget process. Where the process has been applied to historical figures, we must now think about the future, your future, and the best method of keeping things balanced.

CASH MANAGEMENT SYSTEM — TODAY AND IN THE FUTURE

There are those among us for whom the budget process is instinctive, significantly speeding up the process of gathering and processing the data; others fear it and tend to forget about it whenever the chance to do something else comes up. Complications generally arise when there are too many accounts used in maintaining the household. In a surprisingly large number of cases I have dealt with, three or four checking accounts and six to twelve credit cards are being used simultaneously to pay bills and make household purchases. It is no wonder that these clients have no idea what their household expenses are like. Getting on a budget and determining whether or not the budget is working is much easier when a simplified approach to handling deposits and paying household expenses is implemented *and* utilized.

The following simple, twelve-step approach to cash management may be the best way to deal with future budgeting issues. In our discussion, we talk about Sessions. This would be our Session Six. However, in much the same way that Session Five is ambiguous and encompasses one or several meetings, Session Six is everything that happens after the divorce is final. It is important for you to utilize the budget which has been prepared and to periodically update it. The cycle for this system is twelve months long, although it is intended to create spending habits which last a lifetime. The following steps summarize the cash management system:

1. Categorize your expenditures over the last year.
2. Think about your financial future and what you would like your financial picture to look like in five years. What are your goals? Write them down.
3. Forecast your living expenses over the next year and create a 12-month cash flow calendar which will allow you to reach your financial objectives.
4. Identify all sources of income. Determine net income from each source.
5. Add up all fixed expenses and subtract them directly from net income.
6. If you don't already have a money market checking account into which all your income flows, establish one. Hold on to only one checking account. You should also have two separate investment accounts: one for your periodic payments (defined below); and one for retirement and savings.
7. Deposit all income into the main (collection) account. Pay all mandatory living expenses directly from this account and set aside an amount each month in your first investment account which will allow you to make your periodic payments.
8. Keep track of your expenses for at least 12 months. Make sure you are staying within the budgeted amounts.
9. You may want to allocate specific income to specific expenses.
10. Monitor withdrawals from the investment accounts.

11. Review the budget each year to determine whether or not the goals and objectives set forth are being met. Look at in-flows and out-flows in your money market account and identify any excesses or deficiencies. Excess funds are transferred to your retirement/savings account. If there are deficiencies, go to step three.

12. Once the budget has been successfully maintained for 12 months, go out and treat yourself to something fun.

No, you don't need to categorize your expenses again, nor do you need to redefine your financial goals. This system is intended as a follow-up to all the preparation and hard work you've already done. In addition, the system is designed to accommodate changes in living expenses as well as any changes in your financial objectives through periodic reviews and updates.

As suggested in step six, the system proposed in this chapter includes the use of three accounts. The chart below summarizes the structure of the accounts and the flow of funds through them.

You should find yourself a money market account that allows you to write checks and deposit all income you receive into the account. Only two types of checks should be written from the money market account. One check per month is written to you for deposit into your checking account. The amount of the check should equal the total expenses determined at your last budget review minus your periodic payments. The payments occur either once per year or at regular intervals and include things like auto, life and homeowner's insurance payments, property taxes and quarterly income tax payments. Your periodic payments are the other type of check which you should be writing. Pay these expenses directly from the money market account, since it will be much easier to make sure that the payments are made and much more obvious when your budget is working effectively.

The balance in the main money market account should always be at least one half of the total living expenses (from step three above.) required to maintain the home for three to six months. The other half of your emergency funds may be kept in the third account which we haven't yet discussed. This last account is your reserve parachute. It holds the money you intend to spend in reaching your longer-term

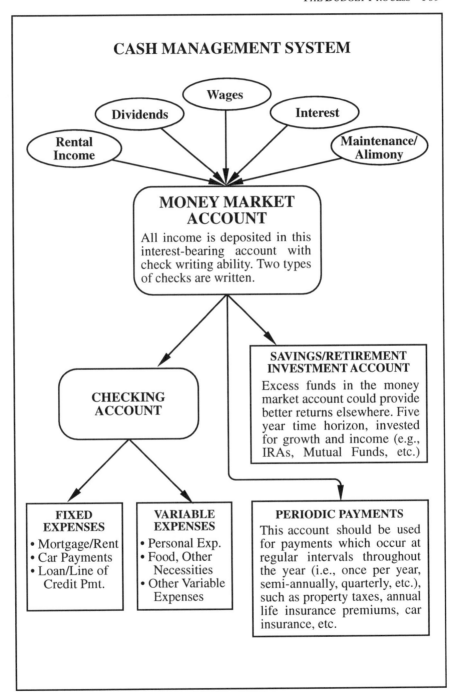

CASH MANAGEMENT SYSTEM

Wages

Dividends

Interest

Rental Income

Maintenance/ Alimony

MONEY MARKET ACCOUNT

All income is deposited in this interest-bearing account with check writing ability. Two types of checks are written.

CHECKING ACCOUNT

SAVINGS/RETIREMENT INVESTMENT ACCOUNT

Excess funds in the money market account could provide better returns elsewhere. Five year time horizon, invested for growth and income (e.g., IRAs, Mutual Funds, etc.)

FIXED EXPENSES

• Mortgage/Rent
• Car Payments
• Loan/Line of Credit Pmt.

VARIABLE EXPENSES

• Personal Exp.
• Food, Other Necessities
• Other Variable Expenses

PERIODIC PAYMENTS

This account should be used for payments which occur at regular intervals throughout the year (i.e., once per year, semi-annually, quarterly, etc.), such as property taxes, annual life insurance premiums, car insurance, etc.

financial objectives, or possibly it holds your retirement funds, or it may mean you set up two accounts, since retirement funds withdrawn early often have a penalty and an income tax consequence.

In either case, you should review the balance in your money market account periodically to see: 1) if the money you spend from your checking account is really enough, and 2) if you have excess money sitting in your money market account. Your excess funds could be providing you with better investment return if you put the money into a mutual fund or other slightly higher risk investment. This higher risk is often acceptable in light of the increased earnings potential. We will discuss this and other types of accounts in the chapter entitled, "What Should I Do With My Settlement?"

You should be setting aside something each month for the achievement of your long-term financial objectives. The question is, how much should be used for goal funding? A good rule of thumb is to deposit the greater of ten percent of net income or one-half of the money you have left after you pay all of the bills and after you spend your budgeted variable expenses such as food, entertainment, clothing, etc. You should set up your budget so that there is some money left, no matter how small, to put in your investment account.

I like to use the example of two investors, call them A and B, both age 35. Mr. A believes that at age 35 he has plenty of time to start saving for his retirement. He spent every dime he made until he was 45 when, realizing he couldn't work forever, he began to put $6,000 per year into his retirement plan (perhaps an annuity) for the next 25 years for a total investment of $150,000. Ms. B decides that now is the time to think about retirement and makes a ten year commitment at the same $6,000 per year level starting now. In ten years, she will have made a $60,000 investment. Assume they both invest in assets which earn eight percent after-taxes or eight percent tax deferred. (Most retirement accounts, pensions, IRAs, annuities, etc., are tax deferred, which means you pay taxes on the earnings when funds are withdrawn after retirement.) The after-tax value of Mr. A's account after his last $6,000 deposit, if he were to take all the money at once is $552,555, while Ms. B has $694,317 in after-tax dollars, with $90,000 less having been deposited in the account! The cost of waiting is evident in this example.

Having discussed the accounts and how funds should flow from them, you should be ready to implement your system based on the concepts I have discussed above. Your plan must constantly be monitored so that the results may be measured against the objectives defined in creating the plan, in addition to helping you stay on your budget. Any time there is a variance it should be investigated, understood, and then either corrected or incorporated into future plans. Reviews should be made periodically so that significant changes may be incorporated, and a major update of the plan should be done at least annually.

Make sure you continue to monitor your spending. Not only is this to make sure that you are following your budget, but to ascertain whether or not any child support being received is sufficient for the needs of the child. Child support figures are adjusted every two years or by agreement, and the ages of the children and the requirements of your household are part of the facts being considered. Your organization of the facts in a concise format will save everyone (including you) time and money.

The cash flow analysis discussed in this chapter really has a dual purpose. On one hand, a legal document is prepared which clearly indicates the cash flow requirements of the household in both the pre- and post-divorce settings, while on the other hand, the identification of the financial goals as well as a potential means of achieving them have been defined. These tools are invaluable in this time of transition, and a clear understanding of your future financial picture can help reduce the level of emotional distress brought about by a divorce.

Judith was not unique in her budgeting process. The family spent most of the money earned each year. Judith did not keep a detailed family budget during her last few years of marriage. The family business paid for many discretionary expenses, such as vacations and meals. When Jake filed for divorce, she was immediately put on an "allowance" with no training to prepare her for the challenges of budgeting and downsizing the family's married lifestyle. Judith and Jake continue their divorce process in Chapter Twelve.

Library Resource Center
Renton Technical College
3000 NE 4th St.
Renton, WA 98056-4195

Library Resources Center
Renton Technical College
3000 NE 4th St.
Renton, WA 98056-4195

CHAPTER SEVEN

CLOSING IN ON DISPARITY

The best career advice to give the young is:
Find out what you like doing best
And get someone to pay you for doing it.
— *Catherine Whitehorn*

In this chapter, I wish to talk about a subject dear to the hearts of women. The subject is disparity of earnings between the male and female. Particularly after divorce, women — often removed from the work force through marriage — start again at a time, and in an employment configuration, that places them far below their former spouse in earnings and in their capability to catch up.

The majority of the material presented here is adapted from an article written by myself, Janice E. Reha, M.A., and Dan Desonier, an attorney. They have given their permission for me to reproduce it in this book.

Disparity between the economic well-being of divorcing couples is a critical problem facing Americans today. Despite career opportunities that opened up for women during the last decade, older women who enter or re-enter the work force in the 1990s after dissolution of a marriage face incredible obstacles.

Statistics point out that women who maintained their careers throughout marriage experience salary discrepancies when they have chosen fields dominated by female workers, such as education, administrative support and other services. Of those women working in male-dominated occupations, few have broken through the "glass ceiling" that exists when men are favored for promotion to the best paid positions.

Closing the gap remains a significant social problem. Treating divorcing couples equitably is a twenty-first-century challenge for lawyers and the courts. The amount of spousal maintenance and the length of time over which such funds shall be disbursed continue to be the subjects of debate.

By combining expertise in divorce law, financial planning, and career development, Janice Reha and I examined the complexity of divorce settlements by analyzing trends, presenting guidelines and simulating models to aid divorce attorneys in the determination of equitable awards and maintenance periods.

Discussion here is based on the premise that the objective of any divorce settlement is to assure that *both parties share equally in the residual economic benefits, responsibilities and losses resulting from the dissolution of the marriage contract.*

The goal is to maintain *equity of lifestyles beyond divorce — not only for the parents but also for any and all dependent children.*

This makes singular, historical baseline strategy obsolete in negotiating settlements. Each case requires relative thinking and creative solutions because of variable economic and career factors.

Looking at this goal single-dimensionally, devoid of time, change or circumstance, a 50/50 split of current assets and liabilities might seem equitable. Isn't this the premise upon which state community property laws and equitable property division were enacted? However, if the wife stayed home during a given period of time to rear the children, the working husband might be asked to contribute a little extra to help her catch up to the work place in the way of job experience, training or education. Perhaps a 60/40 split would be appropriate. Fair enough.

… Or, is it?

Even when other factors — such as layoffs, disabilities, and bankruptcies — are constant, the playing field remains uneven between male and female wage earners. Divorce settlements that offer rehabilitation for women who interrupted or postponed a career during marriage are inadequate.

Compensatory strategies often used today may reimburse the spouse who didn't work full-time outside the home for lost income while they recognize the value contributed to the marriage, family and other spouse's career. That is a step in the right direction. However, future consequences of career decisions made during a marriage must be considered as well. Long-term wage disparity must be addressed not only in terms of the distribution of current assets and property settlements but also in terms of ongoing spousal maintenance.

Consider the graph on the following page, showing pre- and post-divorce wages. We assumed in this case that the husband, as an engineer in managerial positions of increasing importance, earned an income which steadily improved over time. He experienced no interruption in his career. In contrast, we analyzed three common scenarios that would affect the wife's earning capacity. In the first case, we assumed that the wife maintained a teaching career throughout her marriage and beyond divorce to retirement. The wage disparity between a high seniority engineering manager and a teaching career continues to widen over time. As a married couple, these two professionals enjoyed a comparable lifestyle. After divorce, assuming assets were divided equally, the husband would become nearly twice as affluent as his wife.

In the second scenario, we assumed the engineer's wife interrupted her career for 14 years. As is typical for many American couples, the wife worked during the first few years of marriage to increase total household income. Once the husband completed an advanced degree and his salary was established, the couple agreed that the wife should stay at home to help the children through their educational years. After a divorce in 1994, the wife would be unable to re-enter the teaching field without advanced education.

Industries change over time, and the field of education is no exception. Increased competition, demand for higher standards and specialization along with cost controls have contributed to a shift in

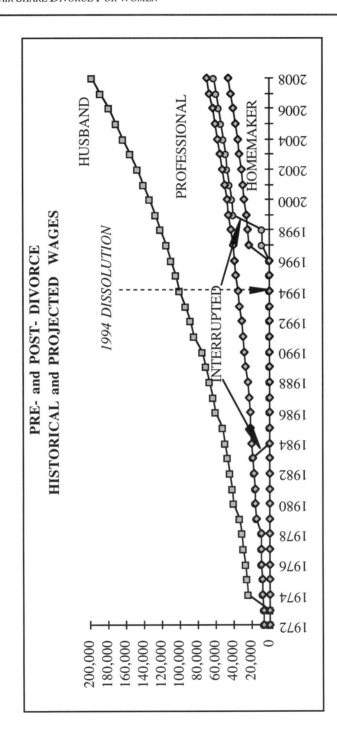

PRE- and POST- DIVORCE
HISTORICAL and PROJECTED WAGES

required teaching credentials and experience. No quantifiable number emerges that indicates just how many years a person must be out of the work force for skills to become obsolete. Even one year of absence from some jobs can result in loss of seniority, credibility and effectiveness. In property settlement planning, any interruption must be analyzed for potential opportunity cost. The general rule follows that the longer the interruption, the greater the loss.

So, the engineer's wife, working with a certified career counselor, developed a plan to go back to school to earn a master's degree in special education, where she could expect to earn about $40,000 annually after a couple of years of part-time work as a substitute teacher while waiting for a permanent opening in special education. An important factor in this case pertains to the difference between what the wife would have earned had she maintained a steady career in teaching and what she would earn by interrupting her career. The difference between the two is lost opportunity, or "opportunity cost." This discrepancy becomes even more dramatic than what is represented on our graph when compared to retirement benefits accrued by the wife, or scenario number one, who maintained a steady career. The wife who interrupted her career gave up her benefits.

Take the homemaker as a third example. In scenario number three, the engineer and his wife agreed that the best use of her time was at home with the kids. By his wife providing emotional support and stability at home, the husband felt he could better concentrate his efforts on his job and excel in his career. The results are seen on the graph.

In this scenario, the wife, who had no previous work experience, faced limited opportunities. With the help of a certified career counselor, she determined that a job as an accountant would provide the optimal match with her personality, style, work habits and expectation, while it offered the best employment and wage opportunities under the circumstances. Because her undergraduate degree was in English, the wife planned to return full-time to college to complete a bachelor of science degree with an emphasis in accounting. Entering the job market at age 46, she would take a temporary position for one year until a full-time opportunity opened up. As an accountant, the engineer's ex-wife could expect to earn less than one-fifth of her former husband's projected wages. Now, compare the opportunity cost between this and what she could have earned had she maintained a teaching position as in scenario number one.

The graph underscores wage disparity (past, present and future) between men and women, husbands and wives. Moreover, the graph emphasizes the opportunity cost of a couple's decision to interrupt or forego one of two careers.

What about the legal perspective? The question before the courts is twofold: If the law mandates equity in divorce settlements, under what circumstances should spousal maintenance be awarded in a dissolution or legal separation case? If an award is appropriate, for what length of time should it be maintained?

Statutory Authority

In Washington, RCW 25.09.090 provides the statutory basis by which spousal maintenance may be awarded; it gives the court full discretion toward spousal maintenance in such amounts and for such duration *as the court deems just,* after considering all relevant factors. These factors include: the parties' financial resources, the needs of the spouse seeking maintenance and the ability to pay of the person being asked to provide the support. It also takes into consideration the education or training necessary to enable the spouse seeking maintenance to find suitable employment; the standard of living established during the marriage and the duration of the marriage; the age, physical and emotional condition, and financial obligations of the spouse seeking support.

Note: Be sure and check the statutes on maintenance in your state.

Theories, Old and New
A. *Transitional / Rehabilitative*

It is not unusual, even in a marriage of modest length, for a trial court to award spousal maintenance of short duration, so as to provide interim financial assistance to a spouse, to aid that spouse in the transition from married to single life, or perhaps, to complete some schooling or training. Terms given to such a support award are "transitional," and "rehabilitative."

At the other end of the spectrum, most family law practitioners are familiar with justifications for an award of lengthy, perhaps even permanent, spousal maintenance in a scenario where a spouse, most typically the wife, is concluding a long-term marriage (e.g., 25 years or longer) primarily as a homemaker with no marketable skills or professional training. Analysis of the case law cited above, however, shows that courts, in awarding spousal maintenance, give increasing recognition and emphasis to the loss of economic opportunity experienced by a spouse who sacrifices or interrupts a career to be a homemaker or takes a less demanding job to further the other spouse's career. The longer the marriage and the longer a spouse is out of the work force, the greater and more permanent is the loss of that spouse's earning capacity. Nonetheless, the length of the marriage ceases to become fully determinative in terms of justifying a spousal maintenance award.

B. Restitution / Compensation

It is not uncommon for a spouse to have interrupted or forestalled professional advancement by doing part-time clerical work or acting strictly as a homemaker, so as to enable the other spouse to complete advanced degrees and establish a career. The expectation is that the parties will eventually enjoy together economic benefits derived from this arrangement. The concept may work if the parties stay married. In the event of a dissolution, however, in the absence of spousal support, the spouse who has interrupted a career is at an economic disadvantage, regardless of the length of the marriage. That spouse often is awarded spousal maintenance on the "compensatory" or "restitutive" theory, to provide payment for the lost economic opportunities experienced during the time when the other spouse was advancing a career.

Of the King County, Washington trial court decisions rendered between July 1, 1992, and June 30, 1993, where spousal maintenance was awarded, three cases come to light in which the awards were based on compensatory theory.

In two of those cases, the length of marriage was 10 years; there were minor children; the husband had adequate income; and the wife was deemed entitled to compensatory maintenance. In one of those two cases, the wife's trial testimony was that she had sacrificed her career advancement to take care of her husband and their children, and she was thus in an economically disadvantaged position compared with her husband. *(The Court Report: The Year of King County Family Law Decisions,* Kathryn J. Kaloosny, J.D. (1994), pp 126 and 189.) In the third case, the the marriage was 31 years in duration; the children were all adults; the husband had significant income; and the court found that the wife had no prospects for rehabilitation or gainful employment and was in need of compensatory maintenance for her years of service to the community and her assistance in making the husband employable. (Ibid. at p. 274.)

Approximately five percent of dissolution cases filed with the court actually go to trial. An analysis of trial court decisions where spousal maintenance is awarded is not necessarily reflective of the considerations used in the other 95 percent of dissolution cases, where spousal support is negotiated via settlement.

C. *Partnership Model*

Long-term marriages can be characterized as "partnerships" in which each spouse has an important role to play. If the wife operated primarily as the homemaker, for example, or worked in low-paying positions, while the husband earned an advanced degree and significant income, those contributions should be considered of similar or equal value. In all three of our scenarios, however, the husband's standard of living will increase after the divorce, while the wife's standard of living will deteriorate sharply unless an equitable distribution of property, and/or spousal maintenance is awarded. When this marital partnership is dissolving, efforts should be made to ensure that the economic hardship created by the dissolution "... be shared equally, or at least fairly and equitably, rather than fall disproportionately on one spouse." *(Judicial Training Materials on Spousal Support: Facilitators' Manual,* is produced by the Women Judges for Justice, and revised by Professor Ellis, contained within the *Family Law Spousal Maintenance Report* from the Superior Court Judges Spring Conference 1992, p. 27.) As Professor Ellis states:

"The partnership notion assumes that both spouses make substantially (although not necessarily identical) contributions to a marriage. If so, they should receive substantially equal benefits from the marriage and should not be left in widely disparate positions after marriage ends." (Ibid, at p. 27.)

In this, the "partnership theory," spousal maintenance should be utilized to level the playing field by providing to the spouse (most often the wife) whose economic position is significantly inferior to the other spouse's ongoing support that, in combination with an equitable distribution of property, places her in a position comparable to that of her husband.

SUMMARY OF THE LEGAL PERSPECTIVE

In examining the appropriateness of spousal maintenance, attorneys should view the length of the marriage as a factor, but not a primary one. Increased attention should be focused on the economic facts and circumstances of the case in the economic positions of each party. In a short-term marriage, neither spouse should have the expectation of financial assistance, and the general focus should be on returning each party to the pre-marital status quo. At the same time, choices, decisions and agreements made in a marriage of relatively short duration may impact what is financially fair and equitable in a dissolution settlement. The longer the marriage, the greater the possible loss of economic opportunity and sacrifice of earning capacity by one or the other of the spouses. At the conclusion of a long marriage, an advantaged spouse may be placed in a position to validate the contribution of the financially disadvantaged spouse by making some economic sacrifices in the form of ongoing spousal maintenance as a tool for the recipient's future comparable economic security.

How do we plan a divorce settlement that offers compensatory awards for opportunity cost and wage disparity so that benefits and losses are equally shared? In addition, how do we measure projected income in terms of future wages, earnings from pensions, IRAs and other retirement investments set aside during a marriage?

A Certified Financial Planner and certified career counselor provide some of the answers which will vary case by case. These experts help attorneys plan settlements that maximize equity based on careful analysis of relevant variables over time. Computer models compare a variety of outcomes in different scenarios, so the optimum settlements can be selected.

Consider, for a moment, two diametrically opposed settlement approaches presented in the following illustration:

	STATIC APPROACH	**VARIABLE/DYNAMIC APPROACH**
Assumption #1: Assumption #2: Assumption #3:	No Wage Disparity Finite State Short-Term (3-8 years)	Potential Wage Disparity Relative Conditions Long-Term (10-15 years)

The "static" approach assumes that parity exists between men and women in the workplace. This perspective may acknowledge that women traditionally have earned less than men, but that the gap can be closed with proper education, training, initiative and hard work. That perspective is rooted in the women's movement of the late 1960s and 1970s.

The "variable/dynamic" approach takes into account that while women entered the work force in record numbers during the last 30 years, their wages are still lower than men's. Overall, a woman earns about 70 cents to a man's dollar. According to the United States Census Bureau, women are not equally represented in all professions. Women continue to be over-represented (77 percent) in clerical, administrative support and service occupations, including education. They are under-represented in production, craft, repair and labor occupations (9.5 percent). Despite good news that college enrollment for women exceeds that of men, and the median earnings of women who worked full-time year-round rose by 1.3 percent between 1991 and 1992, median wages for women were only $21,440 in 1992 compared with median wages for men at $30,358 (unchanged from the previous year).

The median earnings of women aged 25 and older and who were year-round full-time workers was $18,648 for high school graduates in 1992; $24,849 for those with an associate degree; $29,284 for those with a bachelor's degree; and $35,018 for those with a master's degree. Comparable figures for men were $26,766; $32,349; $40,381 and $47,260 respectively.

The static approach to divorce settlement planning operates on the second assumption that a divorce settlement is based on finite analysis, often creating linear projections founded on historical data. The variable/dynamic approach takes into account such variables as economic instability, industry life cycle curves, sex and age discrimination in the work place, a shift from large conglomerates to small, entrepreneurial businesses and the effects of education and training on wages at the individual level. Those dynamic factors influence a person's career decisions and earnings both pre- and post-divorce. Variability must be considered in the settlement plan and allowances made for renegotiating when circumstances change.

Thirdly, the static approach operates under the assumption that the short term is most relevant to settlement planning. The short view assumes that financial awards can offset opportunity costs within three to five years. For instance, if a nonworking wife completes an advanced degree and obtains a couple of years of work experience, it is assumed she will be prepared for financial independence and enjoy a comparable lifestyle to that of her former husband.

Conversely, the variable/dynamic approach recognizes that a longer-term period is more realistic. If equity is to be served, maintenance must be extended to at least 10 years, especially in the case of long-term marriages from which a woman must enter a biased work place, after the age of 40 and with limited work experience.

Unfortunately, awards often are based on outdated "static" models created in the 1970s. They just don't apply to the demands of the 1990s and the twenty-first century. In a society where divorce affects more than half of all marriages, a more "dynamic" approach toward equitable solutions is imperative.

RECOMMENDATIONS

The foundation of any divorce settlement plan should include the following:
1. A career plan that:
   - Analyzes an individual's strength and weaknesses.
   - Evaluates an individual's suitability for various types of work.
   - Identifies appropriate career opportunities.
   - Prescribes necessary training and/or education.
   - Estimates associated costs and projects expected wages over time.

2. A financial plan that includes:
   * Pre- and post-divorce budget planning.
   * A comprehensive list of assets and asset valuations. An income tax and cash flow analysis.
   * A long-term (10 years plus) cash flow analysis.
   * Coordinated retirement estimates and projections for pensions, IRAs and other investments.
   * Tax consequences of liquidating various assets.

Divorce settlements will become increasingly equitable when attorneys implement career and financial planning along with computer modeling to analyze the short- and long-term consequences of alternative awards and spousal maintenance. The simulation of outcomes based on various proposals will help close the gap between divorcing parties and make sure that the benefits and burdens of dissolution are fairly distributed.

The whole problem of the middle-aged woman of divorce has been addressed in numerous publications, and in language less stuffy than the quasi-legal verbiage that typifies law and sociological articles. For the reader of this book, an interview in *USA Today* of Lenore J. Weitzman, a sociology professor at Harvard University who is the author of *The Divorce Revolution: The Unexpected Social and Economic Consequences for Women and Children in America,* pointed out some of the perilous issues facing divorced women, not the least of which may be poverty for herself and her children.

"*USA Today:* Your study of no-fault shows that women and children are hurt most by divorce. Why is that?

"Weitzman: The courts are letting the husbands keep a lion's share of the family property. The whole nature of property has changed. In the past, we had homes, cars and family farms. But increasingly today, people have less tangible forms of property, such as career assets. These include pensions, health insurance, education and professional licenses.

"*USA Today:* Are you saying these assets aren't part of the divorce settlement?

"Weitzman: That's right, and to exclude these things is like promising that they're going to divide all the family jewels, but then leaving the diamonds out of the pile. The diamonds of family property are these career assets which husbands are typically getting.

"*USA Today:* How much is a pension plan worth, for example?

"Weitzman: The typical divorcing couple has about $20,000 to divide at the point of divorce. A pension can pay $20,000 in one year, and it goes on to pay year after year after year. Another good example is something like medical insurance. If you're a 50-year-old woman at the point of divorce and you haven't been employed and don't have any medical insurance — especially if you've had a history of some kind of illness — that medical insurance can be the most valuable thing in the world to you. If that isn't even considered property, you're being deprived of your share of a major marital asset.

"*USA Today:* But isn't it a bit unfair to factor into the divorce settlement the value of a professional education.

"Weitzman: In many marriages, a wife works to support the family while her husband gets a professional degree and license. If they are divorced just at the point where his income is about to take off, it is clear that the major product that the marriage has produced is his professional education and degree. If the court doesn't recognize that as a form of property that's been produced by the marriage and doesn't give her any share in that piece of property, once again, the man is walking off with a major asset of marital partnership.

"*USA Today:* Your research shows that divorced women and minor children experience a 73 percent decline in income, while husbands experience a 42 percent rise. How do you explain this.

"Weitzman: Number one is the way property is defined. Number two is the way property is divided. Number three is child support. There are two problems with child support. Courts typically award very low amounts of child support. In fact the average child support award is less than the cost of day care. These awards are so low that they rarely cover even half of the cost of raising children. Then, there's a very high rate of non-compliance with the child support awards. Also, there is the lack of alimony — 85 percent of the divorced women are not awarded any support."

It seems quite obvious after reading the chilling facts recited by Weitzman that women going into divorce must be more prepared today than at any time in the past to fight for every thing they can fairly, and in justice, derive from a settlement. The consequences of failure to get fair settlement were summed up by Weitzman in this statement:

"One of the key factors in coping is money. The statistics on the middle-class poverty that's been created by divorce gives you an indicator of how tough it is. For example, 40 percent of women in their late 20s are likely to become single parents at some point. About half the children who live in single parent families live in poverty. We have this mythical notion that kids who live in single-parent families are there with unwed mothers. Eighty percent of the children in single-parent families are there because their parents are divorced or separated. So, divorce is the major contributor to child poverty in America today."

I believe there is evidence in our courts and in settlements that the '90s will be a period of change in the concept of spousal maintenance. Courts can't ignore authorities like Weitzman and the consequences to be faced by the children of divorce who turn to violence out of frustration and social isolation. Much of this book centers around the idea of a fair and equitable settlement between divorcing spouses. This means adequate spousal maintenance. It's something I fight for with my clients. A fair and equitable settlement means looking at the social and economic realities that face divorcing couples realistically. Judges can use discretion in this area. As a financial planner, it's my role to provide my clients and their attorneys with the financial tools to graphically illustrate these economic realities. We work directly with a vocational career advisor to quantify these realities in the job place and translate them into dollars.

The changes I advocate are going to come about when judges and the attorneys working with their clients arrive at a better understanding of the economic consequences of divorce and how poorly written property settlements contribute to poverty for women and children in our society.

CHAPTER EIGHT

FINANCIAL AND TAX CHECKPOINTS ALONG THE WAY TO THE PROPERTY SETTLEMENT

Anyone may so arrange his affairs that his taxes shall be low as possible; he is not bound to choose that pattern which will best pay the treasury; there is not even a patriotic duty to increase one's taxes.

— Judge Learned Hand

WHAT WILL MY POST-DIVORCE LIFE LOOK LIKE?

This is a question every person who is a party to a divorce should ask before signing the property settlement agreement.

Each week I meet with clients who bring in their divorce decrees and ask for financial planning help. Too many times, I find they have not met with a competent financial planner. They have relied on their attorney and/or family accountant to provide tax and investment planning advice. These professionals may or may not have the training and information to provide comprehensive financial planning advice, or as is more often the case, a professional was consulted for one part of the divorce, e.g., the sale of the family residence, but was not involved in the analysis of the overall property settlement.

Let's look at the family home as an example. Very often the large family home is awarded to the spouse who has the smallest earning capacity. Because of the expense to support and maintain the residence, the house is often sold within a few years after the divorce. This causes the receiving spouse to bear the entire cost, risk and expense of sale, *and* since a less expensive residence is purchased, income taxes must be paid. If the home has appreciated in value since it was purchased, the income taxes can be substantial.

With a comprehensive financial and long-term cash flow analysis, longer and/or larger amounts of maintenance can be awarded, systematic withdrawals from pension plans can be initiated, or the house can be sold with the expense of sale being shared by both of the parties, and, as is often the case, current taxes can be either substantially reduced or altogether eliminated!

This chapter will cover several important tax, cash flow, investment and retirement planning questions which you will want to understand before agreeing to a final property settlement. The chapter will be divided by major sub-headings with questions you should be asking in each of these financial areas.

SALE OF THE FAMILY RESIDENCE — ARE YOU MONEY POOR AND HOUSE RICH?

Since the family residence is usually one of the major assets which a married couple will be dividing in dissolution, this asset will be the first we consider. The best time to deal with your housing is before the divorce. Part of your cash flow planning and budgeting discussed in a previous chapter centers around your being able to create a "realistic" post-divorce lifestyle. The foundation of this lifestyle is your home and the costs that go with home ownership.

Young couples in short-term marriages of under ten years generally have big mortgages and little equity. It is usually a struggle for either party to keep the house. If the wife is home raising young children, there are generally minimal liquid funds available to be divided. Often, the wife will need to be re-trained to enter the job market or go back to school. Mid-term marriages of 10 to 25 years often are characterized by large homes and large mortgages. The wife most often retains custody of the children, who are often in the later years of high school, and she wants to keep the kids in the school all their friends attend. After the kids leave, she is left with a large house which is too expensive to clean and maintain.

In longer term marriages of 25 years or more, the children have generally left home. In some situations, the wife wants to keep the large residence so the children will have a place to "come home to." Even where there is large equity in the home (market value less mortgage), houses are expensive to maintain. After being in the house for a few years, the spouse decides that it is more than can be handled and decides to sell it. The fact is, barring death or illness, sooner or later we will all sell our primary residence. If it is later, the cost of sale and income tax consequences of the sale are not so important. If it is sooner (one to five years), the timing of the sale can be critical to the long-term financial well-being of the individual.

What are some of the financial considerations of selling a home? Will the sale result in a taxable gain, and if so, how much of a gain? What will it cost to sell the home? What information do you need to assemble for IRS? How long will it take to sell the property? If you find a replacement home and buy it, how will you cover the expenses of two homes if your original home takes some time to sell? What if the real estate market goes down? These are all important questions to be answered in your decision regarding the family home. It is very important to note that unless an asset is to be disposed of incident to divorce, the costs of sale are not considered. The party receiving the asset takes it at the full market value. With the family residence, taxes and costs of sale could represent 10 percent to 30 percent of the gross value of the home. If the home has a mortgage or the mortgage has been refinanced, I have actually seen situations where the costs of sale and income taxes were greater than the equity in the home! Costs of sale and income taxes can materially alter the actual property settlement you thought you were making.

Most homeowners have a general idea of how much their home is worth. With changing market conditions, values of homes go up and down. If you haven't done so, the first recommendation I generally make to a client with a residence is to get two or three real estate agents to do a market analysis. This will give you a better idea of how much your home is really worth. The second recommendation I make is to determine the tax basis of the property. The tax basis is what is used by the IRS to determine if you have a gain or loss when you sell the property. Even if you do not sell your home, it is important to assemble the tax basis. This information will ultimately be needed, and if your spouse has some of the information, it is probably easier to get it now than it will be two or five or ten years from now.

The most common misunderstanding I see people make is to assume that the difference between the mortgage and the sales price is what is taxed. The mortgage is there either because funds were needed for the original purchase or through refinancing, home equity was taken out and used for other purposes. The mortgage has nothing to do with the taxable gain! Basis is generally the original cost of an asset, increased by subsequent costs or improvements, and reduced by certain deductions or prior deferrals. Taxable gain is the difference between the adjusted sales price and the adjusted basis. If the current residence is your first home, the potential taxable gain will be the difference between the adjusted sales price (gross sales price less the expense of sale) and the combination of the original home cost plus subsequent home improvements. Home improvements are generally defined as something that adds value or prolongs the life of the property. Examples would include a new roof, a room addition or remodel, landscaping, storm windows, etc. Repairs and maintenance are not added to the basis of the property.

If you have previously sold a primary residence at a gain, and the gain was deferred (no tax was paid), determining the potential taxable gain will have an additional step. Any gain that was not taxed on the previous sale must be subtracted from the cost and improvements of the current home. If your income tax return was properly prepared in the year your former home was sold, the basis information will be found on *Form 2119 - Sale of Your Home.* The IRS requires this form to be filed each time you sell a home, regardless of gain or loss. For a complete discussion of the tax consequences of a sale of residence, be sure that you see your accountant to discuss the specifics on any potential house sale before signing your divorce decree. There are many complexities in the tax law related to house sales and you do not want to have any surprises around this transaction. To obtain information on how you can do some of the calculations, call the Internal Revenue Service and ask for their guide to filing Form 2119. Sale of residence rules can also be found in self-help books on your personal tax planning/preparation.

If the home is to be sold, effective tax planning can materially change the income tax consequences of the sale. Under the *Internal Revenue Code (IRC) Section 1034,* taxable gain on the sale of a residence can be deferred or rolled over if the following conditions are met:

A. The new residence must be bought or built (and occupied) within 24 months beginning two years before and ending two years after the sale of the old residence.

B. Both the old and new residences must be used as the taxpayer's principle residence during the two year time frame.

C. The cost of the replacement residence, plus improvements made within 24 months from purchase, must total more than the adjusted sales price of the former home.

A taxpayer's principle residence is his or her primary place of abode. The determination of primary place of abode depends on the facts and circumstances of each case. A property may cease to be the taxpayer's residence when he or she vacates it and moves to new accommodations. So if one spouse leaves the marital home while waiting out the divorce or separation, the test for principal residence may not be met. The test is whether the taxpayer *abandoned as a principle residence* the property that is sold. An *intent to return might preclude a finding of abandonment.* Congress has indicated an intent to clarify abandonment in the case of divorce or separation, but as of the date of this writing nothing has been accomplished.

Let's suppose that you and your ex-spouse decide to sell the family home and each purchase a new home. It is important to realize that by agreement, you can divide the sales cash proceeds and the income tax liability disproportionately. In other words, you can receive the majority of the cash yet report less than half the sale on your income tax return. Let's look at the following example to see how this works.

Mr. and Mrs. Client

HOUSE SALE INCOME TAX CALCULATION

Gross Sales Price:	. . . .	$475,000
1st Mortgage/Debt Balance:	. . . .	$175,428
2nd Mortgage/Debt Balance:	. . . .	$22,462
Cost of Sale (%):	7.00%	$33,250
House Tax Basis (Below):	. . . .	$250,394
% Sale Taxable to Wife:	. . . .	40.00%
% Sale Taxable to Husband:	. . . .	60.00%
% Net Cash Proceeds to Wife:	. . . .	25.00%
% Net Cash Proceeds to Husband:	. . . .	75.00%

INCOME TAX ALLOCATION

		Wife	Husband	Total
4	Cost of Replacement Home	$175,000	$250,000	$425,000
5	House Sales Price (A)	$190,000	$285,000	$475,000
6	Expense of Sale (B)	13,300	19,950	33,250
6	**AMOUNT REALIZED (A-B=C)**	**176,700**	**265,050**	**441,750**
7	House Tax Basis (Below) (D)	100,158	150,236	250,394
8	Gain on Sale (C-D=E)	76,542	114,814	191,356
9	Age 55 Exemption	0	0	0
10	Adjusted Gain	76,542	114,814	191,356

11	Fixing Up Expenses	0	0	0
12	Adj Sales Price (F)	176,700	265,050	441,750
13	Replacement Home (G)	175,000	250,000	425,000
14	**TAXABLE GAIN (Lesser of (F-G) or E)**	**1,700**	**15,050**	**16,750**
15	Deferred Gain	74,842	99,764	174,606
16	New House Basis	100,158	150,236	250,394

TAX ON GAIN (28%)	**$476**	**$4,214**	**$4,690**

CASH FLOW ALLOCATION

House Sales Price	$118,750	$356,250	$475,000
Expense of Sale	(8,313)	(24,938)	(33,250)
Tax on Gain (28%)	(476)	(4,214)	(4,690)
Existing Mort/Debt Balance	(49,473)	(148,418)	(197,890)
NET SALES PROCEEDS:	**$60,489**	**$178,681**	**$239,170**

HOUSE TAX BASIS:

House Basis from 1983 Form 2119	$201,584
New Roof - 1987	14,250
Kitchen Remonel = 1990	28,560
Hot Tub	6,000
ADJUSTED TAX BASIS:	**$250,394**

(The numbers down the left side of the example represent the line numbers included on the IRS Form 2119.)

The documents which transfer the interest in the marital home should support the party who intends to defer the gain under IRC 1034. The property should be termed the principle residence and the right to use the property should not be denied to the taxpayer before the actual transfer or sale. Earlier in the chapter, we used an example of a young couple with children. Under these circumstances, for the sake of the children, it is sometimes agreed that for a specified period of time, the couple will continue to own the house jointly.

If this is a consideration for you, be sure you understand how this arrangement will work for you both during the years of joint ownership and at the time of sale. Make sure your property settlement discusses how the cash and taxes at the time of sale will be handled. Who will pay for the upkeep of the house and what is determined to be normal maintenance costs and what constitutes improvements? How are these costs determined? How are costs shared? Is there a trust account set up? Does one party bill the other? How is the agreement enforced if there is a dispute and who pays the legal costs? Can you go to binding arbitration? If you are going to jointly list the house for sale, make sure your agreement discusses how you will handle disputes over price, listing agent, improvements, closing costs, excise taxes, etc. You do not want to become a legal annuity for your attorney to get your agreement interpreted.

Unless you and your ex-spouse can be civil, if not amicable, I would not recommend joint ownership, particularly for the sake of the children. If either spouse is under daily pressure from the costs of operating a home or the sale of a home, the children will feel that tension. In my experience, the children are able to adapt to a lower standard of living up front much easier than witnessing one parent become angry, bitter and over-stressed because he or she cannot handle the home financially, physically or emotionally. Be very careful of any agreement that guarantees one spouse will pay the other a fixed appreciation rate for each year the house is jointly owned. I have seen very unfair agreements in which the equity in the house is inadequate to make this future payment. This could occur when the value in the house has not appreciated at the projected rate, or if the person living in the house has not had sufficient funds to maintain the house in prime condition.

EXCLUSION OF GAIN FOR SELLERS OVER AGE 55

If you are 55 or over at the time of sale, under IRC 121, you may exclude up to $125,000 of the profit from the sale or exchange of your home. To qualify for the exclusion, in addition to your age, the home must have been your principal residence for at least three of the five years prior to the date of sale. This exclusion is available only once in your lifetime.

If you are filing a joint income tax return, only one of the spouses must meet the age, use and ownership requirements. When a couple divorces and each party is over 55, assuming the other requirements are met, it is possible for each to claim the $125,000 exclusion. This could exempt a combined gain of $250,000. To use the double exemption, the divorce must be final before the sale is concluded. For tax purposes, a sale is deemed to have occurred when the sale closes or the purchaser takes possession under a binding contract, whichever occurs first.

If you marry or are married to a person who has previously used the exclusion, you cannot use the exclusion even if the previous exclusion was used prior to your marriage and by a previous spouse. This limitation tells you that if your home has a lot of appreciation and you are planning on selling your home to buy a new one with your new spouse, to take the exclusion you should sell your home before you get married.

IS THE TAX DEFERMENT RESTRICTED TO ONE-FAMILY HOUSES?

You may defer tax on the sale and purchase of a mobile home, trailer, houseboat, cooperative apartment (tied to stock ownership), and condominium apartment, which you use as a principal residence. An investment in a retirement home community does not qualify if you do not receive equity in the property.

WHAT IF THERE HAS TO BE A NOTE TO EQUITABLY DIVIDE THE ASSETS?

In this scenario, the house is awarded to one spouse who then, over time, buys the former spouse's interest in the property. The former spouse effectively becomes the banker to the party that receives the residence. In this situation, under *IRC 1041(c)(2),* the purchase of the former spouse's interest is considered a transfer of property incident to a divorce. Under this section, principal payments to the former spouse are not taxable and payments *do not* increase the basis of the home. The spouse who keeps the home retains the same tax cost basis in the home that the couple had. *(IRC 1041(b)).*

It is more common for these payments to be structured to qualify as deductible home mortgage interest. This requires that the note be secured by the property and meet the $100,000 home equity limitation requirements under *IRC 163(h)(3).* While the principal portion of the payment is a transfer related to the divorce, the interest portion is considered home mortgage interest expense.

In a case in which the non-occupancy spouse owes the additional funds to arrive at an equitable property division, payments are sometimes structured to satisfy the rules of maintenance. While this is not a common practice, it might be used so the the higher-paying taxpayer has the opportunity to get a current ordinary tax deduction for the payments made. In other words, if you are receiving these payments in the form of maintenance they will represent taxable income to you and will be deductible for tax purposes by your ex-spouse.

HOW IS THE TAX BASIS CALCULATED ON REAL AND PERSONAL ASSETS?

Every capital asset you have or will have has a tax basis. This includes stocks, bonds, mutual funds, limited partnerships, real estate, etc. When these assets are sold, there will be a taxable gain or loss. To determine the gain or loss, you must have the information on the tax basis. If you do not obtain this information before the time of the divorce, it may be impossible to accurately obtain the information at a later time. This is your homework assignment. First list all your capital assets. Second, either go to the library or buy a book on taxes, or meet with your accountant to go over the details on which assets have a basis. Third, assemble all the documents and records that substantiate the basis of your assets. The records would include real estate settlement papers, all improvements to real property, stock and bond purchase confirmations, year end statements on mutual funds, canceled checks, etc. At the end of this chapter, I have included a spreadsheet that you can use as a guide for this tracing activity.

WHAT ABOUT MY INTEREST IN THE LIMITED PARTNERSHIPS WHICH WE JOINTLY OWN?

In a limited partnership, limited partners are part-owners of the business but do not have a right to manage or control it. They also are liable only to the extent of the capital they have invested in the partnership. Think of yourself handcuffed to the rail of a cruise ship. You go wherever the cruise ship (general partner) takes you. You may or may not make it back to port and you could run into major weather and mechanical problems along the way. You are together in this to the end. Since there is no active financial market for limited partnerships, it is very difficult to determine their value. Many attorneys recommend to their clients with less financial and economic independence to assign them to their spouse. Doing so could either be giving away a future headache, or you could be throwing out the baby with the wash. Partnerships need to be looked at one by one. On large public partnerships, it may be best to simply divide the investment equally between the parties.

If you are going to have an interest in a limited partnership, you need to have the historical tax information on the investment. I also suggest that you contact the general partner and request current information on your partnership interest. Your annual tax information is reported on a Schedule K-1/Partner's Share of Income, Credits, Deductions, etc. Since tax information from the partnership will be needed to complete your income tax return, and it often takes several months to get the ownership re-registered, you should begin the re-registration process before the ink is dried on your divorce papers.

If your prior year tax returns have been prepared by a professional tax preparer, there should be a record of any passive activity losses with the return. If your spouse has been preparing your return, be sure to obtain the worksheets from his files. This can be a very complicated area of tax, so I do not recommend that you try to get all the answers by yourself. Hire a professional tax accountant.

SALE OF STOCK AND MUTUAL FUNDS

After the divorce, assets have to be retitled into the name of the spouse to whom the asset was awarded. No taxes are due with this transfer as it is incident to divorce. The problems surface when you decide to sell the security. I talked about keeping good records when collecting the financial information in your document round up list in Chapter Five. Make sure that you know what the basis of your security was prior to the divorce being final. Get a copy of the original confirmation from your files, ex-spouse or the brokerage firm. You will then be able to track this paper trail from the original purchase date, transfer between spouses, and sale of a portion or all of the assets.

Because of cash needs, expenses, or risk tolerance, stocks, bonds, and mutual funds are often sold during separation, or after divorce. It is the sharp attorney who details in the decree how these transactions are to be reported by the divorcing parties. Unfortunately, too often it is easier for the attorney to ignore the tax consequences of such transactions and leave it to the clients to argue it out when it comes time to file income tax returns. Make sure the decree states how the capital transactions in the year of the divorce are to be reported.

WHAT ABOUT PAYING INCOME TAXES ON EARLY DISTRIBUTIONS FROM MY QUALIFIED RETIREMENT PLAN, ANNUITY, OR MODIFIED ENDOWMENT CONTRACT? WHAT PART IS SUBJECT TO THE 10 PERCENT EARLY WITHDRAWAL PENALTY?

In general if you receive an early distribution from a qualified retirement plan or annuity prior to age 59-1/2 under *IRC Section 411(a)(11) or 417(e)*, the part of the distribution which is includable in gross income is generally subject to an additional 10 percent tax. The 10 percent additional tax does not apply to certain distributions specifically excepted by the code. One of the exemptions is "distributions made to an alternate payee under a Qualified Domestic Relations Order (QDRO)." Retirement accounts covered under a QDRO must be "employer sponsored qualified retirement plans." IRA accounts do not qualify.

For example, the husband passes part of his company 401(k) plan to his wife as a transfer of property incident to divorce. The wife is able to take a distribution from this plan and not pay a 10 percent penalty on the distribution. The husband cannot qualify for this exemption on distributions from his plan. When the wife receives these funds she will have to pay taxes on these funds as ordinary income. Sometimes this strategy is used to provide liquid cash to one or the other of the spouses to allow for both of them to own a home. If this strategy is used, the income tax obligation is taken into account in the overall property settlement prior to the divorce.

I saw this strategy used effectively in a recent case. The couple had been married for 22 years. They had four children all attending private schools. Both husband and wife were committed to the children's private school education. The couple had been separated four and one half years and during that time the wife had returned to school to complete a masters degree in education. The husband was an engineer and had been with his present corporation for the past 20 years. He received a substantial salary and annual bonuses and was considered to be a senior manager with the engineering firm. She was teaching part-time and looking for a full-time teaching position.

The family residence had a small mortgage which would be paid off in six years. The husband had shared custody of the children and wanted to purchase a home for himself and the children. He had been living in a condominium they had purchased four years previously. However, there was no equity in the property. The couple's assets were primarily in the equity in the house, his 401(k) retirement plan, and his earning capacity.

She initially requested 60 percent of the assets, maintenance for 10 years and a house paid for in six years. He wanted to have a home for himself and the children. He felt he had paid maintenance for four years at a level representing half of his income and bonuses, and had paid for all of costly private school education for the children and his wife's masters program. He was ready to have a home.

With creative planning and the use of the pension plan, we were finally able to settle the case. They continued to share his income and bonuses for the next four years with maintenance decreasing annually. If she found full-time employment, it would decrease sooner. Until she obtained full-time employment, he would continue to pay the children's private school education costs. After she obtained employment, they would share education costs in proportion to their total income. In addition, she would receive 65 percent of his 401(k) plan and make a cash settlement to him. Under the QDRO, she took a lump sum distribution of 15 percent of the plan. After paying income taxes on the distribution, she made a cash settlement to the husband. This strategy saved the 10 percent IRS penalty on early distributions. Since she was in a lower income tax bracket, it saved income taxes, and it provided the cash needed by the husband to purchase a home. It was a win/win financial and tax strategy for each of them.

INCOME TAX RETURNS

There are four possible tax statuses for filing an income tax return. They are:
1. Married Filing Jointly (or Qualifying Widow/er).
2. Married Filing Separately.
3. Head of Household.
4. Single Taxpayer.

You tell the IRS how you are going to file in the block labeled: Filing Status. Your marital status as of December 31 determines your filing options. Neither marriage or divorce come under the jurisdiction of federal laws. You might wonder about this with the nationalization of so many parts of our life today — environments, air traffic control and soon health care. At this time marriage, remarriage, divorce, pre-nuptial agreements and community property rules as they relate to marriage are all deemed to be strictly domestic affairs and therefore tax implications are determined based on family laws in the state of domicile. In navigating your divorce, filing status is another area in which you need to hire a professional or do some research and outside reading. It is typical for me to see clients who have met with their accountant and had several "what if" returns completed in an attempt to find the optimum tax return filing status for the divorcing couple. For example, in November, you may have agreed to and signed property settlement, maintenance and child support documents, but for tax purposes, decide to wait and file your final divorce decree until January 1 of the following year. This would be done where both parties realize it would save tax dollars and they agree as to how the tax savings would be shared. To obtain more complete information on your filing status options, call the IRS and request a copy of their Publication 504.

WHAT IS MY LIABILITY ON PRIOR INCOME TAX RETURNS FILED WITH MY HUSBAND?

If you suspect your spouse of fraud or other inappropriate claims or deductions you may choose to not file a joint return. For tax returns which have been previously filed, there is the possibility of being considered an "innocent spouse." A definition of this is found in *IRC Section 6013(e)*. The section allows for a spouse to be relieved of liability in certain cases. If you suspect your spouse of foul play, you should discuss this with your attorney and/or accountant.

In an earlier chapter, I said that you should have the last five years' tax returns available for your attorney, accountant and financial planner. Pull out a copy of any of your returns and turn to page two of the return. Look for the signature block near the bottom of the page which says: "Please sign here." You have probably never read the small print above the white space for your signatures before signing your name. It reads: "Under penalties of perjury, I declare that I have examined this return and accompanying schedules and statements, and to the best of my knowledge and belief, they are true, correct, and complete."

Unless you can prove that you are an innocent spouse, the IRS holds you liable for any errors, penalties, or interest due on the return. The IRS is looking for the quickest way to collect it's money, and can assign tax liabilities to assets of either party of a jointly filed income tax return. You will then have to go to civil court to dispute payments your spouse should have made.

If your spouse was the one who handled all the business, financial and tax affairs of the household, I strongly urge you to have language put into your decree that holds this spouse financially responsible for any future tax problems. You may have to share in inadvertent mistakes on the returns, but you should have some protection from intentional misrepresentations of which you had no knowledge. While this language may not save you from the IRS taking some of your funds, it will give you recourse against your former spouse.

WHO CAN CLAIM THE CHILDREN AS DEPENDENTS ON HIS OR HER INCOME TAX RETURN?

This issue is normally addressed in parenting plan and child support agreements. If the dependency deduction is not discussed in your child support documents, by default, the deduction goes to the custodial parent. Since the non-custodial parent is generally the one with the highest income, this parent would like to claim the children as exemptions on his income tax return. With the current income tax law, if income goes over a certain level, the dependency exemption is limited. Where this is the case, the parties may agree to share income tax information annually by March 15 and if the non-custodial spouse does not receive a tax benefit from the exemption, it is passed over to the other spouse. Spouses will sometimes alternate the deduction between their returns from year to year.

A limitation I often see in the verbiage for dependency exemptions is that the non-custodial spouse simply needs to have tax savings to use the deductions. Because of the deduction limitations, the deduction could save as little as $1, yet the conditions for claiming the exemption would be met. I prefer to see language that states the deduction must meet a minimum deduction or tax savings.

It is best if you agree on this issue before the divorce is final. However, we know that the financial circumstances change between divorced parents. If you have been given the dependency exemption in your child support agreement and want to release this exemption, use *IRS Form 8332, Release of Claim to Exemption for Child of Divorced or Separated Parents* can change your prior agreement. Instructions on the form permit release for the current year only, for a specified number of years, or for all future years. I prefer to have the annual signing as attitudes and conditions in the future can change. You will need to keep detailed records on the use of your child support money and what money is spent on the children whether you use this form or not. Child support — the payment and collection — is a major problem for single divorced parents. I encourage you to continue the detailed budgeting and accounting of dollars spent introduced in Chapter Six. There will come a time in the post-divorce period where this will be essential.

Often financial conditions change. Where the relationship is not amicable, child support payments may be the first cut in the non-custodial spouse's budget. If you find that you are not receiving the support which was ordered, there is a national law enforcement agency attempting to enforce these collections. Contact your state office if you are having problems.

MAINTENANCE VERSUS CHILD SUPPORT, DOES IT MAKE A DIFFERENCE? OR, HOW DO I DISTINGUISH MAINTENANCE (SOMETIMES CALLED "ALIMONY" OR "SEPARATE MAINTENANCE") FROM CHILD SUPPORT AND PAYMENTS MADE AS PART OF A PROPERTY SETTLEMENT?

Alimony, or maintenance, provides an income tax deduction for your husband's payments and is taxable income when you receive it. Child support and payments made pursuant to a property settlement are neither deductible to him nor taxable to you and are not even reported on your income tax return. In Washington and many other states, there are child support payment guidelines which will be used in determining the amount of child support. Any additional payments you receive will be either property settlement payments, or maintenance (alimony). If your situations falls outside the schedule, you may have to negotiate the allocation of maintenance and child support. Given the income tax considerations of maintenance and child support, you will want to have the lion's share of your payments considered child support, and your husband will want the lion's share to be maintenance; however, since he will be making the payments, and an income tax savings will make more funds available for both of you to share, your negotiations should encompass the tax and cash flow of both of you.

There are five requirements for a payment to qualify as alimony/maintenance:

1. The payment must be in cash (or by check or money order).
2. The payments must be made under a written divorce decree, separation agreement, or similar order such as a temporary alimony/maintenance award. There must be a *legal obligation* to pay via a court document.
3. The payments must cease in the event of the payee spouse's death.
4. The ex-spouse (or soon to be ex-spouse) may not be members of the same household or file a joint return.
5. The payments must not be deemed to be child support.

Your final property settlement will address the amount and duration of maintenance and its taxability. If you have been receiving payments during your separation, and the payments were ordered under a separate maintenance order from the courts, when the above conditions are met, these payments also will be deemed to be taxable to you.

Sometimes the courts will award a specified amount of money to be transferred during separation and state that the money you receive is not differentiated between child support and maintenance. This is done "so that the decree can have some room for negotiation and flexibility." Unfortunately, too often the decree does not address the taxability of the temporary order. Since you will not want the income to be taxable and he will want the income tax to be tax deductible, disagreement will follow. If your separately-filed income tax returns do not list the same amount of maintenance payments, the IRS will then be contacting both of you and you will have to explain the difference.

I do a great deal of post-divorce planning in which a client will come in to see me just before or shortly after signing the final property settlement. It is not unusual for the client to have received maintenance income for several months. Too many times to number the client was taken by total surprise to find that not only does she have a large income tax liability owed on the maintenance income, but that since no quarterly payments have been made, there will be IRS penalties assessed when the income tax return is filed. Unfortunately, no professional ever told her about the tax consequences of receiving maintenance. Don't let this happen to you. If you are receiving maintenance income, taxes will be owed. You should ask your attorney, accountant or financial planner to estimate what the tax obligation will be and when the tax is due without penalty. If taxes being withheld from wages are not sufficient to cover the tax on maintenance income, you will need to either increase the amount of tax withholdings, or make quarterly tax payments (see below). When I am working with a client to complete a financial affidavit, I always make sure there is an allowance for income taxes and provide payment vouchers so that the taxes are paid in a timely manner.

As income taxes reduce the amount of cash flow available to the receiving spouse, it can increase the cash flow of the paying husband. If the same amount of taxes are being withheld from your husband's paycheck after beginning maintenance payments as was withheld after maintenance payments, there could be a big tax refund when he files his tax return. By adjusting the amount of taxes withheld from the wage now, next year's refund is available to the parties for current needs. One other note relative to maintenance is what is called "front-loading." This is where very large maintenance payments are made in the first few years, then drop off dramatically. The IRS sees this as a disguised property settlement and will apply additional taxes. If your maintenance income declines substantially within the first three years of payments, you should be sure your accountant looks at the terms of the agreement.

WHAT HAPPENS IF MAINTENANCE DECLINES SUBSTANTIALLY IN THE FIRST THREE YEARS?

Recapture rules apply when within the first three years of maintenance payments, the annual payment is reduced by more than a certain floor level. The floor level for post-1986 divorces is $15,000. For divorces in 1985 and 1986, the floor level is $10,000.

Exceptions:
1. Payments are made under a temporary support order before the divorce or separation.
2. Payments made over at least three years are a percentage of the business or property income.
3. Payments end due to the death of either spouse, or the spouse remarries within the first three calendar years of payments.

Only a portion of the previously deducted (claimed) maintenance payments are to be recaptured (deducted). In general terms, the amount of maintenance adjustment is equal to the amount by which the maintenance deduction exceeds the floor amount. The formula is fairly complicated and competent professional advice is strongly recommended.

WHEN MUST I FILE MY FORM W-4 WITH MY EMPLOYER AFTER I AM DIVORCED?

While on the subject of income taxes, I am often asked if there has to be a change in the W-4 (Employee's Withholding Allowance Certificate) filed with the employer after the divorce. Technically, an employee must give an employer a new Form W-4 within ten days after a divorce if the employee has been claiming married status, or if a spouse claims his/her own exemption on a separate certificate, or after any event which decreases the number of withholding allowances an employee can claim. Again, this is the case in which an accountant or financial planner can help you. You should check to see if enough tax will be withheld for the year by comparing the total withholding from your pay with what you expect your tax to be. You probably will have too little withheld if you have more than one job at a time, if you are receiving maintenance, or if you have income not subject to withholding. If too much tax will be withheld and you don't want to wait for a refund, decreased withholding by claiming more exemptions is possible.

If you are having too little withheld, you may need to start making quarterly estimated tax payments. These are due April 15, June 15, September 15, and January 15. It is never too late in the year to start making these quarterly payments. If you have missed one or two payments, start as soon as you have the funds available and don't wait for the end of the quarter. To make an adjustment to the W-4, employees must give a new form W-4 to their employers. This form includes three areas of information which the employer uses to figure the withholding amount. These areas are the rate at which to withhold (single or lower married rate), how many allowances the employee claims, and whether the employee wants an additional amount withheld. The deductions and adjustment worksheet which is part of the form can be helpful in determining the number of allowances, but an in-depth tax analysis done with your advisors will be more accurate.

ARE ANY OF MY LEGAL AND EXPERT FEES DEDUCTIBLE ON MY INCOME TAX RETURN POST-DIVORCE?

Section 212 of the Internal Revenue code of 1954 provides, in effect, that except as otherwise stated in the code, no deduction is allowed for personal, living or family expenses. The cost of getting a divorce is considered a personal expense. However, Section 212 allows an individual to deduct all of the ordinary and necessary expenses paid or incurred during the taxable year:

1. For the production or collection of income.
2. For the management, conservation or maintenance of property held for the production of income, or
3. In connection with the determination, collection or refund of any tax.

Provided you itemize your deductions, some of your attorney fees will qualify as a deduction on your income tax return. These fees are Schedule A miscellaneous itemized deductions and are limited to two percent of your adjusted gross income. The fees are deductible in the year paid. Request a letter from your attorney and other experts which will assist you and your accountant in determining the deductibility of fees paid to the legal firm in connection with your dissolution proceeding. The following page shows a format which may be used as a prototype letter indicating the needed information.

In some instances, fees which are not currently deductible under *Section 212* may be treated as a capital expense and added to the cost basis of property awarded to you in the dissolution proceeding. *(Cf. George v. United States, 434 F, 2d 1336 (1970), Regs. 1-211-1(k)(n).)* Ask your accountant if your expenses may qualify.

SHOULD I HAVE MY OWN FINANCIAL PLANNER AND/OR ACCOUNTANT DURING THE DIVORCE PROCEEDINGS AND AFTER THE DIVORCE?

My answer is unequivocally "Yes!" Just as in mediation, you are recommended to seek your own separate legal counsel, the same is true

---

Anderson, Mitchell, Barnes & Williams, P.S.
1717 18th Avenue
Suite 304
Seattle, WA 90000-0000

June 15, 1994

Jane Smith
12345 Oak Street
Anytown, USA 12345

Dear Jane,

I have reviewed my billings and time records in your case and
have determined that the following tax treatment should be
applied to the legal fees paid by you to this firm:

(1) Percentage deductible under Section 212, as being ordinary
and necessary expenses incurred in connection with the
production or collection of income and in connection with
determination and planning as to federal income taxation:
_____%. (This means the fees to produce or collect
maintenance re deductible, fees charged for defending against a
claim to maintenance are not.)

(2) Percentage includable in the base cost or price of the capital
asset for which the services were rendered per Section 212:
_____%.

(3) General tax advice: _____%.

Thank you for affording us the opportunity to be of service to
you. If we can be of service in the future, please do not hesitate
to call us.

Sincerely,

Ellen P. Anderson, P.S.

with important issues about taxes and overall financial matters. This does not mean that you cannot agree to have your family accountant prepare the joint tax return, it simply means that you have your own separate advocate watching out for your best interests. This is a professional who can advise you on the advantages and disadvantages of various compromises. It is better that you know the issues and options up front rather than discovering them too late and facing the expense and arguments of filing an amended return.

I recommended that you have your own separate advisor for taxes and financial matters. I suggest that you contract with that expert directly. I also suggest that you sign an engagement letter in any divorce tax planning situation with these advisors. This letter should affirmatively state that the attorney is the "quarterback" of the divorce team and that the advisor should take directions from the attorney. You should also state that you authorize the attorney to work with your advisors and that you will pay for this work.

You, as the client, want to be sure that your attorney and experts are working together as a team. This is important before the divorce is final and afterwards, because, once the divorce is final, unless he is re-hired for enforcement, the attorney is finished with your case. It is critical that you get competent tax and investment advice post-divorce as you are starting a new life as a single person and you want to start your future with a comprehensive financial plan rather than learning as you go. This book is designed for the pre- and post-divorce planning client. There are checklists provided for you as you make this financial transition. Avoid the pitfalls by taking charge of your financial life.

ESTABLISHING GUIDELINES WITH YOUR FINANCIAL PLANNER AND ACCOUNTANT

Tax laws are changing all of the time, annually at the very least, and when this is combined with the trauma being experienced by your getting a divorce, you need to realize that a tax plan developed today probably won't work tomorrow. Because of these changes, I strongly recommend that you develop a working relationship with the financial planner and accountant prior to the divorce and that you continue with this relationship for at least two years post-divorce. This team of experts will have the background of your case as well as the divorce decree and will be able to work out future problems, e.g., changes in the law.

Below are a few possible situations that could arise:

- An audit from a prior year's income tax return where you filed jointly.
- Modification of maintenance.
- Sale of a family residence.
- Both you and your spouse use the same dependency exemption for the child.
- A limited partnership which you both owned is being questioned by the IRS.
- Treatment of rental property.
- Sale of stock or mutual funds and reconciliation of the report from your broker.

There are a multitude of potentially unresolved issues with respect to the income tax consequences of divorce transactions, and changes in legislative, administrative or judicial authority that may change the contemplated tax consequences of a transaction. I work with our accountant on these types of situations every week. No competent professional will guarantee you a specific result, but rather, will advise you on the strengths and weakness of your position based on current laws and the information you have provided.

STOCKS, BONDS & OTHER ASSETS

	Name of Security	Purchase Date	# of Shares (A)	Cost per Share (B)	Total Cost (A*B)	Total Value	Gain (Loss)
(1)							
(2)							
(3)							
(4)							
(5)							
(6)							
(7)							
(8)							
(9)							
(10)							
(11)							
(12)							
(13)							
(14)							
(15)							
(16)							
(17)							
TOTALS:							

MUTUAL FUNDS

	Name of Fund	Purchase Date	Original Cost (A)	Reinvested Dividends (B)	Total Cost (A+B)	Total Value	Gain (Loss)
(1)							
(2)							
(3)							
(4)							
(5)							
(6)							
(7)							
(8)							
(9)							
(10)							
TOTALS:							

REAL ESTATE

	Name/Location of Property	Purchase Date	Cost plus Improvements	Less Depreciation	Adjusted Cost	Total Value	Gain (Loss)
(1)							
(2)							
(3)							
(4)							
(5)							
(6)							
TOTALS:							

CHAPTER NINE

DIVORCED WOMEN, PENSIONS AND AVOIDING POVERTY IN THE GOLDEN YEARS

From birth to 18, a girl needs good parents.
From 18 to 35, she needs good looks; from 35 to 55, a good personality.
After 55, hard cash.
— Sophie Tucker

The next two chapters address long-term financial security for women. The subjects to be discussed in this chapter include:

- Life expectancy and aging of women.
- Pension and profit sharing plans. What you should ask for.
- Understanding your Social Security benefits and rights. What you can expect.
- Early distributions from an IRA account.
- Military pensions.
- Deferred compensation, stock appreciation rights, stock options.
- Transferring retirement assets under a QDRO.
- Reviewing your insurance needs.
- Adjusting maintenance for inflation.
- Buy or rent a home — what is right for YOU?

- Estate planning during and after the divorce.
- What about a prenuptial agreement?
- Retirement asset transfer checklist.

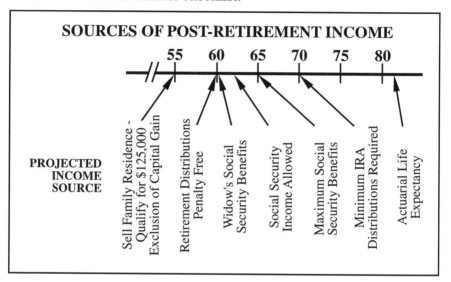

SOURCES OF POST-RETIREMENT INCOME

RETIREMENT BENEFITS ARE NOT WHAT THEY USED TO BE

If retirement benefits, IRA's, Keoghs, defined benefit and profit sharing plans were earned during the marriage, you can expect them to be divided equitably at the time of divorce. I discuss specific rules about taking these funds out of the plan under a Qualified Domestic Relations Order (QDRO) and early withdrawal penalties in Chapter Thirteen.

All women may be at the mercy of their life patterns, but women who divorce in mid-life or later are shoved with sudden force into a vulnerable subset of the female experience. It is the women who have done what was expected of them, led the most exemplary middle class lives who may be the least prepared to face the reduced circumstance in which they will very likely find themselves in old age.

A recent 1994 report by the House Select Aging Subcommittee found that while poverty rates for older men will likely decline over the next three decades, almost half of the elderly women living alone by 2020 will have incomes less than $9,500 in today's dollars.

"Women are 70 percent more likely to spend their retirement in poverty than men," said New York Representative Sherwood Boehlert, senior Republican on the sub-committee. "Over half of elderly women who live alone have incomes below 150 percent of the poverty level. Furthermore, a widowed woman is four times more likely, and a single or divorced woman five times more likely, to live in poverty after retirement than [are] married women."

The 1990 poverty threshold for a single person aged 65 and over was $6,268 per year. This was lower than the level used for the rest of the population "based on the faulty premise that persons age 65 and over need less nutrition and eat less than the general population," the report states.

And where did the subcommittee gather its information? The study was compiled using material from two outside study groups formed by the subcommittee to examine Social Security and private pensions. Overall, the groups found that both systems penalize women for living longer than men, for earning less than men, for getting divorced and for taking time off from jobs to care for children and other family members.

These studies seem to be sending women a strong message about their long-term value as mothers and caretakers of the family, and about their retirement years and financial independence during those years. When my mother married, her commitment was until death, for better or worse, in sickness and health. My mother told me how her father, an immigrant from Germany, gave her the following piece of advice: "Don't marry below your economic-social station in life, work hard, and you will be taken care of for the rest of your life just as I have taken care of you up to this time of marriage."

My mother was raised on a farm; my grandfather did not mean to say she would not work hard. She married a farmer and raised six children, so there was hard work, but there was also a promise of financial security. Both the study I've mentioned and experts in pensions and divorce say changes in matrimonial law since 1970, when California became the first state to allow "no-fault" divorce, generally have not worked to the benefit of women. Where the courts once used alimony/maintenance and tangible assets to punish *and* reward, they now focus on distributing property fairly. They have expanded the definition of property to include intangibles, like potential earning power and pensions, and in the process women have come to receive alimony/maintenance less often and for shorter periods.

The last thing the woman may be thinking about as she contemplates the sinking trend line of her post-divorce income is a pension that won't come home to roost for several years. I have found that women with children, especially, may have other priorities. They choose to solve a three-year problem at the expense of a ten-year problem.

Too many times I see women ignore the pension issues in their property settlements without realizing the economic impact. The pension and retirement issues are very important in the divorce process. You need to be thinking about the pension benefits which were earned from a defined benefit plan and accrued during your marriage years. These pension benefits — though earned by the husband — are a marital asset and can be handled as a lump settlement to you, or you can share in the income provided at retirement alongside your husband. However, you also need to be aware of the risks of anticipated changes such as remarriage or the death of your ex-husband which could occur before his retirement and nullify your agreement, leaving you with nothing.

What are the messages we are giving out today in our society with the rising divorce rates and increasing poverty for our women? The major one I hear loud and clear is: marry rich and stay married as long as possible, or go to work but don't leave the work force to raise your child or care for an elderly parent, or your contribution to Social Security and a future pension will be meaningless.

Social Security came about in the 1930s and was sold to voters as a supplement to retirement for those who needed help. At that time the American family consisted of a wife who stayed at home to raise the children and a wage-earning husband. Today, Social Security benefits are the foundation of many women's retirement and long-term financial security.

By 1988, however, just one in five families fit this traditional description; now, about 43 percent of families have two wage earners.

The survivor of a two-earner couple, usually the widow, almost always gets a lower Social Security benefit than a one-earner couple with the same total earnings, the subcommittee report found.

The report went on to warn women to beware of the "Widow's Gap" in Social Security. Because of outdated job skills and age discrimination, women under the age of 60 are more likely to be collecting spousal benefits early. This decreases their lifetime benefits by as much as 30 percent.

The subcommittee study also showed how Social Security also discriminated against divorced women. A divorcee is entitled to benefits as long as her former husband is receiving them and the marriage lasted at least a decade. But there are no benefits awarded if the marriage dissolved without reaching a 10th anniversary.

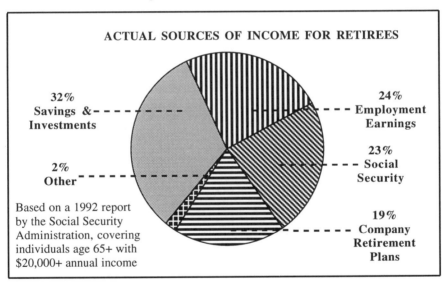

ACTUAL SOURCES OF INCOME FOR RETIREES

32%
Savings & Investments

2%
Other

Based on a 1992 report by the Social Security Administration, covering individuals age 65+ with $20,000+ annual income

24%
Employment Earnings

23%
Social Security

19%
Company Retirement Plans

There are also problems with private pension plans. The odds are stacked against a woman's long-term financial security because female workers are more likely to hold low-wage, service, part-time or non-union jobs where coverage for retirement is less likely.

Many people are arguing for an overhaul of the Social Security system. That is not the subject of this book. However, I will say that I believe there are going to be significant changes to this system in future years for women. Already, plans are afoot to advance the date of retirement incrementally toward age 67 by the year 2027, and Social Security benefits are being taxed in cases where recipients have income above certain levels ($25,000 for a single person and $32,000 for a married couple filing jointly).

Women are living longer. This is a reality of life as we approach the twenty-first century. As recent census data clearly shows, longevity is a reality and women are the leaders in the trend. At the beginning of this century, American men and women could expect to live to be about 47 years old. Today the average life expectancy at birth is 72 years for men and 79 for women. As baby boomers reach retirement age, the number of women 85 and older is expected to mushroom from 2.2 million today to more than 10 million by mid-century.

It is not clear why women are living longer but even more unclear is whether or not living longer is really an advantage to them. "Women's longevity is not all good news," says Nancy McConnell, who is studying the issue for the National Institute on Aging. "It is frequently 10 years of poverty and declining health."

Cynthia Tauber, a demographer with the U.S. Census Bureau who has recently authored a study on aging women, says, "Most women should be planning and financing to live into their mid-80s or longer, often alone ... The life that one leads as a younger person greatly affects the life one leads as an older person." Getting your fair share on the pension is going to be a major part of your financial security if you are 50 or older today and getting a divorce. In many middle income families pensions are the most valuable marital assets to be divided, sometimes exceeding the equity which the married couple has accumulated in a family home.

Some basic terminology will be helpful to you in figuring retirement income benefits, and planning for them. This information comes from an article I read in *The Matrimonial Strategist,* a publication for divorce practitioners.

BASIC TERMINOLOGY

The following list consists of terminology which every divorcing woman needs to know:

1. Defined Benefit Plan:
A defined benefit plan promises the employee a specified benefit, usually a function of the years of service and salary level.

2. Defined Contribution Plan:
A defined contribution plan promises the employee that specified contributions will be made to the plan, but does not commit to payment of a specified benefit. The employee and employer can contribute to this plan. A 401(k) plan, for instance, is a defined contribution plan.

3. Vested Interest:
Benefits are vested when they are not subject to forfeiture upon the termination of employment, whether by voluntary act of the employee or by employer discharge. Otherwise stated, once the benefits are vested, the only further precondition to their receipt is that the employee survives until retirement age.

4. Non-vested Interest:
The employee's interest is non-vested when it is contingent upon continuation of employment with the employer sponsoring the plan.

5. Unmatured Benefit:
Benefits may be unmatured, even though vested. They are matured when the employee has "an unconditional right to immediate payment of the benefits upon retirement."

6. Contributory Plan:
A plan funded by contributions from both employer and employee.

7. Non-contributory Plan:
A plan funded entirely by employer contributions.

Before I get into specific planning opportunities about retirement, pensions, Social Security and specific retirement plans, I am going to give you a checklist of pension questions for you to complete. Get the answers to these questions in writing and document the answers whenever possible. This is one area of investigation where you must "TRUST, BUT VERIFY." Start early with your investigation. There are many bureaucratic rooms for your to pass through on the way to your answers.

ASK YOURSELF

1. How much Social Security will I receive? To get an estimate of future Social Security Benefits, call (800) 772-1216 and request a Personal Earnings and Benefits Estimate statement.
2. What are our annual earnings from investments? This includes dividend and interest income. Check Schedule A on your income tax return, and look at all brokerage, savings accounts, and credit union statements for information. You may or may not have this annual income distributed to you.
3. Is my pension or my husband's a defined-benefit plan, which pays a set amount based on salary, or a defined-contribution plan, like a 401(k)?
4. When are you eligible to retire?
5. How will these benefits be paid? Lump sum, annuitized?
6. Is there a survivor benefit for the divorced spouse?
7. What is the earliest date you can qualify under this plan?
8. What are the lifetime costs if you retire early?
9. How many employer plans have you or your husband been participants in, and can you locate the pension information from all the jobs held?
10. Is there a military pension?
11. What documents have you signed previously relating to these pension benefits?

ASK YOUR EMPLOYER AND YOUR HUSBAND'S EMPLOYER

1. Ask for an individual benefit statement and a summary plan description from each plan in which either of you have been a participant.
2. Do you have copies of your annual summary benefits statement? Get them for as many years back as possible on your and your husband's plans.
3. Do I or does my spouse participate in the employer-sponsored plan? Are we each vested in our plans? If not, what are the requirements?
4. Is the pension guaranteed by the federal government (Pension Benefit Guaranty Corporation)?

5. By what amount are the benefits reduced for early retirement?
6. Is the pension integrated with Social Security? If it is integrated with Social Security you will not receive the full amount of the pension as Social Security benefits will be subtracted.
7. Is the pension benefit amount guaranteed as formulated on the length of service and/or average earnings?
8. Is there an automatic cost of living adjustment (COLA) in my retirement benefits?
9. Can you be away from your job or have a break in service for months or years and not lose pension credits?
10. How will the retirement benefits be paid out?
    a) in monthly payments?
    b) in a lump sum?
    c) in an annuity (a monthly payment until death)?
    d) a choice from above determined later or at retirement?
    e) survivor benefit for divorced spouse?
11. How are the 401(k) dollars invested?
12. Are the 401(k) funds invested properly for my goals?
13. How often can the investment allocation be changed on these funds?

ASK YOUR SPOUSE
1. What is the death benefit on all of our life insurance policies, both those at work and our privately owned policies?
2. What will I receive at your death as long as we are married?
3. What percentage of our pension will I receive at your death?
4. What kind of disability insurance do you have from work?
5. Will I get a benefit if you die before you retire? How much?
6. What are the terms of your military retirement?
7. Is there any life insurance death benefit from the military since your retirement?

The purpose of this chapter is to provide you with information and questions to ask about your retirement benefits in a dissolution. The topics are grouped by subject areas and special situations. I hope to provide you with planning tools which you and your attorney can apply to your divorce. It is my intention to give you decision-making models and ideas which you can apply to your own situation in the following examples and client stories. Try and understand what your retirement benefits are as a worker, ex-spouse or divorcee, and/or as a widow.

VALUING A PENSION BENEFIT

The two primary methods of allocating pension income benefits include (1) preparing a present value calculation and (2) allocating the future pension benefit as either a fixed dollar amount or as a percentage of the ultimate benefit.

Present Value

The primary purpose of a present value calculation is to account for the effects of inflation on funds to be received in the future. Since a loaf of bread will cost more tomorrow than it does today, a present value calculation attempts to estimate how many loaves of bread money received at some point in the future will purchase.

The present valueof a pension is generally calculated by an actuary, an accountant or other financial expert. Assumptions needed to make the calculation include (a) an actuarial life expectancy of the employee, (b) an acceptable discount rate (generally the rate of inflation), and (c) the future pension benefit. Given these assumptions, you can determine what a future stream of income is worth today.

The present value calculation works best when you know exactly how much the monthly benefit will be. For those with several years left in the work force, present value calculations aren't as meaningful since any major event, such as prolonged illness or disability, will impact the ultimate pension benefit. Even slight changes in the monthly benefit or in any of the assumptions used can have significant effects on the present value of the benefits.

I will use Thomas and Gina as an example of a present value calculation. They have had a 35-year marriage, and Thomas has been employed with his company since the year they were married. He has a significant accrued pension benefit. In their case, a present value analysis would be presented as follows.

In making this calculation, the following assumptions were used:
- Retirement Date: January 1, 2002 at Thomas's age 65.
- Valuation Date: January 1, 1993 — their date of separation.

- Accrued monthly benefit: $6,500.
- The number of years for which the benefit is to be received is based on the unisex actuarial table included in IRS Publication 590 and is based upon the age at the birthday nearest the valuation date. Thomas has an actuarial age of 20.0 years at age 65.
- Discount rate (expected rate of inflation) of 5 percent per annum (approximately equal to the fifteen year average increase in the consumer price index of 5.36 percent), compounded monthly.

Based on the above data and assumptions, the value of Thomas's pension at retirement age is $984,914.53. However, this will need to be discounted (adjusted for inflation again) to reflect the value of the pension on January 1, 1993. The present value of Thomas's pension on January 1, 1993 is $628,596.63. This benefit could be allocated to one spouse or the other in the property division, providing that the value is agreed upon. Now, do you see how important a pension can be in a divorce settlement?

Let me give you another example of this present value calculation in which I demonstrate the importance of which actuarial chart is used in calculating the present value of a pension. In the following case I am looking at a teacher's retirement pension in the Washington State Teacher's Retirement System.

Susan Thomas is 41 years old and plans to retire from teaching at 65. Her actuarial life expectancy past the age of 65 is 12.9 years, according to the Washington mortality tables. If you use the IRS unisex actuarial table, her life expectancy past 65 is an additional 20.0 years.

Using the IRS table results in over $11,000 in additional present value, or over 25 percent more, due to the assumption that Susan will live an additional 7.1 years past her retirement. See the calculations on the following two pages. If you change the annual discount rate, even just a little, the values in our example again change dramatically.

Suppose inflation is assumed to be 6 percent. Now the pension benefits will be worth only $23,213 under the Washington State tables, compared to $30,675 using the original 5 percent rate. With so many unknown variables which are beyond anyone's control, present value

PRESENT VALUE OF PENSION BENEFITS

Client Name:	Susan Thomas
Date of Birth	10/13/53
Current Age	41
Annual Discount Rate Employed:	5.0%
Current Year:	1994

WASHINGTON STATE ACTUARIAL TABLES

Actuarial Life Expectancy Past 65:   12.9

Year	Age	Annual Pension	Value @ Retirement
2,018	65	$10,104	$10,104
2,019	66	10,104	9,623
2,020	67	10,104	9,165
2,021	68	10,104	8,728
2,022	69	10,104	8,313
2,023	70	10,104	7,917
2,024	71	10,104	7,540
2,025	72	10,104	7,181
2,026	73	10,104	6,839
2,027	74	10,104	6,513
2,028	75	10,104	6,203
2,029	76	10,104	5,908
2,030	77	10,104	5,626
Total Income		*$131,355*	

Total Discounted Value @ Retirement   **$99,661**

1994 PRESENT VALUE   **$31,234**

PRESENT VALUE OF PENSION BENEFITS

Client Name:	Susan Thomas
Date of Birth	10/13/53
Current Age	41
Annual Discount Rate Employed:	5.0%
Current Year:	1994

IRS ACTUARIAL TABLES

Actuarial Life Expectancy Past 65:   20.0

Year	Age	Annual Pension	Value @ Retirement
2,018	65	$10,104	$10,104
2,019	66	10,104	9,623
2,020	67	10,104	9,165
2,021	68	10,104	8,728
2,022	69	10,104	8,313
2,023	70	10,104	7,917
2,024	71	10,104	7,540
2,025	72	10,104	7,181
2,026	73	10,104	6,839
2,027	74	10,104	6,513
2,028	75	10,104	6,203
2,029	76	10,104	5,908
2,030	77	10,104	5,626
2,031	78	10,105	5,359
2,032	79	10,106	5,104
2,033	80	10,107	4,862
2,034	81	10,108	4,631
2,035	82	10,109	4,411
2,036	83	10,110	4,201
2,037	84	10,111	4,001
2,038	85	10,112	3,811
	Total Income	*$212,225*	

Total Discounted Value @ Retirement	**$136,041**
1994 PRESENT VALUE	**$42,635**

calculations are a decreasingly popular method of valuing pension benefits.What does this tell you? Get an expert or actuary to value your pension.

Allocation of Future Pension Benefit

In the allocation of future pension benefits, there can be an allocation of either a fixed dollar amount, or an allocation of a percentage of the ultimate pension benefit. Traditionally, a fixed dollar amount was allocated to the non-employee spouse. More recently there has been a trend toward the participatory allocation method.

Fixed dollar amount allocation

Under the normal defined benefit pension plan, the final pension benefit is calculated by multiplying the average annual compensation by the average annual final salary which is multiplied by a certain percentage. If the fixed dollar amount method is used in allocating the pension, the non-employee spouse is not fully compensated for the years that the parties were married.

Consider the following pension income example: Assume Sally and Harry are married. Harry retires after 30 years of service with an average annual final salary of $70,000. Let's say the annual pension benefit would be $42,000, or $3,500 per month. Sharing the pension benefit equally, under the fixed dollar allocation method, the non-employee spouse would receive a monthly income of $1,750.

Jim and Martha are also married, but get divorced after Jim has 20 years of employment service. Assuming Jim would also be earning $70,000 per year after 30 years of employment, with a 5 percent rate of inflation, his salary at the end of 20 years would be only $43,000 per year. With 20 years of service and an annual average salary of $43,000, the earned pension benefit would be $17,200 per year or $1,433 per month.

Martha receives only $716.50 per month while Jim receives $2,783.50 per month. Although Martha participated in two thirds (20 years of the total 30 years of service) of the years of accrued pension benefits, her pension benefit is only 20 percent of the total pension income.

PARTICIPATORY ALLOCATION

In the State of Washington, the Bulicek case is an attempt to equalize the disparity of a fixed dollar allocation of future pension benefits. Also referred to as the participatory allocation method, the ultimate pension benefit is allocated to the divorcing parties based on the percentage of the benefit earned during the marriage versus before or after marriage.

Under the participatory allocation method, the formula used in the calculating the allocation of benefit is as follows:

$$\text{Wife's \% of Asset Allocation} \quad X \quad \frac{\text{Community Yrs. of Serv.}}{\text{Total Years of Service}} \quad X \quad \text{Final Pension Benefit} \quad = \quad \text{Wife's Part of Husband's Retirement Benefit}$$

Using this method of pension allocation, refer to the above case of Jim and Martha. After 30 years of service, Jim's final pension benefit is \$3,500 per month. Of the total years of employment, Jim and Martha were married for 20 years, so 67 percent of the final pension is considered earned by the marriage. With an allocation of 50 percent of

$$50\% \quad X \quad \frac{20}{30} \quad X \quad \$3,500 \quad = \quad \$1,166.67$$

the marital property and benefits, Martha would receive a monthly pension of \$1,166.67 (\$3,500 monthly benefit X 2/3 community portion X 50 percent allocated to Martha) or \$456 per month more than by using the flat pension benefit method! Under the participatory allocation method, Martha would receive 33 percent of the pension income rather than 20 percent. If the pension is received over 15 years, Martha would receive an additional \$82,080.

This is an important concept for you to understand. In Washington and across the country, we are seeing more cases settled using this method to calculate the shared retirement pension benefit. Ask your attorney to provide you with a copy of the Bulicek case or one similar in your state so that you can get a better understanding of how this works.

Once the divorce decree is filed and your sharing of the pension benefit is determined, a Qualified Domestic Relations Order (QDRO) is filed with your ex-spouse's company. Your benefit formula will segregate your future pension benefit from this point forward. You will need to call the corporate pension office annually to get an updated estimate of the pension benefit or request this information in writing. Some corporate benefit offices are more responsible than others. It is important that you notify your husband's employer's office of any change of your address so they can contact you regarding the distribution of this pension benefit in the future.

Social Security benefits — what can I expect?

Once the change in federal law went into effect in 1983, it became much easier for a divorced person (married for ten years or more) to receive benefits on former spouse's work record regardless of whether the worker has retired and taken benefits for him/herself or has chosen to continue working.

In order to receive one half of your ex-husband's Social Security benefits at retirement you need to be at least 62, and must have been married for at least ten years, and you must not have remarried when you claim your benefits. These rules do differ if you are disabled or if your ex-spouse has died. More and more I see women who don't get the benefits they earned in their first marriage, often because they have remarried, making them ineligible or because the spouse in the second marriage did not earn as much as the first.

If you qualify, you can start getting reduced benefits as early as age 62. People retiring now get full retirement benefits at age 65. However, starting in the year 2000, for people born in 1938 or later, the full retirement age will be increased in bi-monthly steps until 2027 when it reaches age 67 for people born after 1959. By claiming benefits early, you are penalized. At age 62, your benefits are permanently reduced about 20 percent; at age 63, 13 percent; and at age 64, the reduction is 6.5 percent.

A woman was in my office a few weeks ago concerned that her ex-husband was struggling financially over their property settlement.

He is a physician, she is a therapist. Let's call them John and Sheila. John earns an average of $210,000 per year and she will make up to $35,000 in a good year (these are their three-year averages). Sheila earns money only if she is working, billing on an hourly basis for her time or her supervision of others.

John owns a building and is in a partnership in a small local medical practice. She received 52 percent of the property and three years of maintenance. Part of her maintenance was designed to be paid as a settlement note from the business valuation on his medical practice. It was advantageous to pay her this money as maintenance so it would be tax deductible to him (Note: the other side of this scenario is that the maintenance is taxable income to her). She is in the 31 percent marginal income tax bracket so she is giving up about 30 percent of this maintenance in taxes.

They have two grown children. One is now employed and the second daughter has two more quarters before she is out of school. They are sharing the tuition costs on a pro-rata basis of their gross wages. Money is tight for him while he pays her the maintenance, payments on the property settlement note and the daughter's remaining college costs. She has agreed to defer the property settlement payment until the daughter is out of school. Sheila is afraid he will stop paying his share of the tuition otherwise. They have been separated for four years and divorced one year.

I am telling you this story because I believe it shows that Sheila is still responding to John's emotional manipulation. She is worrying about him and submitting to his anger and rage over the divorce. He hates her attorney and her for uprooting his life and causing him short term financial setbacks. This whole situation is all her fault. He is the victim.

At this point I pulled out the post-divorce cash flow and income tax spreadsheets which I had prepared for Sheila a few months earlier. This was the kick start that Sheila needed to get a grip on her finances and her responsibility for John's future. John was making choices and getting on with his financial and personal life. She couldn't change anything about his life and choices, but certainly she could look at her own. Sheila was very nervous about her finances and the need to make money in order to meet her financial obligations. She knew she had to be at work to earn money and was frightened about becoming ill and taking care of herself. Sheila knew that she would eventually receive a substantial inheritance from her mother's estate. However, she was concerned about the interim years. She had credit card debt since the divorce and this made her nervous. Her son had married and her share of the wedding costs was a lot more than anticipated.

Sheila and I reviewed the facts. She had come in to see me to discuss cash flow management for the next year: what debts to pay off and with what funds. The money was scheduled to come in from various investments over the next three years. She would be okay. Sheila also wanted to discuss her giving up part of her Social Security benefits. She did not understand how these benefits worked for her and John. Let me explain.

We did some post-divorce planning and I showed her each of their post-divorce lifestyles in three years. The disparity of income between them has not gone away. Now you might ask me, what does this have to do with her Social Security benefits at age 62? I was telling her that at her age 62 she would be able to qualify for 100 percent of her eligible benefit or 50 percent of his benefit, whichever is greater. She understood that this 50 percent benefit would reduce his benefit to 50 percent. This is not the case. He would get his 100 percent and she would get her 50 percent, or 150 percent paid out. She was feeling bad that she was going to be a burden for the rest of her life. Remember, that since the 1983 law change, you and your ex-husband each qualify separately for your Social Security benefit.

If you feel you are taking financial advantage of your ex-spouse and have the urge to step back into your role as the caretaker, look at the disparity between your earnings and try and put a value on your time at home raising your children. One sobering method to use in this process is to write to the Social Security office nearest your home and request a Personal Earnings and Benefit Estimate Statement. Order one for yourself and your husband. Each of you need to sign your own form. It takes the Social Security office about 6 weeks to process this report. Samples of sections of this report are in Chapter 13 for Barbara Hudson which show her earnings record and estimated Social Security income.

HOW TO REACH IRA MONEY WITHOUT A PENALTY TAX

In some situations this can be an effective negotiation strategy to help make the settlement a win/win for both parties. Sometimes I work with clients who have been savers their entire lives. They find themselves in their mid-50s with their house nearly paid for and a large retirement fund at the corporation where the husband has worked for the past 25+ years. It may make sense for the non-working spouse to start taking a distribution from the husband's qualified plan prior to age 59$\frac{1}{2}$. Here is how it works. A portion of his qualified plan is rolled into an Individual Retirement Account (IRA) for her. She starts taking an early distribution. The rules are that she must take the same distribution for the greater of five years or until age 59$\frac{1}{2}$, whichever is greater. There are three methods allowed by the IRS in calculating this distribution amount. Let me give you some examples.

Method 1

An account holder may determine the payment according to the rules for determining required minimum distributions under *IRC Section 401(a)(9)*. Generally, payments may be based on the joint life expectancy of the account holder and a designated beneficiary or the account holder's single life expectancy.

EXAMPLE: An account holder has an IRA balance of $100,000. He and his spouse, who is the designated beneficiary, are both age 50. Therefore, their joint life expectancy is 39.2 years. According to the required distribution rules, he determines his payment by dividing $100,000 by 39.2 which is $2,551 per year.

Method 2

An account holder may determine the payment by amortizing the account holder's IRA balance over either the joint life expectancy of the account holder and a designated beneficiary or over the account holder's single life expectancy. A reasonable interest rate determined on the date payments commence must be used.

EXAMPLE: A 50-year-old individual has a life expectancy 33.1 years and an IRA balance of $100,000. Assuming an interest rate of 8 percent, the individual could withdraw $8,679 per year. Note that amortizing an account balance is different than dividing the balance by a life expectancy figure.

Method 3

An account holder may determine payments by dividing the IRA balance by an annuity factor. The annuity factor is the present value of an annuity of $1 per year beginning at the individual's age attained in the first distribution year and continuing for the life of the individual. The annuity factor must be derived using a reasonable mortality table and using an interest rate that is reasonable on the day payments commence.

EXAMPLE: If the annuity factor for a $1 per year annuity for an individual who is 50 years old is 11.109 (assuming an interest rate of 8 percent and using the UP-1984 Mortality Table), an individual with a $100,000 account balance would receive an annual distribution of $9,002 per year ($100,000 divided by 11.109).

How long will my IRA account last?

The answer to this question is dependent on several factors: your age, the rate of return you are getting on the investment, how long you live, and what level you withdraw from the account. You are required to take a minimum distribution from an IRA account when you are 70 1/2. The amount you are required to withdraw is based on your actuarial age or how long you are expected to live per the IRS actuarial tables.

What if I have so many legal bills from this divorce that I need to take money from my IRA to pay off my debt?

As discussed above, incident to divorce and pursuant to a Qualified Domestic Relations Order (QDRO), you are allowed to take a distribution penalty-free from your IRA. I discussed the income tax implications and rules regarding this withdrawal in an earlier chapter. You will still be required to pay income taxes on this distribution. In other words, this income will be added to other taxable income for the year in which the IRA funds are withdrawn.

Sometimes this is the only realistic debt reduction plan which a client may have when she comes to see me. If you find yourself in this situation, be sure and see a financial and tax advisor so that you handle this withdrawal in such a way as to minimize your overall income tax liability. Don't forget to pay your quarterly estimated taxes after taking this withdrawal.

MILITARY PENSIONS

If there is a military pension as part of your property settlement I strongly urge you to choose an attorney who is familiar with this type of retirement plan and how you go about dividing these benefits. As an example, the Survivor Benefit Plan (SBP) is an annuity which allows retired members (either active duty or reserve) to designate a beneficiary to continue receiving up to 55 percent of the member's income after the member's death. The benefits are funded by non-taxable premium payments drawn from the retiree's paycheck. Payments to a member's spouse will cease upon the member's death without this SBP coverage.

A married active service member must make the SBP election at or before retirement. Reservists can make the election upon the completion of 20 years of creditable service or upon reaching age 60. This decision to participate is irrevocable. State courts can order a member to elect SBP coverage. A current spouse will be notified of the election to provide coverage for a member's former spouse, but he/she cannot veto that election.

This is only one of many special features of the military pension. If a military pension is part of your settlement, write for a copy of the following document for you, your attorney and your financial planner if they don't already have the publication: *A Guide for Military Separation or Divorce*, EX-POSE, P.O. Box 11191, Alexandria, VA 22312.

In this publication, you will find excellent information on topics of benefits to which an ex-spouse may be entitled under the Uniformed Services Former Spouses Protection Act. Also particulars about the Survivor Benefit Plan I discussed earlier are explained, as well as how to prepare for divorce court, the complete survivor benefit plan, miscellaneous benefits available to you, and other pertinent information.

You also will want to contact the military finance centers listed below relating to the appropriate branch of service for their guidelines and information regarding your rights as a former spouse:

Army   Defense Finance and Accounting Service
                 Attn. FINCL-G
                 Indianapolis, IN 46249

Navy   Defense Finance and Accounting Service
                 (Code DG)
                 Celebrezze Federal Building
                 Cleveland, Ohio 44199-2055

Air Force   Defense Finance and Accounting Service
                 ATTN: JA
                 Denver,Colorado 80279

Marine Corps   Defense Finance and Accounting Service
                 (Code DG)
                 Kansas City, Missouri 64197-0001

Coast Guard   General Law Division
                 (G-LGL)
                 United States Coast Guard
                 2100 2nd Street, S.W.
                 Washington, D.C. 20593

DEFERRED COMPENSATION

Don't forget to look at deferred compensation packages. The employer may have given your husband the opportunity to defer current income. This money is backed by the full faith and credit of the company for which he works when deferred compensation is elected as a "non-qualified" retirement benefit.

The major objective of a deferred compensation plan is to postpone the tax on compensation to a year in which you will be in a lower tax bracket. The IRS will generally treat amounts paid under a nonqualified deferred plan as taxable to the person who earned the compensation, rather than the person who receives it.

A recent private letter ruling, LR9340032, shed some light on the tax treatment of payments made to an ex-wife from the ex-husband's deferred compensation plan. The ruling involved a major league baseball player who had participated in his team's unfunded and nonqualified deferred compensation plan. Under the plan, a portion of his salary was not paid in the year it was earned. Instead, it was allocated to a deferred compensation account, from which it would be paid to him at a later date. His rights to the account were solely as an unsecured creditor, with no rights to assign or otherwise convey the benefits, as is the usual case with an unqualified plan.

The ballplayer and his wife were divorced in 1990, and the wife received a percentage of the marital estate, including the deferred compensation account. Pursuant to the divorce decree, the wife was to be liable for taxes on the withdrawal of money held in the account; furthermore, she was obligated to reimburse her husband if the IRS found him liable for the taxes even though the payments were made to her.

The baseball team issued the wife a W-2 for the deferred compensation and withheld income taxes at the husband's rate. The wife's attorney requested the letter ruling from the IRS as he wanted the income paid to her, rather than to her husband, and taxed at her tax rate.

The QDRO does control the tax treatment of certain property transfers such as the division of a qualified pension or profit-sharing plan. However, it does not apply to all property transferred in the divorce. Stock options and non-qualified deferred compensation are two notable exceptions which will generally be taxed to the earning spouse rather than the recipient spouse, regardless of any court order. Therefore, the ballplayer's wife was entitled to receive the difference between her portion of the benefits paid and income taxes on this portion at his rate.

There are terms and conditions that go along with this deferred compensation. Be sure that you get an interpretation about how this money can be shared with you. Ask about the taxation aspects: who pays? What are the restrictions on when it is paid out and can it be paid to you, the spouse, or only to the employee?

Recently I saw a case where the attorney tried to transfer an interest in a deferred compensation plan to a spouse with a QDRO. The money was distributed by the plan administrator, and income taxes were withheld with the balance being sent to the wife with a 1099-R form reporting the transaction to the wife, and to the IRS. The husband was the administrator and trustee of his own plan internally. Her CPA, upon doing her tax return for the year of the distribution, found that this was not done correctly and was invalid under a QDRO. The plan administrator had to re-issue the check to the wife for the original $75,000 without taxes, the husband had to pay income taxes on the distribution, along with a 10 percent penalty. The wife was pleased, and her husband was furious.

WHAT ABOUT STOCK APPRECIATION RIGHTS?

Stock Appreciation Rights (SAR's) are a form of cash bonus tied to an increase in the price of the employer's stock. Each SAR entitles an employee to cash equal to the excess of the fair market value of one share on the date of exercise (the date you choose to cash in on this appreciation) over the value on the date the SAR was granted. For example, assume a stock is worth $30 a share and you get 100 SAR's exercisable within five years. Two years later, when the stock has increased to $50 a share, you exercise the SAR and receive $2,000 ($50 current price - $30 exercise price = $20; $20 times 100 shares = $2,000). You are taxed when you receive the cash.

CHAPTER TEN

MORE ABOUT DIVORCED WOMEN, PENSIONS, AND RETIREMENT

What lies behind us and what lies before us are tiny matters,
compared to what lies within us.
— Ralph Waldo Emerson

Though it may seem dull, as well as complicated, the business of what you are entitled to in a divorce may very well affect your retirement years, your level of income, and your opportunities after divorce. Looking back with regret because you failed to act aggressively in your own behalf to secure your future is one of the saddest acts of nostalgia. The whole purpose of this chapter and the one before is to give you the information you need to act in your own behalf to get your fair share of all the assets in your marriage.

WHAT ABOUT STOCK OPTIONS AND RESTRICTED STOCK?
Under this type of asset you have qualified incentive stock options, employee stock purchase plans, non-qualified stock options, non-qualified employee stock purchase plans, and restricted stock. You will want to have all of these analyzed to determine their value as a

marital asset. There are more new court decisions on the division of these marital assets each month. If you own any of these as part of your marital assets, be sure and see a tax expert and securities analyst to determine the value of the stock.

Each of these has restrictions on the holding period, taxation, and ownership. For example, a corporation may provide its executives with Incentive Stock Options (ISOs) to acquire its stock (or the stock of its parent or subsidiaries). These ISOs are not taxed when granted or exercised. Instead, the gain (if any) is taxed when the employee decides to sell stock options which have already been exercised. The ISO agreement will usually indicate the holding period required for an appreciation in stock value to qualify as a capital gain (usually taxed at a lower rate) or whether it should be treated as ordinary income. The corporation issuing the ISOs will also have restrictions regarding the transfer and exercising of these options.

Start early gathering information on these marital assets. In my experience, I have found this area to be a difficult one in which to get a fair settlement. There is a great deal of disagreement on valuing these assets and then dividing them equitably as they stay with the employee and are typically non-transferable. However, these forms of compensation are the incentives of the '90s. If you have any of these types of assets in your marriage be sure you ask your attorney about his experience in dealing with them. You will want an experienced attorney arguing on your behalf. Current statutes are changing monthly on the division of these assets.

REVIEWING YOUR INSURANCE NEEDS

The following is taken from an article in *Financial Planing Perspectives,* a weekly column produced as a public service by the Institute of Certified Financial Planners. I was interested in the information in connection with evaluating readers' insurance needs.

Many people think of having life insurance, yet not everyone needs it. For example, an older, divorced woman without children at home, or other beneficiaries, and with a modest estate, might not need life insurance, but she may need long-term care insurance to help replace lost income and pay estate taxes.

The first step in determining what types of insurance you need is to identify and analyze possible risks in your life. Second, how much insurance might you need to cover those risks, and how much of the risk are you willing to carry yourself? What property and assets do you own? Do you face potential estate taxes? Are you a partner in a business in which you may need to buy out the heirs of a deceased partner?

Some types of coverage will be obvious. If you own one or more cars, you'll need auto insurance. The same for a home. But have you thought about coverage for rental property you own, or for a particularly valuable collection of jewelry or works of art? Do you provide child care at your home or do you work out of your home?

People often overlook personal liability coverage over and above that offered by your auto and homeowner's policies. These policies are relatively inexpensive and they cover not only for accidents involving your property, but for claims usually not covered by other policies such as libel, slander, or invasion of privacy.

Many people buy life insurance but not disability insurance because they know they'll die someday but don't think they'll become disabled. Yet you are at least four times more likely to be disabled for at least 90 days before age 65 than you are to die. Social Security benefits typically won't be enough, if they are available at all. Disability insurance will provide monthly income during that disability period.

When assessing your insurance needs, don't determine them piecemeal. Work with your Certified Financial Planner to see where each type of insurance fits into your overall plan — post-divorce. Health insurance is also a major consideration for you. Under the Consolidated Omnibus Budget Reconciliation Act of 1983 (COBRA), you are allowed to continue on your husband's policy for three years, however, you must pay the conversion premium cost. Health insurance is under major reform currently and you will need to do your research to determine what the best health insurance alternative is for you.

Check with more than one provider and get quotes on your coverage so that you know your facts when it comes time to negotiate the property settlement. No one is going to know the basics of your situation better than you.

One area that I encourage very careful documentation of is uninsured medical costs. What have they been historically, who is to pay them in the future, and what is the method of payment?

I recently helped a woman purchase life insurance on her ex-husband as their divorce was being settled. She is 57 years old and has worked only part-time during her 30-year marriage. Meredith was married to a doctor who had been in and out of the military three times over their marriage. They had lived in 24 different houses and in several states during the course of the marriage. Finally at age 60 he retired from the military and, at the same time, from their marriage.

Meredith was devastated emotionally. Prior to her husband's departure from the military with full retirement, Meredith had signed a waiver of any pension benefit coming to her in the event of his death. This was an irrevocable election. Her property settlement provided that Robert split his pension income with Meredith for the remainder of his life on a 50-50 basis. At his death, the pension benefit would stop. All during the divorce proceedings Robert insisted he wouldn't live to be 70, even though he was in very good health. He argued against the life insurance saying that, "I don't want Meredith to become a rich widow at my expense."

Meredith was concerned about a major portion of her pension income disappearing with his death. Robert also would receive two times the Social Security benefit of Meredith, as he had maximum earnings under Social Security and Meredith had only little on her own poor work record of inferior jobs during their marriage. Robert had never wanted her to work. To Meredith's credit, she had maintained a part-time position with an airline over the years, earning minimum wages and enjoying some travel benefits.

As part of the final property settlement, Meredith did negotiate for the right to purchase a term insurance policy on Robert's life. The premium was fixed for the first 15 years, after which the premium cost would begin to rise dramatically. Keeping the policy beyond the term would not be cost effective. Meredith is the owner of the policy and the beneficiary and Robert is the insured, the person on whose life the insurance contact was written.

Women often ask me if they should buy term insurance or permanent coverage. Obviously, in Meredith's case, she sought to protect her pension income from Robert through insurance. In essence, she was betting that he wouldn't outlive the term of the policy.

It took several months for her to get the policy in place. Typically, people who have divorced are not interested in cooperation and communication, particularly with the attitude that Robert had regarding life insurance in the first place. He saw no breach of trust on his part when he encouraged Meredith to waive her rights to a future pension when he signed his military pension paperwork.

Robert then remarried his first wife, "The woman with whom I shared my history," said Meredith. The first wife and Robert have a son. Meredith and Robert have a daughter who is 31. I believe, as Meredith does, that Robert had a definite plan in mind when he asked Meredith to sign off on the military pension, for less than one month after the divorce was final he took a new job and within a year had remarried his first wife from whom he had been divorced 36 years previously. For whatever reason, he had tried to thwart Meredith's plan to guarantee her portion of his pension beyond his death by insurance.

I currently have a case where the spouse was awarded life-time maintenance and an assignment of her husband's state pension at his retirement. Since there is no survivor benefit if he dies prior to retirement, she is totally unprotected in the event of his death. We are now negotiating for her to purchase an insurance policy on his life, and to have him pay the premiums as maintenance until he retires. She will have the option to terminate the coverage after his retirement as the additional maintenance will cease and she will receive one half of the pension benefit — whatever the amount. My client came to me after the divorce was final and she and her attorney discovered our state pension structure does not have a provision to pay the divorced spouse a survivor benefit if the employee dies prior to retirement, even under a QDRO.

I cannot emphasize too strongly you need to get "all the facts" before your divorce is final.

ADJUSTING MAINTENANCE FOR INFLATION

Inflation can seriously erode the value of a maintenance award, especially one that is long-term and compensatory in nature.

Check to see if maintenance awards have an escalation clause in your state. In my research, I have found that this varies from one state to the next. That doesn't mean that you and your husband are not free to make your own agreement on this issue.

In the two charts below, and in the historical data on price inflation on page 183 I would like you visualize why it is important to

EFFECT OF INFLATION ON THE PURCHASING POWER OF $1

Year	Inflation Rate							
	3%	4%	5%	6%	7%	8%	9%	10%
1	1.00	1.00	1.00	1.00	1.00	1.00	1.00	1.00
2	0.97	0.96	0.95	0.94	0.93	0.92	0.91	0.90
3	0.94	0.92	0.90	0.88	0.86	0.85	0.83	0.81
4	0.91	0.88	0.86	0.83	0.80	0.78	0.75	0.73
5	0.89	0.85	0.81	0.78	0.75	0.72	0.69	0.66
6	0.86	0.82	0.77	0.73	0.70	0.66	0.62	0.59
7	0.83	0.78	0.74	0.69	0.65	0.61	0.57	0.53
8	0.81	0.75	0.70	0.65	0.60	0.56	0.52	0.48
9	0.78	0.72	0.66	0.61	0.56	0.51	0.47	0.43
10	0.76	0.69	0.63	0.57	0.52	0.47	0.43	0.39

EFFECT OF INFLATION ON $3,500 MAINTENANCE PAYMENT

Year	Inflation Rate							
	3%	4%	5%	6%	7%	8%	9%	10%
1	3,500	3,500	3,500	3,500	3,500	3,500	3,500	3,500
2	3,395	3,360	3,325	3,290	3,255	3,220	3,185	3,150
3	3,293	3,226	3,159	3,093	3,027	2,962	2,898	2,835
4	3,194	3,097	3,001	2,907	2,815	2,725	2,637	2,552
5	3,099	2,973	2,851	2,733	2,618	2,507	2,400	2,296
6	3,006	2,854	2,708	2,569	2,435	2,307	2,184	2,067
7	2,915	2,740	2,573	2,415	2,264	2,122	1,988	1,860
8	2,828	2,630	2,444	2,270	2,106	1,952	1,809	1,674
9	2,743	2,525	2,322	2,133	1,959	1,796	1,646	1,507
10	2,661	2,424	2,206	2,005	1,821	1,653	1,498	1,356

ANNUAL RATE OF PRICE INFLATION IN THE UNITED STATES

Year	Consumer Price Index		Year	Consumer Price Index
1974	11.0%		1984	4.3%
1975	9.1%		1985	3.8%
1976	5.8%		1986	1.1%
1977	6.5%		1987	3.7%
1978	7.7%		1988	4.4%
1979	11.1%		1989	4.7%
1980	13.5%		1990	5.4%
1981	10.4%		1991	3.1%
1982	6.1%		1992	2.9%
1983	3.2%		1993	2.9%

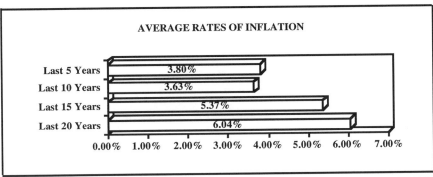

AVERAGE RATES OF INFLATION

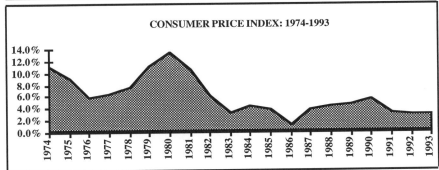

CONSUMER PRICE INDEX: 1974-1993

Source: Bureau of Labor Statistics

become familiar with the concept of maintaining your purchasing power over time. When you see the Hudson and Jessup cases in upcoming chapters, you will note that I have used a 4 percent annual rate of inflation, a little more than the ten-year average.

LONG-TERM MARRIAGE: CHILDREN NO LONGER HOME — A MOVE TO A TOWNHOUSE TO BE OWNED FREE AND CLEAR OR SHOULD I RENT?

In a short- or mid-term marriage, especially one where the children are still living at home, keeping the family residence or purchasing a comparable replacement home may be the best alternative. But when the children have left home and are living independently and the wife is in the family home, it may make more sense to move and to downsize. Consider the case where the decision to downsize has already been made and the only questions involve the issues.

Richard and Celeste are at this point in their proceedings. Through joint efforts of saving and paying down the mortgage over the past 25 years there is a small balance remaining on the property. Both parties want to sell the house. He is over 55 and is eligible to use his one time exclusion of the first $125,000 of gain when the house is sold. They agree to go ahead with their divorce, hold the house as tenants in common, then sell it. He will take the exclusion on his share of the house sale and she will take a lesser share of the tax liability.

Often, you can structure this deferral of gain between the husband and wife in such a way that neither party must pay income taxes with the sale of the residence.

In this scenario, I will assume there is no income tax liability for either party at the time of the sale. For the husband this is due to his qualifying for the exclusion provision and his purchase of a replacement home, and her portion of the gain is deferred since she is purchasing a new townhouse as well. Their property settlement says that Richard will be reporting 55 percent of the sale on his tax return and Celeste will report 45 percent on hers.

The sale of the house resulted in a price of $475,000, with a $150,000 mortgage and $28,500 (6 percent) in expenses relating to the sale. Richard and Celeste had a tax basis of $220,985, which included the initial purchase and several improvements to the home. In her final settlement, Celeste received 85 percent of the cash proceeds of $296,500, or $252,025. She came to see me to discuss whether she would be better off buying or renting with her cash settlement.

From a purely emotional point of view, my client wants to have a home that she owns. She has been a homeowner for 29 of her 30 years of marriage. She has been looking at smaller houses and has found one that she likes. In planning sessions with Celeste, we determined that she should purchase a house for $205,000 with no mortgage. Celeste wanted to have living expenses which she could manage from her employment income. She had worked hard during the marriage to have a home free and clear at retirement and with the downsizing of her home post-divorce she was able to achieve this goal.

The decision whether to buy or rent is different for every divorce case. When there are children, I almost always see a home purchase for the wife, often a home that is smaller and which requires less mainte-nance than the family residence during the marriage. Usually the mother and children want to stay in the same school district. This can sometimes pose a problem if the family has lived in an upscale suburb. There may not be houses within her price range.

GUIDELINES — PURCHASE OR RENT?

I would like to provide readers with some guidelines for deter-mining whether buying or renting is in their best interests.

1. Is the "total return" on the purchase of the house as good as other investments?

This means you evaluate the purchase of the home from a purely financial perspective. When you rent there is no large down payment, real estate taxes, improvements and mortgage or homeowner's insur-ance payments (you may elect to obtain renter's insurance coverage). The real question is what kind of a return do you get on the money you have saved monthly by not making the down payment. I disagree that a renter has nothing to show for her investment at the end of her lease. She has the return on the money that has not gone into the home mainte-nance and payments.

2. What about the tax savings that I am giving up?

These tax savings may not be as big as you think. It is true that your mortgage interest and local real estate taxes can be used as a deduction on your income taxes and that renters do not have these deductions. These deductions are of benefit only to the extent that they exceed the standard deduction ($6,350 for married couples who file jointly, $3,175 for married couples filing separately, $3,800 for singles, and $5,600 for head of household in 1994).

In the example above, the tax savings between renting and carrying a mortgage of approximately 30 percent of the value of the home purchase is $3,008 annually. It is true that this woman could leverage her purchase where she only put 10 percent to 25 percent down, instead of 70 percent of the purchase price in my example.

But let's look at another example of how this risk can be greater than you think. Let's suppose you buy a house for $300,000 and put $50,000 as a down payment. If home prices go up and the house is worth $400,000 you have just made $100,000 on a $50,000 investment. If you had invested the same $50,000 in a non-leveraged investment and it similarly increased in value by 25 percent, you would have made only $12,500.

If prices go down, however, the fact that your investment is highly leveraged means that your equity can be wiped out quickly. If you make a $50,000 down payment on a $300,000 house and prices drop 20 percent, your equity is gone. This is a real possibility. I have seen many people who bought in the '80s highly leveraged and who lost big. I have seen many women try and keep their houses with insufficient cash to maintain the home. They defer the maintenance of the home, and, forced to sell later due to cash flow problems, they end up losing big. This loss is attributable to the lower sales price, a capital gains tax and the full share of the closing and settlement costs at the time of sale.

OTHER QUESTIONS TO ASK YOURSELF ABOUT BUYING VS. RENTING

- What kind of a neighborhood are you living in?
- Are there a lot of houses up for sale?
- What will this neighborhood be like in five years if there is a recession or downturn in the economy?
- What kind of improvements will this house require in the next five years?
- Will these improvements enhance the resale of your house or will they be considered normal maintenance to the new buyer?
- Do you put money in a new deck or in a treasury bill? Ask yourself which one will give you your principal back plus interest in five years.
- How long do you want to live in this large house? Until the children are out of school, until you finish school?
- Where are you likely to find a job after your education and training?
- Owning a home can be a way for you to build equity over time. You can systematically pay down your mortgage by using your excess cash and not spending this money. How will you spend any excess funds?
- If you have a fixed mortgage, your payments remain the same, where an adjustable rate mortgage or rent will probably be going up over time. Which situation is right for your circumstances?
- How close are you to age 55? Can you take a one time exclusion of $125,000 in taxable gains on the sale of your personal residence?
- Is it right for you to rent for a year after selling the family home, complete your education and find employment before purchasing a home? You have two years from the date of the closing to defer any gain into a new home purchase.

These questions are intended merely as a guideline to help you make an objective financial decision regarding your living situation. Because it is your situation, you must make the ultimate determination as to what works best for you. Ask your Certified Financial Planner to model the specific numbers on a purchase versus rent scenario in your situation. She/he will be able to show you the bottom line or cash flow impact of owning versus renting in your specific situation.

ESTATE PLANNING DURING AND POST-DIVORCE

Many women feel that they don't really need a will since they only have a few assets, such as a home, a car and some personal effects. Regardless of whether you own these and potentially many other things, you do need a will, because if you don't have one you will die intestate. The court then appoints an administrator to handle your affairs, and your property is distributed to your heirs based on a formula fixed by state law. After the payment of taxes, debts, funeral expenses and administrative costs, the property goes to the surviving spouse, children and/or other relatives. The laws are very specific about how property is to be distributed, including which relatives have priority and how the inheritance is divided.

Over the past fourteen years of dealing in the divorce planning area I have watched what has happened to divorcing and divorced women's estates when there has been no will or other estate planning documents. I have seen suicides, accidental deaths, and deaths from illnesses. You might say to yourself, "I will wait until the divorce is final to change my will." You need to realize that if your surviving spouse is named as your beneficiary, any assets designated to him as a surviving spouse in your will becomes his property.

A will only controls the disposition of an individual's (testator) separate property at death, and one-half of any community property owned by the testator and his spouse. It does not control the disposition of non-probate assets.

Non-probate assets include pension benefits, life insurance or assets held in joint tenancy with right of survivorship. I have worked with several clients whose husbands have died while in the divorce process. In all of the cases, these male spouses had changed their wills to govern how these assets were to be shared at their death. Trusts, outright gifts and special bequests have been included in their wills. The pension and survivor benefits as well as the beneficiaries on life insurance policies have stayed as they were when the spouse filed for divorce and these assets passed directly to the wife at the husband's death.

In one recent case, more than $2 million dollars in non-probate assets passed to the spouse, including the family residence, vacation home, life insurance proceeds, a pension, profit-sharing plan, deferred compensation and company stock. The husband tried to have the beneficiary changed but was unable to lawfully do this until divorced. He died before he divorced.

During this divorce process check the owner registration of all of your marital assets. Based on how the assets are registered, think about what would happen if you or your husband died while in the process of getting a divorce.

You do not need to have a large estate to plan and prepare a will. Anyone who owns property, whether personal, like cash, stocks, jewelry or furniture, or real property, such as land and any improvements (a house is considered an improvement), should plan and prepare a will. If you are separated or in the process of getting a divorce, I still recommend revising your will for the time of separation. For your post-divorce estate, I would recommend additional revisions where appropriate.

As part of your will, you will name an executor or personal representative who is appointed in the will to fulfill your directions and requirements. Choose someone who is competent and willing to serve you. Also, name an alternate representative if this person is unable or unwilling to serve as your personal representative.

The personal representative is responsible for settling your financial affairs and disposing of property according to the provisions of your will. This will mean assembling and inventorying assets as well as paying any debts, expenses and taxes. If required, the executor will submit a final accounting to the beneficiaries and to the probate court.

I have been involved with the heirs (adult children) and mother in situations in which there have been serious disagreements with the decisions of the personal representative who tries to carry out the wishes of the deceased, particularly if the deceased was the father or mother of the representative. A father who wishes to bypass the mother in favor of the children may leave his family with fuel for resentments, anger and legal costs to satisfy the will.

In the case I'm thinking of, the adult children argued back and forth regarding the issues facing the mother whose husband died prior to his divorce. The mother had legal rights to marital assets as well as the non-probate assets.

If you find yourself in this situation, you will need to start working with an estate planning attorney immediately. The Certified Financial Planner can be invaluable in helping you inventory the assets and work with the heirs in creating a win/win strategy for the family estate. This is the time to inform all the parties about what legal rights belong to whom, as a beneficiary, personal representative, and spouse. There are several legal terms used in estate planning which will help you to become informed about your rights.

DURABLE POWER OF ATTORNEY

I believe everyone needs to have this document filed safely with other personal papers. The durable power of attorney provides an individual of your choice, upon your incapacitation or incompetence with the power to act on your behalf to handle your legal and financial affairs. This document only becomes effective if there is sufficient evidence and two doctors' signatures to support a claim of incompetence. Name someone you trust to handle your financial affairs.

DIRECTIVE TO PHYSICIANS

This is a document signed by a competent individual stating his or her wishes regarding medical care should she/he become incapacitated. In addition to specifying acceptable forms of treatment, it provides for the withdrawal of life-sustaining procedures in terminal cases. Be sure that the language of your living will conforms to the laws of the state in which you reside. In Washington, state law requires that two physicians certify that a patient's condition is terminal and that life-sustaining procedures "would serve only to prolong artificially the moment of death." In Washington the directive must be signed by two witnesses, neither of whom may be related to the patient or entitled to any part of that person's estate. Some other individuals are also prohibited from serving as witnesses. Among those excluded are the attending physician and employees of the health care facility where the person is hospitalized.

A copy of the directive must be filed with the patient's doctor and it can be revoked by its maker at any time.

QUESTIONS TO ASK IN PLANNING YOUR ESTATE
Can a spouse be cut out of a will?

A spouse cannot be disinherited. If a will gives a surviving spouse less than the state inheritance laws would provide (which is at least one third to one half of the estate), the spouse can appeal and seek the state's minimum allowance.

Should I create a trust as part of my will?

A trust is an agreement under which money or other assets are held and managed by one person for the benefit of another. Different trusts can be created to accomplish specific goals. Each kind of trust may vary in the degree of flexibility and control it offers.

Among the common benefits that trust arrangements offer are:
- Providing personal and financial safeguards for family and other beneficiaries;
- Postponing or avoiding unnecessary taxes;
- Establishing a means of controlling or administering property; and
- Meeting other personal goals.

There are many good reasons to consider creating a trust as part of your will. Remember, the assets must be part of your probate estate to be considered for a trust. The non-probate assets often make up a large part of one's estate. Unless you change the registration of some of your assets, you may find they do not pass to your heirs as directed by the will and that they cannot be part of a trust.

Eleven of the most common mistakes I see among my clients in estate planning are:

Mistake 1	Failure to have a will.
Mistake 2	Failure to coordinate other estate planning techniques with the will (i.e., registration of assets).
Mistake 3	Failure to deal with business succession.
Mistake 4	Failure to deal with incapacity or incompetence.
Mistake 5	Illiquidity — lack of cash to pay estate taxes.
Mistake 6	Leaving everything to a spouse.
Mistake 7	Wrong choice of three key players (executor, trustee, guardian).

Mistake 8   Treating all beneficiaries the same.
Mistake 9   Failure to educate the would-be survivors.
Mistake 10   Failure to review and update the estate plan.
Mistake 11   Failure to deal with non-citizenship issues.

See an attorney who specializes in estate planning to determine what documents are most appropriate for your circumstances.

PRE-NUPTIAL AGREEMENTS — PRACTICAL TIPS

Marriage and divorce are the most important financial transactions in anyone's lifetime. I believe a contemporary woman needs to be informed about both of them. Divorce is the one business deal that puts virtually everything which a couple owns on the table.

Planning for the contingency that a marriage may end in divorce is not romantic, but if the statisticians are correct approximately 50 percent of all present marriages will end in divorce. If a woman were in any other business enterprise with an attrition rate that high she would certainly protect herself. If you have sizable wealth, a closely held business or are entering into a second marriage, you will probably want a pre-nuptial agreement.

In a pre-nuptial agreement you will negotiate the financial terms of your marriage and each partner's role before saying the vows. Financial issues include: bill paying, earnings, career goals, short and long-term financial goals, estate planning in the event of death or divorce. Other issues include how income taxes will be paid. Who will pay to defend a tax audit? Who will pay for specific expenses and obligations in a divorce (certain levels of support may be promised after a certain number of years of marriage, or perhaps a percentage of income may be shared per an agreed upon formula)? How should a pension be shared? You can't waive rights to pension benefits if you are not married, so this may require a post-nuptial agreement where you waive the pension rights in lieu of some other asset.

Some people dislike the concept of a pre-nuptial agreement, believing that the execution of such an agreement takes the romance out of the marriage. It is true that negotiating and executing a pre-nuptial agreement during the last week or two before the wedding does not add to the festive atmosphere surrounding the wedding preparations. If you wait too long to discuss the issues, it may also make it more difficult to enforce the agreement later on.

There are several useful purposes for a pre-nuptial agreement other than planning for a dissolution. These could include the following:

1. Establishing a written record of each party's separate property and its value and determining the procedures to assist you in maintaining it as separate property.

2. Defining each person's debts and protecting the other person's property and earnings from liability (e.g., a hold harmless clause regarding prior income tax return liabilities or debts from a closely held business).

3. Reducing the fear that one spouse is marrying the other for his/her money.

4. You may be giving up alimony/maintenance from a former spouse when remarrying and want some financial security for this action.

5. Planning for the disposition of property upon death, including preserving an existing estate plan and ensuring that each party's children are provided for and that certain family assets (especially family business interests) remain in the bloodlines.

Just because there is a pre-nuptial agreement does not mean that it is enforceable. I see judges rule against pre-nuptial agreements regularly. The issue of separate property is taken into account directly or indirectly when a property settlement is reached. Some of the reasons they are not enforceable include:

- The agreement is interpreted to be unfair to one spouse, (e.g., you waive the right to alimony or maintenance upon dissolution).
- Both parties did not enter into the agreement voluntarily, with independent legal advice and with full knowledge and understanding of the document's content.
- There was not full disclosure of all the assets and liabilities at the time the pre-nuptial agreement was signed.
- The timing of the signing of the pre-nuptial agreement did not allow for an informed decision. Allow plenty of time to create the pre-nuptial agreement, time for all of the above factors to fall into place, and time for a thorough investigation of all assets and liabilities.

Your attorney will work with you to determine whether he believes your pre-nuptial agreement is enforceable. Some clients prefer not to sign a pre-nuptial agreement at the time of marriage or re-marriage, but they attempt to maintain separate property through the registration of the assets and through their estate plan.

If you want a pre-nuptial agreement and the other party is reluctant to comply consider revising your estate plan to include new wills, a buy-sell agreement, powers of attorney or a Qualified Terminable Interest Property Trust (QTIP) to accompany the pre-nuptial agreement. Remember that with or without a pre-nuptial, you should use some care in how you title your assets. Changing a title to joint ownership can create marital property, subject to a property settlement in much the same way that commingling assets in a bank account or brokerage account may jeopardize the separate property characteristics of the assets. Regardless of how you handle these financial affairs, keep careful and accurate records. I have several clients who maintain these and other similar records in their safety deposit box.

CHECKLIST FOR TRANSFER OF RETIREMENT ASSETS POST-DIVORCE

In this chapter I have discussed retirement issues and your long-term financial independence. I have focused on what assets to look for, questions to ask establishing their marital value, and taking care of the assets you receive. Another area I believe is important to discuss is the timely transfer of these assets to your name. Your divorce decree and property settlement will summarize the assets you are to receive. If there are pension and retirement assets these will be transferred by a QDRO.

Once your decree is final, create a spreadsheet for yourself which chronicles the transfer of all of these assets. These transfers can take several weeks to complete before the account and funds are re-registered in your name.

Let me give you an example. Recently I had a client come to me from an attorney and was asked to help her transfer 401(k) funds from her husband's account in a local bank. The divorce decree specified that the transfer would be authorized via a QDRO. There was no QDRO

STATUS OF ASSET TRANSFERS

ASSET DESCRIPTION	OLD ACCT. # / NEW ACCT. #	DECREE VALUE / TRANSFER VALUE	FORMER CONTACT / NEW CONTACT	OLD PHONE / NEW PHONE	AMOUNT OF TRANSFER	PAYMENT REC'D	NOTES
EXAMPLE	1234567 / 2345678	11,215 / 11,710	John Doe / Joe Smith	444-5555 / 555-6666	(5,855) / 5,855	☐ / 7/14/94	Joe called to confirm receipt of funds at Great Northwest
						☐	
						☐	
						☐	
						☐	
						☐	
						☐	
						☐	
						☐	
						☐	
						☐	
						☐	
						☐	

Assets to include: Bank Accounts, Mutual Funds, Brokerage Accounts, Insurance and Annuities, Partnerships, Retirement Accounts, and other assets.

with the final divorce papers so we had to have one drawn up which met the legal requirements and that would be accepted by the administrator of the bank plan.

This took two weeks. Then we sent the request for transfer of these funds on the form from her new IRA custodian to the bank custodian. Remember, you do not want to have these funds sent directly to you as there are adverse tax consequences. The bank did not accept the wording of the first QDRO and it had to be revised by the attorney's office. It took four months for these funds to be transferred and several phone calls from me to finally accomplish the transfer. The divorce decree stated a dollar amount that was to be transferred from my client's ex-husband's account to her IRA. However, it did not state that this was a minimum dollar amount to which any appreciation on the assets since the valuation date would be added. These clients had been separated nearly a year before the divorce was final and then another five months had passed. The original value in the decree was as of the date of separation. During this sixteen-month period the husband had control of how the funds were invested in the plan. He had the funds invested 50 percent in a bond account and 50 percent in an aggressive stock fund. The market was down at the end of March when she finally was able to transfer the funds to her account and there was an 11 percent decrease in the value of her account from the date of separation.

If we had been able to accomplish this transfer sooner, she probably would not have experienced the loss. We would have worked together to create an investment strategy that fit her risk tolerance and then gradually invested the money. Some of this could have been avoided if the attorney had prepared the QDRO in a timely manner. The QDRO also should have stated that there would be a minimum dollar amount transferred plus a pro rata share of any increase since the date of separation.

I always meet with my clients after the divorce and discuss transfers and their income tax liability as soon as they have a divorce decree and property settlement in writing. I have found that what is written and what the woman thinks she is getting are sometimes quite different. I also work with a number of attorneys who ask that I review the wording in the property settlement and make changes as appropriate.

Remember, the attorney is your legal advisor and may not have a practical understanding of money issues.

Long-term financial independence is something we all strive for, personally and as a partner in a marriage. Understanding the comprehensive pension, retirement and Social Security benefits of both parties in the marriage is essential when dividing the marital assets. Women who have not had a career outside marriage or who have interrupted their career to stay home and raise a family need to be objective when looking at benefits and how they can be shared. See the Hudson case in Chapter Thirteen to examine a specific application in which the couple have a long-term marriage.

Difficult cases in which to assess the division of retirement are the mid-term marriages where one spouse is returning to work or entering the job force for the first time. There is a disparity of earnings between the spouses, the wife is going back to school to upgrade her skills, she has teenage children at home, she is in direct competition with her children for college funds. Typically, these families have a good start on their retirement funding. However, the maximum funding years typically come when the clients are 50 or older.

Read this and the former chapters carefully, use the spreadsheets and apply the information here to your own life. Try to be creative when you come up with your plan to share marital retirement assets.

REFERENCES

For additional information about retirement and the problems and opportunities of aging, contact:

- **American Association of Retired Persons.** They offer free four helpful booklets: *Focus Your Future: A Women's Guide to Retirement Planning* (#D14559); *The Social Security Book: What Every Woman Absolutely Needs to Know* (#D14117); *Women, Pensions and Divorce*, a survey of pension issues with a section of proposed reforms; and *A Woman's Guide to Pension Rights.* To order, write to AARP Fulfillment, 601 E Street N.W., Washington, D.C. 20049.

- *Your Pension Rights at Divorce: What Women Need to Know,* by Ann Moss. To order, write Pension Rights Center, 918 16th Street N.W., Suite 704, Washington, D.C. 20006. ($16.50)

- To receive a free packet of information on pensions from the **Older Women's League,** send a self-addressed, stamped envelope to the league at 666 11th Street N.W., Suite 700, Washington, D.C. 10002. A women and pensions edition of the league's newsletter has several short articles and a list of resources. Call 800-825-3695 for the current price.

- To get an estimate of your future **Social Security Benefits,** call 800-772-1216 for your Personal Earnings and Benefit Estimate Statement.

CHAPTER ELEVEN

EQUITABLE PROPERTY DISTRIBUTION AND NO-FAULT DIVORCE

You need to claim the events of your life to make yourself yours.
— Anne-Wilson Schaef

In Chapter Seven, I discussed income disparity between divorcing partners in a marriage and how the courts are beginning to make settlement awards which take into account the loss of economic opportunity by the spouse who has stayed home as the anchor for the family. In this chapter we're going to look at equitable property distribution and no-fault divorce. In some respects part of this material overlays income disparity information which I presented earlier. But since equitable distribution is so important, I'll risk repeating some thoughts to make a whole of the important concept of *Fair Share Divorce*.

Divorce is fraught with myth and misinformation. Perhaps nowhere is this more apparent than in the area of equitable distribution. Before 1970, the division of property in divorce was a simple matter. Common law states recognized legal title and the title holder received the property. Community property states divided marital property equally between the spouses.

Now all common law states have moved to equitable distribution. Only three community property states retain the 50/50 division, while the majority have adopted an equitable standard. Although state statutes vary, the principles of equitable distribution are fundamentally the same in common law and in community property states.

The following chart is worth taking a glance at because it reflects the state of community property in the 50 states, as reported in the *Family Law Quarterly:*

	COMMUNITY - PROPERTY STATES[1]	DUAL - CLASSIFICA- TION STATES[2]	ALL - PROPERTY STATES[3]
TITLE	No bearing[4]	No bearing	No bearing
GIFTS & INHERITANCE	Not subject to division[5]	Not subject to division6	Subject to division[7]
PROPERTY ACQUIRED BEFORE MARRIAGE	Not subject to division	Not subject to division	Subject to division[8]
COMMINGLED ASSETS	Subject to division	Subject to division	Subject to division
BUSINESS OWNED BY EITHER SPOUSE	Subject to division if started during marriage	Subject to division if started during marriage	Subject to division
PENSIONS[9]	That portion earned during marriage subject to division	That portion earned during marriage subject to division	All funds subject to division
IRAs	Same as pensions	Same as pensions	Same as pensions
FAMILY HOME[10]	If acquired following marriage, subject to division	If acquired following marriage, subject to division	Subject to division
PERSONAL PROPERTY	If acquired following marriage, subject to division	If acquired following marriage, subject to division	Subject to division
OTHER PROPERTY ACQUIRED DURING THE MARRIAGE	Subject to division	Subject to division	Subject to division
SOCIAL SECURITY	Not subject to division	Not subject to division	Not subject to division

	COMMUNITY - PROPERTY STATES[1]	DUAL - CLASSIFICA- TION STATES[2]	ALL - PROPERTY STATES[3]
PROFESSIONAL LICENSE, ADVANCED DEGREE	Not considered property, treated as a factor at division	Not considered property, treated as a factor at division[11]	Not considered property, treated as a factor at division
APPRECIATION ON PROPERTY ACQUIRED BY GIFT, INHERIT- ANCE, OR BE- FORE MARRIAGE	Appreciation is subject to division only if result of effort by non-owner spouse	Appreciation is subject to division only if result of effort by non-owner spouse[12]	N/A - All property is subject to division

Source: "Family Law in Fifty States: An Overview," Family Law Quarterly, Vol. XXIV, Number 4 (Winter 1991).

1. Arizona, California, Idaho, Louisiana, Mississippi, Nevada, New Mexico, Texas, Washington, and Wisconsin.
2. Alabama, Arkansas, Colorado, Delaware, Georgia, Illinois, Kentucky, Maine, Maryland, Minnesota, Missouri, Nebraska, New Jersey, New York, North Carolina, Oklahoma, Pennsylvania, Rhode Island, South Carolina, Tennessee, Virginia, and West Virginia.
3. Alaska, Connecticut, Florida, Hawaii, Indiana, Iowa, Kansas, Massachusetts, Michigan, Montana, New Hampshire, North Dakota, Ohio, Oregon, South Dakota, Utah, Vermont, and Wyoming.
4. Except in Mississippi.
5. Except in Wisconsin.
6. Except in Delaware, Georgia, and Nebraska.
7. Except in Iowa.
8. Contribution an important factor, most likely to result in unequal distribution of property.
9. At least two states, Colorado and Kansas, do not divide military pensions.
10. Some states give preference to custodial parent.
11. Except New York. New York statutes extend definition of marital property to include professional license, advanced degree, and enhanced earning capacity.
12. Pennsylvania and Colorado treat all appreciation as marital property. The cause of the appreciation is a factor considered at the property-division stage.

I'm sure by the time you've reached this point in my book, you are asking yourself exactly what is equitable?

The law does not provide a definition. Despite the fact that the courts have been making decisions on equitable distribution for two decades, there is no standard or formula. Case law provides precedents, but with the infinite variety of factors which may occur, the final definition is at the discretion of the court. The trial court is charged with the duty to apply a fair and reasonable standard to several relevant criteria or factors found in state statutes. Whether negotiated, mediated, or mutually agreed upon, property settlements must have a recognized authoritative standard to establish guidelines for the negotiations. Statutes within each state and case law provide that standard.

While there is no agreement on a definition for equitable, there is uniform agreement, in both common law and community property states on the application of partnership theory to the division of marital property. Under partnership theory, each partner has an interest in the property of the partnership. The extent of the interest is based on each partner's contribution. Contributions in the context of marriage and divorce encompass both direct, economic contributions as well as the non-economic contributions of a non-working spouse. The length of the marriage and needs of the divorcing spouses are also taken into account.

DIVORCE PLANNING — EQUITABLE DISTRIBUTION

Below is a list of general factors which are used to determine equitable distribution. However, these factors are NOT necessarily used in the community property states (Arizona, California, Idaho, Louisiana, Nevada, New Mexico, Texas, Washington, and Wisconsin). Equitable distribution is the division of the assets of a married couple in the process of divorce with the intention of arriving at economic parity. The following list represents some of the factors to be used in determining what is equitable distribution in your divorce. These are items you may want to be aware of in today's high-divorce-rate society. Be prepared to discuss these points with your attorney and other experts. You've seen a similar list in a previous chapter, but placed here it serves as a reminder. The information on this list represents the evidence a court will examine to determine equitable distribution in your marriage.

QUESTIONS LIKELY TO BE ASKED BY YOUR PROFESSIONAL TEAM:
1. What is the duration of the marriage?
2. What is the age, physical and emotional health of the parties?
3. What is the income or property brought to the marriage by each party?
4. What is the standard of living established during the marriage?
5. Are there any written agreements made by the parties before or during the marriage concerning an arrangement of property distribution (pre-nuptial agreements or post-nuptial agreements)?
6. What are the economic circumstances of each party at the time the division of property is to be made?
7. What is the current income and future earning capacity of each party, including educational background, training, employment skills, work experience, length of absence from the job market, custodial responsibilities for children? Also, what is the period of time and the expense necessary for the least trained party to acquire sufficient education to enable her to become self-supporting at a standard of living which reasonably resembles the standards enjoyed during the marriage?
8. What has been contributed by each party to the education, training or earning power of the other?
9. What has been contributed by each party in the acquisition, dissipation, preservation, depreciation or appreciation in the amount or value of the marital property, as well as the contribution of one party as homemaker?
10. What are the tax consequences of the proposed distribution to each party?
11. What is the present value of all property?
12. Is it better for the parent who has physical custody of a child to own or occupy the marital residence and use or own the household effects?
13. List the debts and liabilities of each party.
14. Is there a need for creation now, or in the future, of a trust fund to secure reasonably foreseeable medical or education costs for a spouse or child?

15. Were any community property agreements signed during the marriage?
16. Are there buy/sell agreements funded with life insurance in closely held businesses?
17. Are there stock options and unqualified retirement accounts funded by employers?
18. Are there any other factors which the court may deem relevant?

Behind each one of these items you should have a written history of the facts, documents to back up the text, dates, and names. By writing this information out for yourself, you will begin to see a pattern and increase your understanding of the facts. You are the person who is most concerned about these facts. It is your life, your money, and your future.

I am assuming that at this point you know what your assets are, the values of your assets, and your position as to whether they are separate or community property. You have a position about which assets you would like to keep, how they are to be shared, and the income which can be generated from the division of assets. The next area of discussion is how do you share the income: How much and for how long? I am going to discuss spousal maintenance, what it is, how the courts allocate it, and how it is taxed.

1. What is spousal maintenance?

By now you should recognize that it is supplemental income paid from one spouse to another.

2. What factors determine the amount of maintenance?

The duration of the marriage — short-, mid-term or long-term. In Washington, a long-term marriage is usually considered to be one of over 25 years duration.

Earning power of one spouse developed during the marriage can be considered an asset under property division. Specifically, the case in which a couple has structured their marriage to allow one spouse to develop a skill, experience, or education which has created a greater earning ability than the other spouse, has created awards of property and maintenance to address the imbalance. As I stated, I've addressed this issue earlier, but since it is vital, I'll go into it deeper here.

A maintenance award is fair only when all of the relevant factors have been considered. Each divorce case is unique, so the list of relevant factors for all cases is infinite. However, generally speaking, the need of the spouse receiving maintenance and the ability of the spouse paying support are considered first. One study, which is often quoted in Washington law regarding divorce and maintenance, comes from former King County Superior Court Judge Robert Winsor. In a 1982 *Washington State Bar News* article he suggested that marriages be viewed in three categories and that Washington state law should consider the length of the marriage when awarding property and maintenance. He felt that in the case of a short marriage (1 to 5 years), the parties should be placed in an economic position as closely parallel to their pre-marriage state as possible. In long marriages (25 or more years), he advocated a forward economic appraisal and an awarding of property or maintenance which would provide as equal a financial position for both parties as possible. In mid-range marriages (5 to 25 years), he argued for an evaluation and rehabilitative maintenance when necessary to assist the less-skilled partner in acquiring the necessary training for employability.

SUPPORTIVE DATA FOR MAINTENANCE IN MARITAL DISSOLUTION CASES — THE NO-FAULT DIVORCE

The statistics show the marked financial inequities which exist under present no-fault dissolution laws. The no-fault law is based upon the concept of rehabilitative maintenance with temporary spousal support. This concept is an idea that works well in selected cases. However, in many situations it is unrealistic to expect that parity in earning capacity can be obtained.

The March 1981 Current Population Survey, Bureau of the Census provides the following significant data:

"About one half of all families below the poverty level in 1980 were maintained by women with no husband present. The poverty rate for such families was 32.7 percent, compared with 5.3 percent for the married couple families and 11 percent for families with a male house-holder present, no wife present."

Before no-fault divorce came into vogue, one spouse had to prove wrong-doing by the other to end a marriage. While the move to no-fault divorce eliminated the occasional need to invent a guilty party to fit the law, it also did away with a bargaining chip women used to negotiate settlements, some lawyers say. This all suggests an increasing need for factual data at trial regarding a spouse's ability to provide for herself after the dissolution.

If you are receiving maintenance over a period of time, I recommend that you ask for insurance on your ex-spouse's life for the time period you are to receive maintenance. Whenever possible, I also request that the payer have disability coverage as well.

Most maintenance awards are modifiable. This means that if the financial circumstances change for the person paying the maintenance, relief may be sought from the court. If your maintenance is non-modifiable, then there's not much you can do. In either case, bankruptcy does not eliminate a maintenance obligation. Enforcing your divorce settlement is an altogether different matter.

In marital dissolution cases involving a financially disadvantaged spouse (usually the wife), the use of a career specialist may be a necessity. The career specialist can give a financial appraisal of the income potential of the spouse, an assessment of the loss of income potential resulting from non-marketing years, current employability, long-range financial prospects, and other factors to determine what type of maintenance is required. A career specialist can provide accurate testimony as to the likelihood of future employment and can help substantiate the woman's case for rehabilitative maintenance and/or long-term maintenance.

The purpose of maintenance, then, is to offer reasonable economic parity between the parties after the divorce. In Chapter Twelve the vocational report in my case study of the Jessups provided the basis for my analysis of various property and maintenance awards. The information in the vocational report of the Hudson case in Chapter Thirteen, also proved helpful.

WHEN TO USE THE CAREER SPECIALIST?

The candidate for vocational counseling typically falls into one of three economic classifications: (1) the unemployed but employable person who lacks career direction and/or employable skills, (2) the unemployable or marginally employable person who is physically handicapped, or has restricted employment potential due to a prolonged absence from the labor force, and (3) the under-employed person who will be unable to support herself in a fashion similar to the economic position she enjoyed during the marriage due to a lack of skills and/or education.

In addition, if the client is employed and the lawyer and financial planner determine that the salary earned cannot realistically support the client and any children, or if there is no reasonable chance for economic parity between the parties when assets, child-rearing expenses and earning potential are analyzed, then a career specialist may be needed.

SELECTION OF THE CAREER SPECIALIST

The career specialist must provide effective assistance to the client by developing a concise, practical, and desirable plan to become economically self-sufficient. Equally important is the capability of presenting information to the court in a precise and practical manner so that maintenance needs are clear.

The specialist should have the educational background, usually at least a masters degree in counseling or psychology, and experience to adequately determine the client's aptitudes, interests, and values through the use of standardized, well-researched career and psychological tests and counseling techniques. The specialist also must be versed in the local employment market and available training program options, (including the educational costs, length of training, employment outlook and expected wages of program graduates). With this knowledge, the career expert can adequately prepare the spouse for the future. In addition, the career expert needs to be sensitive to the client's psychological and physical requirements and must make appropriate referrals to other specialists when additional assessment and/or therapy is needed.

When a client chooses to be retrained or believes retraining is needed, the lawyer and career specialist and financial planner need to ask the following questions:

1. Can the client reasonably be assured of an adequate supply of job openings upon completion of the program?
2. Will the pay be adequate to meet basic income needs?
3. Is a career ladder possible with the hope of eventual economic parity with the husband?
4. Does the client have interests, patterns or personality traits which make it likely that she will be reasonably satisfied and successful in the proposed career field?
5. Does the client have the emotional, learning and/or physical abilities to successfully complete the training program?

THE VOCATIONAL REPORT

The career specialist's report must summarize the counseling process and vocational goals. The report should include pertinent information and be tailored to the client's case. The following areas should be addressed in a vocational report:

A. Personal History.
  • Name, address, date of report.
  • Client age.
  • Personal background family status (children, marriage length, economic status, etc.).
  • Educational background.
  • Work history including volunteer experience.
  • Review of any physical/psychological handicaps (including age) or learning disabilities.

B. Counseling Process.
  • Review of all assessment instruments, including their purpose and results.
  • Review of the counseling process, including client's desires, role in selection process.

C. Summary of Results of Process.
  • Discussion of the proposed vocational choice, including the job outlook, income potential, entry requirements, career ladder, or,
  • A review of the client's history which supports the recommendation that the client is unemployable, or only marginally employable.
D. Conclusion.
  • A concise review of the data which supports the logical out come of the report.

The career consultant must examine all aspects of the client's case, from a physical perspective and from the practical review of employability. The specialist's report must contain data on the probability of a client's success in a proposed career as well as the economic potential of the choice. When the advice of other experts has been used, their recommendations must be incorporated into the report. The psychologists, physicians, financial planners and other experts referred to in the report may be needed as expert witnesses if the case should come to trial.

WHERE DO YOU FIND A CAREER SPECIALIST?
Usually your attorney will give you the name of a career specialist which he or she has used and would recommend. It is a good rule of thumb to interview at least three qualified experts prior to your selection. Make sure you are compatible with this person. Also be comfortable in his or her ability to provide expert witness testimony for your case. More and more local community colleges are offering courses for the displaced homemaker. This type of course would be an excellent starting point for you. These programs do not offer extensive, in-depth services for specific career planning and expert witness services. Qualified experts help to ensure greater equity in determining spousal maintenance and property awards.

SOME TRENDS WHICH I SEE FOR WOMEN IN THE 1990S

I saw a statistic on the news recently which conveyed the fact that 40 percent of all homes which are owned in this country are free and clear. For the most part they are owned by those over 55. This group saved money and paid off the mortgage. This is not as likely to happen with our current mortgage holders. With divorce, job changes, credit cards, we are seeing fewer people reach the "American Dream." Many young people are waiting for an inheritance as their windfall.

Change the dream is my advice. Join forces. No longer will every middle class family be able to have the home in the suburbs with the dog, white picket fence and a bedroom for each child. If these women want to stay in their homes, I suggest they consider sharing the home with another family — create their own co-op, sharing day-care expenses and car pooling responsibilities.

For some women with young children, child support isn't even enough to pay for day care. They simply do not earn enough money to offset these costs. Pressure to find a different kind of work arises. There are plenty of women out there who need a "hired wife" to assist them. There is also a large group of ex-husbands in need of these services to help with the children during their visitation times. This might be an opportunity. Try creating a new type of job for yourself. Don't always look at the traditional concept of work.

All the news for divorcing women is not bad. Women are narrowing the paycheck gender gap. The progress is slow, but they are making strides when it comes to taking home man-sized paychecks.

During the 1980s the average pay for women compared with men rose significantly, and younger women appear to be doing the best, according to an analysis of recently released census data. In 1979, the average full-time working woman was paid just 61 cents for every $1 earned by men. By 1989, that figure rose to 71 cents. But paychecks of mothers lag well behind those of childless women.

The gap between pay for men and pay for women exists mainly because women tend to hold jobs which pay less. Most top executives are men, despite women's attempts to break through the glass ceiling which frequently blocks their advancement to the top echelons.

Some women's gains are artificial because they were calculated without regard to younger men's average wages, which adjusted for inflation, dropped in the 1980s. But real gains by women in their 20s and early 30s also narrowed the gap. In 1989, women in their 20s with no children averaged 90 percent or more of what men in their 20s earned. A decade earlier, women in their 20s averaged 80 percent or less of men's pay, but the gap grows with age and motherhood.

For example, the average 26-year-old childless woman working full-time was paid about $19,800 in 1989, or 92 percent of what an average 26-year-old man made. But in the same year, childless women in their mid-30s were down to the mid-80 percent range, and the average 25-year-old mother in 1989 earned about $14,900, or about 74 percent of what a 25-year-old man did. By their mid-30s, men with high school educations earned more on average than women with college degrees.

The pay gender gap is biggest in industry, smaller in government and non-profit groups. Women in Rust Belt states fared the poorest; women in Pacific Coast states did the best.

Heidi Hartman, a labor economist and director of the Washington-based Institute for Women's Policy Research, said the real test of women's earning power is yet to come. "Until these younger women who seem to be doing so well hit middle age," she said, "we won't know whether what happened to their mothers will happen to them."

I also see a trend with younger women having children, which has resulted in several observations. First of all, many of these women are getting established in their career before they start a family. Once the children are born they are trying to continue to work in their chosen field part-time, job sharing whenever possible. Many of these women are also hiring help at home and staying in their careers full-time.

I also see the dual-career couple facing new challenges of marriage in the 1990s. Mark and Judy have been married for ten years and have two children, ages six and eight. Judy recently was transferred to the West Coast with her company. Mark left a $75,000-a-year job to follow her and the children. After a year, he couldn't find another job in

Library Resource Center
Renton Technical College
3000 NE 4th St.
Renton, WA 98056-4195

his field and found himself staying home with the children after school and asking his wife for spending money. Like Mark, many American men feel torn between traditional social values and some demands of modern life, but few are torn more brutally than those who are following their wives as the women ascend the managerial ladder. And the numbers of such displaced men are growing rapidly.

Women accounted for about 18 percent of corporate moves in 1992, up from five percent in 1980, the Employee Relocation Council says. By the year 2000, some experts say, a third of transferees will be female, and one in four trailing spouses may be men, up from 15 percent in 1990 and about seven percent in 1985.

As the numbers of trailing husbands increase, more and more men, even those accustomed to a wife with a successful career, are finding themselves caught in an awkward sex-role reversal. The strain tends to intensify when a relocated husband can't find a new job and must depend on his wife's paycheck.

In the current unemployment-plagued economy, a trailing husband typically has a harder time finding work than a trailing wife does. He is usually looking for a relatively high-paying job, and many traditionally male jobs, whether blue-collar factory work or white-collar middle management positions, are harder to find and less portable than many traditionally female jobs, such as nursing and clerking.

I see more of these marriages break up because of the stress. It is responsible for the displaced husband syndrome. Women are paying maintenance, both rehabilitative and transitional. The husbands are seeking the primary custodial responsibility of the children. Big corporations are now taking a serious look at this phenomenon and are starting to assist the husbands in finding work at the new location before the wife is transferred. They feel they have invested a great deal of money in the woman going up the managerial ladder and want her stress level to be kept at a minimum. Job aid packages are being developed. Marriott Corporation and AT&T have developed these out-placement services for their employees.

More and more couples will be asking each other, "Who has the most marketable resume in our dual career family?" Many of the young college graduate women in the job market today are unwilling to back away from their careers to pursue a family full-time. They have witnessed how the divorce courts and society have failed to support these women when a divorce occurs after their being out of the job market for 10-15 years. You just don't re-enter and build where you left off. The times are changing.

Les Krantz wrote in his book, *America by the Numbers: Facts and Figures From the Weighty to the Way Out,* that women own 28 percent of U.S. businesses, 5.4 million companies, and employ 11.7 million workers, as many as the Fortune 500 Companies. The Fortune 500 companies cut their work forces by 250,000 last year, while female owned businesses increased their payrolls by 350,000.

Look at the demographics of the country. Many of these women are creating jobs in fields which were not established ten years ago. As the yuppie movement drove the '80s, and work environments have become bereft of emotional and spiritual content, I believe we are moving back to the creative expression of the '60s. People are looking for balance and health, and putting less importance on the size of the paycheck. Work is changing in our society.

When one of the women I work with asked me how should she respond when she tells a prospective employer that, at 48, she has never worked for a paycheck a day in her life. I tell her she has been working, probably harder than those of us in the job market. She has been raising children, running a household, juggling fifteen things at once, and these experiences have allowed her to develop many skills she would not have learned if she had been in the traditional workplace. I remember one woman who used to get very irritated when someone asked her, "Do you work?" She is at home taking care of the family. Her response is "No, it's a volunteer position and I work for room and board." And yes, sometimes the person who owns the "bed and breakfast house" sells it right out from under you. The marketplace calls it progress, we call it divorce.

If you have the opportunity to take a transition course at your local university to transition back into the work force, do so. If not, take yourself through the process of defining your skills, transferring them into the job market, and finally into the form of a resume. You just might surprise yourself. You can acquire the technical skills, the common sense and the ability to work under pressure from experience. Don't undersell yourself. Let people know in your community that you are looking for work. Go back to the people where you have become known as an excellent volunteer worker, leading and organizing. You just might find a paying job by networking within this group.

WHAT IS THE LEVEL OF SOCIAL AWARENESS ABOUT DIVORCE?

What about the spiritual and social side of marriage? Recently Roman Catholic bishops in the U.S. created a document on marriage which encouraged Roman Catholics to move beyond the sexual stereotypes they grew up with. From the growing men's movement and the changing society, they encouraged Catholics to strive for equality of the sexes in dividing household and parental responsibilities.

"Marriage is a partnership of a man and a woman equal in dignity and value," the bishops said in *Follow the Way of Love: A Pastoral Message of the U.S. Catholic Bishops to Families.* Women and men are in transition. Their historical role models are no longer working in our contemporary society. The younger women only need to look at their "older sisters" and their divorce settlements to realize they must be prepared to take care of themselves.

I do agree with the courts that marriage should not be a ticket to a perpetual pension. Many men are fighting back on the issue of long-term or permanent maintenance and arguing that when a woman elects motherhood and family she is making a choice not to work in a career and with that choice comes some responsibility.

Is permanent alimony making a comeback in the courts? I would say that, in some instances, yes it is. The change reflects the fact that, despite the push for equality between the sexes, the economic reality for middle-aged housewives is that their career opportunities are limited and their earning power is poor.

Is a woman in her late 40s or 50s going to go back to school and become a doctor or a lawyer and compete with her husband at the same earning level? I don't think so, and I don't expect that many people would disagree.

Already state laws are shifting back toward permanent alimony or maintenance. A few years ago New York strengthened its law by spelling out that courts may award permanent maintenance, and Pennsylvania passed similar legislation four years ago. In addition, equitable distribution of property sometimes gives wives a larger piece of the pie than they might have gotten when distribution was determined primarily by who held title. However, equitable distribution has been viewed by many courts as a substitute for maintenance.

This trend, however, is beginning to change. If you are a woman who lost 20 years of work and pension, dividing up property equitably doesn't make up for that. Even if you go into the job market, you'll make less than you would have made in the first 20 years. Indeed, the experience of the past 20 years has shown that older women often suffer a severe drop in their standard of living after a divorce. Such women often lack the skills and even knowledge of the contemporary workplace. Moreover, they often face age and sex discrimination.

The courts are beginning to take those factors into account. Several states are now beginning to show reversals of trial courts that limit maintenance for long-term marriages. Look at the state statutes where you live. What do you see coming out of the courts?

Divorce is the biggest financial decision of your life. Be sure you are prepared with your financial and vocational data. Have experts on your side.

As a side note, it is never too late to develop marketable work skills for yourself. If you are a woman under 40, this is particularly important. One of the reasons I am hired by attorneys for their clients is to graphically show the economic consequences of various property settlements, including the division of income over time through an award of maintenance. This joint working relationship is making a difference for a lot of women.

CHAPTER TWELVE

THE DISPLACED HOMEMAKER —
HOW DO I SURVIVE WHEN MY SPOUSE'S EARNINGS
HAVE BEEN WITHDRAWN?

In the middle of difficulty lies opportunity.
— Albert Einstein

In the previous chapter, I discussed the displaced homemaker and how she is treated by divorce in our courts in relationship to equitable property distribution. In this chapter, I've presented the case of a woman in divorce, following her through the process and examining her future economically, sociologically, psychologically and legally. It is a study worth examining because it is a chapter out of real life.

I believe there is evidence in our courts and in settlements that the '90s will be a period of change in the concept of spousal maintenance. I've said this before, but it's worth repeating. Courts can't ignore the consequences to the children of divorce who turn to violence out of frustration and social isolation. Much of this book centers around the idea of a fair and equitable settlement between divorcing spouses. This means adequate spousal maintenance. It's something I fight for with my clients. A fair and equitable settlement means looking realistically at the social and economic realities that face divorcing couples. Judges can use discretion in this area. As a financial planner, it's my role to provide my clients and their attorneys with the financial tools to graphically illustrate these economic realities. I work directly with a vocational career advisor to quantify these realities in the job place and translate them into dollars.

The changes I advocate are going to come about when judges and attorneys working with their clients arrive at a better understanding of the economic consequences of divorce and how poorly written property settlements contribute to poverty for women and children in our society. So, this chapter is principally a study of John and Mary and Jake and Judith. By examining their divorces and their property settlements, we can begin to appreciate first-hand how important fair and equitable justice is to the woman who most usually loses in the legal dissolution process.

The entire question of spousal maintenance can be traced back to the concept of marriage and the marriage contract. I am a second generation American. I can clearly remember my grandmother telling me that I should marry for love but, also be aware of the business aspects of the marriage. She definitely viewed marriage as a long-term (presumably life-time) commitment and that each partner had the responsibility to protect and be provided for by the other partner.

Mary may have been slightly better off than some women of divorce facing a new future, but only to the extent that she had a profession delayed by her marriage to John.

Mary and John are both attorneys. They are each 45 years old. Mary worked as a lawyer in the public sector and John had a private practice in a law firm where he was a partner. Mary had worked for seven years full-time until the couple adopted their first child. They agreed that it was important for the child to have a stay-at-home mother and she consented that she should be the one to stay home, partly because of his greater earning capacity in the private sector. Also, Mary's desire to be a mother after many years of unsuccessful pregnancies was a big factor.

It was Mary's strong belief that her marriage was secure and that John was as committed as she to the future of the child they had chosen to adopt. She told me that one of the reasons that she and John were chosen by James's biological parents over other adoptive candidates was the fact that they appeared to have a stable, financially secure future together. The same judgment was made of them when they subsequently adopted their daughter Emily.

While being a mom, Mary has worked part-time, on an as-needed basis, as a hearing examiner for two local cities near her home. The time she devoted to work varied between a few hours and 40 hours per week. She consulted out of a home office. When she had to leave her home base she was often able to take her children with her. If that was impossible, she scheduled appointments while the children were in school.

James was ten years old in the fourth grade and Emily was six and in kindergarten when I first saw Mary. In the early stage of Mary's separation from John, he wanted to have her stay home with the children. Then, he changed his mind as he realized the arrangement would cost him money in the short and long-term. Later, John believed that if Mary planned to enter a full-time practice, her earnings would soon equal his and might very well exceed his in the long run. Mary did not agree. She did not believe the facts supported his evaluation. Mary had gone to the library and studied the statistics concerning the legal job market and those relating to women re-entering the job market after a ten year hiatus. They did not support the idea that a woman can easily or quickly make up the gap. She also believed that her experience in the public legal sector was not as lucrative as her husband's private practice.

Our firm completed an analysis that showed what Mary would be earning today had she stayed in her prior position. About $78,000 was the figure and that would probably be as a judge. This salary also was verified by other attorneys she knew from her employment in the public sector who had not had a break in service.

Mary's other serious concern about returning to the work place was that she would not have enough time to devote to a full-time career and mothering as well. She believed that her children rightfully had the expectation of a mother at home. Both she and John had always believed that day-care was not the place for their children.

Mary's additional worry centered on the fact of the children's adoption. She talked with an adoption counselor and was told that often children who are adopted face extra trauma with divorce when they become old enough to realize that they have been relinquished by their birth parents and then abandoned by an adoptive parent. Mary was very concerned that the children not have this burden placed on them suddenly and she wanted maintenance for five years while she gradually re-entered the legal marketplace full-time. Her career plan was to open a private law practice initially from her home. She did plan to move out of the family residence as it was much larger and more costly than she could afford. She and John agreed to the sale, but Mary felt resentful that she was the one to stay behind to get the house ready for resale. John was living with a new friend and at the beginning of their divorce was helpful in maintaining the former home, but as time passed, his involvement became almost nonexistent. In the divorce settlement, Mary wanted start-up cash for her home-based law practice of $40,000. This would cover a minimal legal library, computer software, insurance, a secretary-receptionist, office supplies and equipment.

Perhaps most bitter to Mary was John's abandonment of the commitment he had made to her and the children after 23 years of marriage. She had altered her career track to be the home-parent to their children. As a devoted mother, she believes she cannot simply return to her pre-mother career track. She believes that John is successful today because of his ability and hard work, but also because she sacrificed her career freedom to enable him to pursue his professional obligation content with the knowledge that the children had a loving mother at home.

To Mary, John's abandonment of their marriage was a breach of a contract and she should be compensated with damages. She was aware that this type of breach is not recognized in dissolution law in our state, but insists that it should be. Mary did not believe, nor do I, that no-fault divorce law has helped women economically over the long-term.

It is so easy to marry in our society today. In a few hours with a few dollars you can have a license to marry and to influence another person's life for years to come. It is too easy to move from one partner to the next. No-fault divorce was designed to avoid litigation over grounds for granting divorce. Too many times, no-fault divorce is being interpreted as a means for avoiding damages and costs for breach of the marriage contract on which the non-breaching spouse has unwittingly relied to her detriment. Almost overwhelmingly, the women are the ones who have suffered with no-fault divorce.

In the Winter 1993 *Family Law Quarterly,* Margaret Brinig reviewed a book by Allen M. Parkman entitled *The Law And Economics Of No-Fault Divorce — A Review Of No-Fault Divorce: What Went Wrong?* In her review she points out that Parkman argues that "no-fault divorce should be awarded only if both spouses want the divorce, the divorce initiating-contract breaking-spouse should 'buy out' the other spouse." He notes that "even in a contract terminable at will, the parties anticipated performance, but they recognized each party had a right to break the contract subject to the requirement of compensation."

Will we return to the notion of no-fault divorce in the '90s? I don't think so. I do think, however, that there will be legal provisions in the future to compensate women for loss of earning power they will never regain.

In the next section of this chapter you will meet the Jessups and you'll be able to see for yourself the economic impact of their proposed property settlement.

DIVORCE SETTLEMENT ANALYSIS

This is not a full written report, but a summary of my analysis work including a few of the spreadsheets used in the negotiations for a property settlement between Jake and Judith and their attorneys. This is what their agreed settlement looked like in its final form. They each had made a settlement proposal during the dissolution, then spent eight hours in mediation to finally reach the property settlement which I describe in this chapter.

These decision-making models are tools to assist you and your attorney in reaching a fair and equitable property settlement. When I work with you in the property settlement negotiations, it is my role to model the economic impact of various settlement proposals. Almost no one gets everything they want. Divorce means compromise, and these economic models will help you understand your compromises, including what they cost you today and in the future.

Background

Jake Jessup was born on February 19, 1948 and graduated from high school in 1966. He was accepted at Seattle University and completed his BA in management in July 1970. Judith was born on April 2, 1951 and graduated from her high school in Minnesota in 1969. She was also accepted at Seattle University and moved to the Northwest in the fall of 1969. It was during her first year that she met Jake. They started dating, and in 1973, having finished her BA in physical education, she decided to complete her fifth year teaching certification while Jake worked at his father's company, Northwest Systems, Inc.

They dated for two years, and in 1975 Jake and Judith moved in together. Judith began teaching physical education courses in the Bellevue School system in 1974, and in 1978 Jake and Judith were married. One year later, their first son, Sam, was born, and, in the same year, Jake purchased Northwest Systems, Inc. from his father. At the time, the company had about 11 employees, annual sales revenues of approximately $750,000 and net income of $125,000. Jake and Judith agreed that she should make the family her primary responsibility. Their second child, Jacob, was born in July 1981. Judith did volunteer work for the school district on and off during this period, and in 1985 decided to go back to work part-time as an aerobics instructor. She became good friends with another instructor, who, one year later, asked Judith to go into business with her as an instructor and personal trainer. J & W Aerobics lasted for five years, producing less than $5,000 per year in income for Judith, since her time commitment could only be about 12 hours per week. In 1988, the couple's youngest son, Francis, was born.

Jake paid the balance on the loan used to purchase the business in 1989. Then, in 1991, the "W" in J & W moved to the Midwest. In 1991 Judith decided to work, as she does now, for the local community college as an aerobics instructor, earning as much as $33 per hour two years later. She also continues to teach an additional class each week at a local athletic club.

The characteristics of this divorce are as follows:
- Mid-term marriage (16 years).
- Judith and Jake each are in their primary working years, with 20+ years to retirement.
- Judith and the children are competing for future education costs.
- Judith wants to be the primary caretaker of the children, working part-time outside the home while the children are at home. However, her divorce circumstances make delaying her move into the work force unrealistic.
- Disparity of earnings between Jake and Judith.
- Increasing erosion of Judith's married standard of living.

The summary sheet on the following page is intended to serve as a quick reference to the facts regarding the Jessup's income, work skills, ages, financial issues, etc. For the first two months of the separation Jake gave Judith $3,000 per month for living expenses and paid the home mortgage.

Jake wanted to settle the divorce in 90 days. He wanted Judith to take the house and he would keep the business. They would split the retirement 50-50 and he would pay her three year's of maintenance at $2,000 per month plus $1,000 per month of child support. It is not unusual for the person who is planning the divorce to have a settlement plan in mind when he files for divorce. Judith was not in agreement with Jake and experienced emotional trauma about facing the economic responsibilities of raising the family and finding full-time employment. She needed time out to evaluate her position and to create a career and financial plan. She was not willing to be rushed into a divorce settlement.

Judith filed her financial declaration which resulted in $3,000 per month in maintenance and $1,500 per month in child support under a temporary order. Judith's attorney recommended that she come to see me after the realization that she had understated many of her budgeted expenses. We worked together to show how the family of five had spent money historically. From this information, I created the historical budget analysis you saw in an earlier chapter. From my report, we were

SUMMARY OF JESSUP FAMILY

Husband: **Occupation:** **Education:** **Age:**	Jake Jessup Self-employed owner of family business BA in Business Management 46
Wife: **Occupation:** **Education:** **Age:**	Judith Jessup Homemaker - Teacher for 5 years after marriage BA in Physical Education, 5th year certificate 43
Children:	Sam, age 15 - 10th Grade Jacob, age 13 - 8th Grade Frances, age 6 - 1st Grade
Duration of Marriage:	16 years, plus 3 years of cohabitation pre-marriage
Husband's Salary:	$165,000 including a $15,000 bonus in 1994
Wife's Salary:	$8,500 in 1994
Annual Retirement Contributions:	Jake contributes the maximum in his 401(k) plan - $9240 in 1994, Judith contributes $2000 in her IRA
Issues:	1. Sale of family residence 2. Purchase of two new residences 3. Judith's career and education plan 4. College funding 5. Retirement funding 6. Valuation of Northwest Systems, Inc. 7. Disparity of earnings 8. Sharing of bonus 9. Maintenance 10. 1994 Income Tax Filing Status 11. 5-year Cash Flow and Tax Analysis 12. 5-year General Living Expense Detail 13. 5-year Net Worth Comparison

able to initiate a motion for reconsideration which resulted in an increase in Judith's support payments to $4,500 per month for alimony/maintenance and the same $1,500 per month for child support. Judith was to pay the mortgage payment out of these funds. Over the next six months Judith and Jake worked on the other financial issues in their divorce settlement, including the parenting plan.

By August of 1994 they had each been provided valuations on the marital assets from their experts. Jake made an initial property settlement offer, Judith countered and this went back and forth for more than a month. They were scheduled for trial in November of 1994. What follows is their final property settlement agreement. The economic impact of this settlement is analyzed for both Jake and Judith for a five year period. There were several areas of disagreement between Judith and Jake. However, through negotiation and mediation they were able to come to an agreement.

The cash flow, living expense detail, income tax analysis, and net worth spreadsheets were used to help them come to a final settlement. I was able to model both of their proposals and help them compromise on the various financial issues. I have prepared a timeline of their married life which you may want to refer to as you read through the analysis.

Timeline for Jake and Judith Jessup's Married Life

Jun.	1966	Jake graduates from high school and begins undergraduate coursework at Seattle University in the fall of the same year.
Jun.	1969	Judith graduates from high school, begins her studies at Seattle University, where she meets Jake.
Jul.	1970	Jake completes his BA in management at Seattle University. He begins working with his father in the family business, Northwest Systems, Inc.
Jul.	1973	Judith finishes her BA in physical education.
Jul.	1974	Judith completes her fifth year certificate and begins teaching physical education in the Bellevue Junior High School system; she also coaches three sports.

Aug.	1975	Jake and Judith move in together.
Feb.	1978	Jake and Judith are married.
Apr.	1979	Their first son, Sam, is born. Jake agrees that Judith should stop teaching to take care of Sam.
Dec.	1979	Jake buys the family business from his father. Annual revenues were less than $750,000.
Jul.	1981	Jacob is born. Late in the year, Judith begins part-time volunteer work for the school district.
Jan.	1985	Judith decides to work part-time as an aerobics instructor. In 1986, she opens J & W Aerobics.
May	1988	Francis is born.
Sep.	1989	Jake pays off the balance of his debt on the business.
Mar.	1991	Judith's business partner moves away; Judith takes on part-time work teaching aerobics, which she continues to do.
Sep.	1993	Judith and Jake separate.
Nov.	1993	Jake files for divorce.
Dec.	1993	Temporary maintenance and child support orders are started. Judith receives $4,500 in maintenance and $1,500 in child support.
Jan.	1994	Judith and Jake list the house for sale.
Jun.	1994	House sells on June 30, 1994. Judith and Jake decide to rent until the divorce is final and a property settlement is agreed upon.
Sep.	1994	Judith starts her coursework at the university full-time.
Oct.	1994	Divorce is finalized, property settlement agreed upon.
Jan.	1995	Jake buys $175,000 house with $140,000 mortgage at 8.5 percent for 30 years.
		Judith buys $175,000 house with $125,000 mortgage (same rate, also 30 years).
		Jake also begins the settlement note payments of $880 per month (see cash flow analysis below).
		Maintenance and child support do not change post-divorce.

FINANCIAL ISSUES:

1. Sale of Family Residence

Initially Jake wanted Judith to take the house and he would keep the business. Once they had gone through the initial phase of the budgeting and the temporary maintenance/alimony and child support levels were set by the court and a careful analysis of the family's historical spending was completed, they both agreed that the current home was too costly for either of them to maintain individually.

Judith wanted to focus on her career and education plan and not worry about how to make house payments and maintain a large home. Jake did not want to pay any more money in maintenance than the current level and definitely not for more than three to five years.

Both Judith and Jake agreed that the current residence should be sold and they listed the house for sale in January of 1994. The house sold more quickly than they had anticipated and the transaction closed in June of 1994. Judith and Jake were still in disagreement about their overall property settlement and decided to put the house sales proceeds into a blocked account until they had finalized the entire property settlement and parenting plan. They each moved into a rental house and signed a six-month lease. Jake paid $1,100 per month while Judith, with the children, had rental payments of $1,375.

2. Purchase of Two New Residences

In the final property settlement they agreed to purchase two homes. Each would look for a home valued at $175,000. Jake would take out a mortgage for $140,000 and Judith $125,000. Both chose fixed mortgages at 8.5 percent. They each moved into their new homes on January 1, 1995.

Over the duration of the Jessup's marriage, Judith's role has primarily been as a homemaker. Therefore, although she has been both a business owner and an employee at several area health clubs, she has no significant employment history, which was borne out by the vocational report on her career assets.

Early in the divorce proceedings, Jake made a request for joint custody of the children. He wanted them to live with him at least 50 percent of the time. He was concerned that he would lose his relationship with the children in the divorce process unless he protected his time with them. He was willing to hire a housekeeper/driver to assist him in sharing the responsibilities of the children.

Judith was very upset with Jake's request to have the children for half of the time. She was angry and felt that her mothering skills were being questioned, that Jake was "hiring a wife" to replace her, that he was the one who left the marriage and broke his vows, that he was more concerned about money than the children.

Jake, Judith and the children did see a court-appointed child evaluator who talked with all of them about their situation and what would be best for the children. The evaluator gave her report to the attorneys just as the certified financial planner, business valuator and career advisor had done in this case. In the end, the children remained with Judith in her primary custody, however, Jake had generous visitation and sharing rights and responsibilities. Once the intense emotions were diffused, everyone was satisfied with the outcome.

In the end, they agreed on a parenting plan that allowed the children to be with Jake every other weekend, two afternoons and nights a week and half of the holidays each year. Therefore, Judith and Jake purchased homes in the same school district so that the children would have less disruption when going back and forth between the two homes. They agreed to re-evaluate their parenting plan in another year and to have family meetings with the children through counseling to discuss the workability of the parenting plan.

3. Judith's Career and Education Plan

For the past three years Judith has worked part-time as an aerobics instructor at a local health club. She has always been active in sports and was committed to her own physical fitness, as well as that of Jake and the children.

Judith liked teaching aerobics, but she knew that it would not provide enough income as a career. Within three months of Jake filing for a divorce, Judith started working with a career advisor about a career plan for herself. An excerpt from that report showed that Judith would have to invest in her future with education expenses and with an adjustment to the realities of a new career. The career evaluator, Janice E. Reha, summarized Judith in the following manner:

"Ms. Jessup is a competent, energetic woman who is entering the job market at mid-age. Typical of women in her age group, she lacks consistent paid work experience. In addition, Ms. Jessup is entering the job market during a recession. Many employers are currently hiring part-time and temporary workers to avoid paying expensive benefits and retirement. Ms. Jessup's present employment symbolizes this trend.

"Since the job market is extremely competitive, Judith would benefit greatly by obtaining additional skills and knowledge to sell to an employer. If she were to teach physical education in the high school, her age would likely be a handicap. Also, Judith is concerned about her ability to cope with the physical stamina needed in this position. For this reason, Ms. Jessup is seeking an occupation more suitable to her present and future financial needs.

"According to the results from the inventories, Judith shows strong inclinations toward more enterprising occupations including sales. Because she has not thoroughly researched this option, Judith intends to gather more information about this broad field and simultaneously, begin to take business-related classes to gain a more theoretical basis as well.

"I believe that Judith has the determination and motivation to achieve her goals. In the past she has performed well in her educational endeavors. Once she has reached more resolution emotionally about this divorce, I think that Judith will be ready to achieve her goals of economic self-sufficiency. In the interim, she will need financial support to help her overcome both the internal and external obstacles that impede this process. I strongly encourage her to seek counseling to help facilitate her in bridging the transition from marital to single status."

The complete vocational report, which begins on page 247, was used by attorneys and by Judith as a guideline for her anticipated college expenses, her re-entry into the job market as a basis to determine her future earnings.

4. College Funding

Jake and Judith agreed to share in the funding of their children's college education based on a pro rata (proportional) share of their gross wages. Each of the children have $10,000 in a college fund provided by their grandparents. Jake and Judith have agreed to fund up to $10,000 per year in today's dollars for each child's undergraduate education. This funding includes tuition, books, lab fees, travel, an allowance and miscellaneous expenses. Both Jake and Judith want the children to pay for part of their own education.

5. Retirement Funding

Jake sees funding for his retirement coming from the following sources:

- The company funds up to 15 percent of employee compensation in a profit sharing plan. This contribution is voluntary and is paid only if there are profits in the company and management (Jake) makes that determination.
- Northwest Systems, Inc. also started a 401(k) plan five years ago and Jake has been contributing the maximum allowed into this plan.
- A cash bonus from Northwest Systems, Inc.
- Growth of Northwest Systems, Inc. Jake hopes to sell the business to his son in a few years, or to an outside person when he retires.

Judith will fund a $2,000 per year Individual Retirement Account (IRA) and will participate in whatever form of pension or retirement benefits are available once she obtains employment.

Jake and Judith recognized that Judith's ability to fund her retirement from her earnings would be limited, therefore, she received their current retirement assets in the property settlement.

6. Valuation of Northwest Systems, Inc.

Jake and Judith each hired their own expert to value the family owned business. The valuations differed by $75,000 and they agreed to split the difference.

7. *Disparity of Earnings*

Jake and Judith, and particularly Judith, are aware of the difference in their future earning power. The disproportionate share of assets to Judith and five year's of maintenance were given as consideration for this disparity. It is a reality for both of them.

8. *Sharing of the Bonus*

Jake did not wish to share his bonus with Judith, and in defense insisted that there was no guarantee that the company could afford a bonus each year. He argued that 1994 was going to be a tough year as he has been preoccupied with the divorce and has been unable to put needed time into the business. He doesn't want to work as hard as he has in the past, and he complained that the economy was unpredictable.

Jake's argument is a common one when a couple goes through a divorce. I have found the judges to be skeptical of this line of reasoning. If the divorcing couple can come up with a formula for sharing the bonus, these arguments typically go away.

Jake and Judith did not agree about the bonus sharing and she wanted to share in the growth of Northwest Systems, Inc. as she had shared in the building of the company during the marriage.

They finally agreed to assume that Jake's cash bonus would be $15,000 per year for the next five years for purposes of calculating their individual cash flow, taxes and net worth. Jake would keep all of this bonus but agree to pay maintenance for five years (the first three years are non-modifiable) and all of Judith's college expenses outlined in her vocational report.

9. *Maintenance*

Maintenance (or alimony) is a part of the Jessup settlement. Jake will pay this maintenance as follows:

Year	Monthly Maintenance Amount		Months		Total Annual Maintenance
1	$4,500	X	12	=	$54,000
2	4,500	X	12	=	54,000
3	4,000	X	12	=	48,000
4	3,000	X	12	=	36,000
5	2,000	X	12	=	24,000
			TOTAL		$216,000

Note, also, that the income is taxable to Judith and tax deductible to Jake.

10. 1994 Income Tax Filing Status
The Jessups did not file jointly in 1994 as their accountant showed them there was a cost savings in finalizing the divorce in 1994 and filing separate returns.The income tax savings comes from utilizing the lower tax brackets twice, and, since Jake has deductible maintenance payments, his marginal tax bracket drops. Judith's marginal tax bracket increases, but not enough to offset the benefits of filing separately.

11. 5-Year Income Tax and Cash Flow Analysis
A five year income tax and cash flow analysis was completed for the Jessups based on assumptions that were discussed in the property settlement negotiations. See the assumptions for this analysis below for more detailed information.

12. 5-Year General Living Expense Detail
In an earlier chapter I showed you how to complete a comprehensive analysis of your historical spending and used the Jessup family as our example. We then created a temporary budget for Judith Jessup which was used as a basis for her revised maintenance and child support request. Finally, we have created a post-divorce budget for Judith based on her changing economic circumstances.

We have provided Jake and Judith with a proposed post-divorce budget which included other new living expenses. These budgets are meant to be used as a guideline by both Jake and Judith in their post-divorce budget planning and are designed to show Jake and Judith that it is possible to create a fair and equitable post-divorce lifestyle for each of them. They will have realized, having gone through this process, that things are going to be different for each of them in the long-term. Judith's adjustments are likely to be greater than Jake's over the long-term. That is a reality.

13. 5-Year Net Worth Comparison

In this analysis I was trying to quantify the future net worth of both Jake and Judith in five years. The assumptions used in this analysis are conservative. They represent the "what if" scenario, incorporating all the financial information prepared throughout the financial analytical process. The goal is to create a win/win strategy for Judith and Jake. Judith has time to complete her education and find full-time employment. We believe a five year projection is realistic for a 16-year (or mid-term) marriage in addition to their three years of living together. By the time the divorce is final, Judith and Jake have been together financially for over 20 years, nearly all of their adult lives.

**TABLE OF CONTENTS FOR
SPREADSHEET ANALYSIS ON JESSUPS**

Assumptions For Reallocation of Assets

A list of the Jessup assets is provided. They agreed upon an overall 55/45 split. Jake would owe Judith $72,520 in a settlement note. He would pay no interest on this note in year one and thereafter pay 7 percent interest only each year. The remaining note principal will be due at the end of the sixth year.

Jake & Judith Jessup

REALLOCATION OF ASSETS

COMMUNITY ASSETS

Reference Number	Assets	Present Position	Encumbrances	Net Equity	Jake	Judith
CASH						
1	Checking & Savings	$4,500	-	$4,500	$ -	$4,500
2	Money Market Fund	41,000		41,000	19,250	21,750
RESIDENCE						
3	Home Value	475,000	320,000	155,000	30,000	125,000
4	Expense of Home Sale	-	33,250	(33,250)	-	(33,250)
FAMILY BUSINESS						
5	Northwest Systems, Inc.	315,000	-	315,000	315,000	-
RETIREMENT						
6	Co. Profit Sharing Plan	104,000		104,000	-	104,000
7	Company 401(k) Plan	60,000		60,000	-	60,000
8	IRA - Jake	4,380		4,380	4,380	-
9	IRA - Judith	5,670		5,670	-	5,670
PERSONAL						
10	91 Dodge Caravan	18,000	12,000	6,000	-	6,000
11	Mirage Ski Boat	22,000	10,500	11,500	11,500	-
12	Personal Propety	32,000		32,000	10,000	22,000
SETTLEMENT NOTE						
13	Settlement Note				(72,520)	72,520
	TOTALS:	$1,081,550	$375,750	$705,800	$317,610	$388,190
	Percentage Allocation:			100.00%	45.00%	55.00%

Assumptions for Historical and Projected Wages

The only assumption for this model is in the projection of income. Both parties have an assumed wage growth rate equal to our assumed inflation rate, or 4 percent.

Jake & Judith Jessup
HISTORICAL & PROJECTED WAGES

Wage Growth (Inflation) 4%

GROSS WAGES

Year	Jake Salary	Jake Bonus	Judith Salary	Total	Jake	Judith
1991	$86,000	$14,000	$3,000	$103,000	97%	3%
1992	112,000	18,000	4,000	$134,000	97%	3%
1993	140,000	10,000	8,500	$158,500	95%	5%
1994	150,000	15,000	8,500	$173,500	95%	5%
1995	156,000	15,000	3,000	$174,000	98%	2%
1996	162,240	15,000	3,000	$180,240	98%	2%
1997	168,730	15,000	28,000	$211,730	87%	13%
1998	175,479	15,000	32,000	$222,479	86%	14%
1999	182,498	15,000	35,000	$232,498	85%	15%
2000	189,798	?	36,400	$226,198	84%	16%
2001	197,390	?	37,856	$235,246	84%	16%
2002	205,285	?	39,370	$244,656	84%	16%

SUMMARY OF HISTORICAL & PROJECTED WAGES

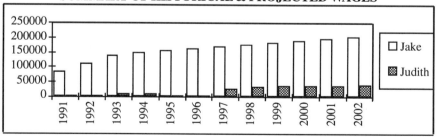

NOTES:
(1) Both parties have agreed to an estimated annual bonus of $15,000 per year for the next 5 years.
(2) Judith has agreed to give up any share of future bonus compensation in exchange for him paying her college expenses, tuition, books, lab fees,

Assumptions for General Living Expense Detail

Judith and Jake have agreed on the figures as proposed for their post-divorce general living expenses. In comparing the temporary budget to the post-divorce budget, note that the mortgage payment is now included only in the income tax and cash flow analysis. In addition, I have included expenses for items for which Jake and Judith are assuming responsibility, such as Judith's future anticipated health insurance expenses. Note, also, that both Jake and Judith have adjusted their expenses to reflect their current requirements based on their estimates in their new living environments. For instance, Judith has adjusted her budget for her gas heat from $100 per month down to $75 per month, based on an estimate obtained for her new residence.

In each subsequent year, most living expenses increased by my assumed inflation rate of 4 percent. However, it is assumed that medical expenses increase by 8 percent per year to reflect current trends in the industry. Since Judith and Jake have agreed that all other expenses grow with inflation, I made no additional rate assumptions. I could also vary the growth rate for real estate taxes, which also tend to differ from inflation, should there be a need for multiple projections.

The sum of all general living expenses for each year is carried into the cash flow analysis presented above. Therefore, the growth rate on general living expenses may differ from that of other income and expense items.

GENERAL LIVING EXPENSES DETAIL
Jake & Judith Jessup

Annual Growth Assumptions

Expenses 4.00%
Medical Expenses 8.00%
Real Estate Taxes 4.00%

GENERAL LIVING EXPENSES	1995		1996	
	Jake	Judith	Jake	Judith
5.1 HOUSING				
1. Mortgage/Rent	Incl. in Cash Flow analysis		----------	
2. Improvements				
3. Furniture, Appliances	1,200	600	1,248	624
4. Tax & Insurance	2,000	2,000	2,080	2,080
5. Yard Care & House Repair	600	600	624	624
Total 5.1 HOUSING	$3,800	$3,200	$3,952	$3,328
5.2 UTILITIES				
1. Heat (Gas & Oil)	960	1,080	998	1,123
2. Electricity	900	900	936	936
3. Water, Sewer, Garbage	600	840	624	874
4. Telephone	900	1,200	936	1,248
5. Cable	420	420	437	437
6. Other (Specify)				
Total 5.2 UTILITIES	$3,780	$4,440	$3,931	$4,618
5.3 FOOD & SUPPLIES				
1. Food	3,600	5,400	3,744	5,616
2. Supplies	600	1,200	624	1,248
3. Meals Eaten Out	3,600	3,000	3,744	3,120
4. Other - Pet Care		720		749
Total 5.3 FOOD & SUPPLIES	$7,800	$10,320	$8,112	$10,733
5.4. CHILDREN				
1. Day Care/Babysitting				
2. Clothing		3,600		3,744
3. Tuition				
4. Other Child Related Exps	6,000	12,000	6,240	12,480
Total 5.4 CHILDREN	$6,000	$15,600	$6,240	$16,224
5.5 TRANSPORTATION				
1. Payments or Leases				
2. Insurance and License		1,206		1,255
3. Gas, Oil, Maintenance		1,500		1,560
4. Parking	120	420	125	437
5. Other: Repairs		720		749
Total 5.5 TRANSPORTATION	$120	$3,846	$125	$4,000
5.6 HEALTH CARE				
1. Insurance		$2,100		$2,184
2. Uninsured Dental, Ortho, Med	3,000	480	3,240	518
3. Other - Counseling		2,880		2,995
4. Prescriptive Drugs	600	600	624	624
Total 5.6 HEALTH CARE	$3,600	$6,060	$3,864	$6,322
5.7 PERSONAL EXPENSES				
1. Clothing	2,400	2,400	2,496	2,496
2. Hair Care/Personal Exps	600	1,200	624	1,248
3. Clubs, Recreation	1,200	1,380	1,248	1,435
4. Education				
5. Books, Newspapers, Magazines	300	480	312	499
6. Gifts	600	1,200	624	1,248
7. Other - Vacat., Ent., Misc.	900	1,800	936	1,872
Total 5.7 PERSONAL EXP.	$6,000	$8,460	$6,240	$8,798
5.8 MISCELLANEOUS				
1. Life & Disability Insurance	720		749	
2. Other: Bank & Credit Card Fees	120	120	125	125
3. Other: Donations	800	500	832	520
4. Other: Professional Fees				
Total 5.8 MISCELLANEOUS	1,640		$1,706	$645
TOTAL EXPENSES	**$32,740**	**$51,926**	**$34,170**	**$54,667**

1997		1998		1999	
Jake	Judith	Jake	Judith	Jake	Judith
----------		----------		----------	
1,298	649	1,350	675	1,404	702
2,163	2,163	2,250	2,250	2,340	2,340
649	649	675	675	702	702
$4,110	$3,461	$4,274	$3,600	$4,445	$3,744
1,038	1,168	1,080	1,215	1,123	1,263
973	973	1,012	1,012	1,053	1,053
649	909	675	945	702	983
973	1,298	1,012	1,350	1,053	1,404
454	454	472	472	491	491
$4,088	$4,802	$4,252	$4,994	$4,422	$5,194
3,894	5,841	4,050	6,074	4,211	6,317
649	1,298	675	1,350	702	1,404
3,894	3,245	4,050	3,375	4,211	3,510
	779		810		842
$8,436	$11,162	$8,774	$11,609	$9,125	$12,073
	3,894		4,050		4,211
6,490	12,979	6,749	13,498	7,019	14,038
$6,490	$16,873	$6,749	$17,548	$7,019	$18,250
	1,305		1,357		1,411
	1,622		1,687		1,755
130	454	135	472	140	491
	779		810		842
$130	$4,160	$135	$4,327	$140	$4,500
	$2,271		$2,362		$2,457
3,499	560	3,779	605	4,081	653
	Stops after 1996				
649	649	675	675	702	702
$4,148	$3,480	$4,454	$3,642	$4,783	$3,812
2,596	2,596	2,700	2,700	2,808	2,808
649	1,298	675	1,350	702	1,404
1,298	1,493	1,350	1,552	1,404	1,614
324	519	337	540	351	562
649	1,298	675	1,350	702	1,404
973	1,947	1,012	2,025	1,053	2,106
$6,490	$9,150	$6,749	$9,516	$7,019	$9,897
779		810		842	
130	130	135	135	140	140
865	541	900	562	936	585
$1,774	$671	$1,845	$697	$1,919	$725
$35,666	$53,760	$37,233	$55,933	$38,873	$58,194

Assumptions for Income Tax Analysis

1. Jake files as a single taxpayer and Judith as Head of Household.
2. Jake earns $165,000 in total wages and Judith $8,500.
3. Jake pays Judith $54,000 in maintenance/alimony starting in 1994, the year of their separation and continues to pay maintenance on a declining schedule for the next five years.
4. Jake and Judith have minimal interest income.
5. Jake continues to fund his 401(k) plan with his maximum contribution allowed and Judith funds a $2,000 per year contribution to her IRA.

INCOME TAX ANALYSIS
Jake & Judith Jessup

INCOME: / Year	1995 Jake	1995 Judith	1996 Jake	1996 Judith
Wages	$156,000	$3,000	$162,240	$3,000
Bonus	15,000	-	15,000	-
Taxable Investment Income	200	5,623	200	5,214
Maintenance (Payment)/Income	(54,000)	54,000	(54,000)	54,000
Other Income	-	-	-	-
401(k) Contributions	(9,610)	-	(9,994)	-
IRA Contributions	-	(2,000)	-	(2,000)
Long Term Capital Gains	0	0	0	0
Taxable Social Security Income	-	-	-	-
Adjusted Gross Income:	107,590	60,623	113,446	60,214
PERSONAL EXEMPTIONS:	*(3)*	*(2)*	*(3)*	*(2)*
Personal Exemptions	(7,350)	(4,900)	(7,350)	(4,900)
Personal Exempt Adjustment	-	-	(147)	-
DEDUCTIONS:				
Deductible Taxes	2,000	2,000	2,080	2,080
Home Interest Expenses	11,951	10,671	11,774	10,512
Charitable Contributions	200	300	200	300
Misc Deductible Expenses	-	-	-	-
High Income Adjustment	-	-	(150)	-
Itemized Deductions (or)	(14,151)	(12,971)	(13,904)	(12,892)
Std Ded (if greater)	-	-	-	-
TAXABLE INCOME:	$86,089	$42,752	$92,339	$42,422
Federal Income Tax:	$22,077	$8,006	$24,015	$7,913
Capital Gains Tax:	0	0	0	0
NET FEDERAL INCOME TAX:	**$22,077**	**$8,006**	**$24,015**	**$7,913**
Marginal Tax Bracket	*31%*	*28%*	*31%*	*28%*
Filing Status:	*S*	*H/H*	*S*	*H/H*

6. Jake claims two of the children and Judith one child.
7. In 1994 Jake takes the interest deduction for the boat and Judith takes the deductions for the house and car.
8. Minimal charitable contributions are made by Judith and Jake. Jake contributes through his corporation.
9. Future itemized deductions are based on the appropriate mortgage interest and taxes for their individual residences and vehicles.
10. Income tax savings comes from utilizing the lower tax brackets twice, and since Jake has deductible maintenance income, his marginal tax bracket drops. Judith's marginal tax bracket increases, but this not enough to offset the benefits of filing separately.

	1997		1998		1999	
	Jake	Judith	Jake	Judith	Jake	Judith
	$168,730	$28,000	$175,479	$32,000	$182,498	35,000
	15,000	-	15,000	-	15,000	-
	200	4,770	200	4,290	200	3,769
	(48,000)	48,000	(36,000)	36,000	(36,000)	36,000
	-	-	-	-	-	-
	(10,394)	-	(10,809)	-	(11,242)	-
	-	(2,000)	-	(2,000)	-	(2,000)
	0	0	0	0	0	0
	-	-	-	-	-	-
	125,536	78,770	143,869	70,290	150,456	72,769
	(3)	*(2)*	*(3)*	*(2)*	*(3)*	*(2)*
	(7,350)	(4,900)	(7,350)	(4,900)	(7,350)	(4,900)
	(882)	-	(2,058)	-	(2,352)	-
	2,163	2,163	2,250	2,250	2,340	2,340
	11,673	10,422	11,563	10,324	17,628	15,739
	200	300	200	300	200	300
	-	-	-	-	-	-
	(513)	-	(1,063)	-	(1,260)	-
	(13,523)	(12,885)	(12,950)	(12,874)	(18,908)	(18,379)
	-	-	-	-	-	-
	$105,544	$60,985	$125,627	$52,516	$126,550	$49,490
	$28,108	$13,111	$34,865	$10,740	$35,198	$9,892
	0	0	0	0	0	0
	$28,108	**$13,111**	**$34,865**	**$10,740**	**$35,198**	**$9,892**
	31%	*28%*	*36%*	*28%*	*36%*	*28%*
	S	*H/H*	*S*	*H/H*	*S*	*H/H*

NOTE:
Wages are increased annually by 4%.

Jake and Judith Jessup
CASH FLOW ANALYSIS

CASH INFLOW:

Source / Year	1995 Jake	1995 Judith	1996 Jake	1996 Judith	1997 Jake	1997 Judith	1998 Jake	1998 Judith	1999 Jake	1999 Judith
Wages	$156,000	$3,000	$162,240	$3,000	$168,730	$28,000	$175,479	$32,000	$182,498	$35,000
Bonus	15,000	-	15,000	-	15,000	-	15,000	-	15,000	-
Taxable Investment Income	200	5,623	200	5,214	200	4,770	200	4,290	200	3,769
Maintenance (Payment)/Income	(54,000)	54,000	(54,000)	54,000	(48,000)	48,000	(36,000)	36,000	(36,000)	36,000
Child Support Income (Payments)	(18,000)	18,000	(18,000)	18,000	(18,000)	18,000	(18,000)	18,000	(13,200)	13,200
Settlement Note Receipts	-	-	(5,076)	5,076	(5,076)	5,076	(5,076)	5,076	(5,076)	5,076
Social Security Income	0	0	0	0	0	0	0	0	0	0
TOTAL CASH INFLOW:	$99,200	$80,623	$100,364	$85,290	$112,853	$103,846	$131,602	$95,366	$143,422	$93,045

CASH OUTFLOW:

Source / Year	1995 Jake	1995 Judith	1996 Jake	1996 Judith	1997 Jake	1997 Judith	1998 Jake	1998 Judith	1999 Jake	1999 Judith
Federal Income Taxes	$22,077	$8,006	$24,015	$7,913	$28,108	$13,111	$34,865	$10,740	$35,198	$9,892
Social Security Tax (6.2%)	3,757	186	3,757	186	3,757	1,736	3,757	1,984	3,757	2,170
Medicare Tax (1.45%)	2,262	44	2,352	44	2,447	406	2,544	464	2,646	508
Mortgage (Rent in 1994) Payments	12,918	11,534	12,918	11,534	12,918	11,534	12,918	11,534	12,918	11,534
General Living Expenses	32,740	51,926	34,170	54,667	35,666	53,760	37,233	55,933	38,873	58,194
Judith - College Expenses	7,080	-	7,080	-	-	-	-	-	-	-
Jessica - College Expenses	-	-	-	-	-	-	-	-	9,692	2,128
401(k) Contributions	9,610	-	9,994	-	10,394	-	10,809	-	11,242	-
IRA Contributions	-	2,000	-	2,000	-	2,000	-	2,000	-	2,000
TOTAL CASH OUTFLOW:	$90,444	$73,695	$94,286	$76,343	$93,290	$82,546	$102,127	$82,654	$114,326	$86,425
DISCRETIONARY CASH FLOW:	$8,756	$6,928	$6,078	$8,947	$19,564	$21,300	$29,475	$12,712	$29,096	$6,620

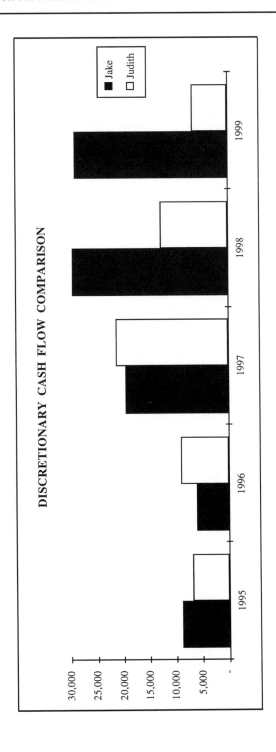

Assumptions for Cash Flow Analysis

1. Jake and Judith each have their base wages increasing at 4 percent annually, our assumed rate of inflation for these reports.
2. Judith works part-time while going to school working as an aerobics instructor. She earns $3,000 per year for two years.
3. Judith starts working full-time in 1997. Based on the vocational report above, we assume that Judith will be able to find employment with a mid-range, entry-level salary of $28,000. Based on market factors discussed with the career specialist, we expect Judith to earn $32,000 and $35,000 in years two and three, respectively.
4. Child support payments continue at $1,500 per month for all the years covered in this analysis. In reality, the child support schedule will be reviewed in two years.
5. Both Jake and Judith have mortgages that start in January of 1995.
6. Judith will start receiving interest only on the settlement note in 1996.
7. Jake pays Judith's college expenses from his earnings.
8. Jake and Judith share in the college funding for Jessica starting in 1999.
9. Jake contributes the maximum to his 40l(k) plan annually (assumed to increase with the wages at 4 percent annually) and Judith contributes $2,000 to her IRA account and into whatever retirement plan her employer may provide.
10. Jake and Judith have 1994 ending balances on all assets, except the residence, equal to those listed on the Reallocation of Assets sheet, inclusive of any retirement contributions made in 1994 and any excess or deficit cash flow from 1994.

Assumptions for Net Worth Estimates

Real Estate/Other Asset Growth Rate	4.00%
Retirement Asset Growth Rate	8.00%
Investment Assets	6.00%
Business Interest Growth Rate	4.00%
Inflation Rate	4.00%

Jake and Judith Jessup
NET WORTH ESTIMATES

Asset: / Year	1995 Jake	1995 Judith	1996 Jake	1996 Judith	1997 Jake	1997 Judith	1998 Jake	1998 Judith	1999 Jake	1999 Judith
Real Estate/Other Assets:	$175,000	$175,000	$182,000	$182,000	$189,280	$189,280	$196,851	$196,851	$204,725	$204,725
Mortgage Balance:	(140,000)	(125,000)	(139,033)	(124,137)	(137,890)	(123,116)	(136,645)	(122,004)	(135,290)	(120,794)
Retirement Assets:	53,830	187,404	80,048	204,396	107,314	222,748	135,672	242,567	165,163	263,973
Taxable Investment Assets:	(53,508)	94,504	(44,752)	101,432	(38,674)	110,379	(19,110)	131,679	10,366	144,392
Business Interests:	327,600	-	340,704	-	354,332	-	368,505	-	383,246	-
ADJUSTED ASSETS:	362,922	331,908	418,966	363,691	474,363	399,291	545,274	449,093	628,211	492,296
Excess/(Deficit) Cash Flow:	8,756	6,928	6,078	8,947	19,564	21,300	29,476	12,713	29,096	6,620
Total Assets:	**$371,678**	**$338,836**	**$425,044**	**$372,638**	**$493,927**	**$420,591**	**$574,750**	**$461,806**	**$657,307**	**$498,916**

NET WORTH ESTIMATES

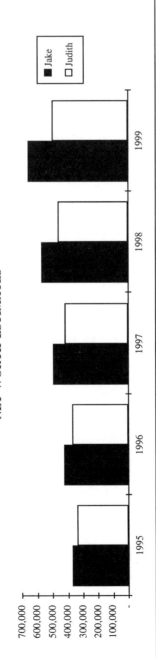

NOTES TO NET WORTH ESTIMATES:

(1) Real estate and retirement assets are increased by the stated growth rate. The return on investment assets is reflected in the income tax and cash flow analysis. Excess cash flow is added to the taxable investment assets.

(2) Beginning balances on retirement assets are based on the proposed property settlement. Judith will contribute $2,000 to IRA; Jake will contribute the maximum allowed to his 401(k) plan each year in addition to profit sharing at 10% of his gross wages.

Conclusion

The net worth analysis is the summary of all of the assumptions made in these reports for the five-year projections for the Jessups. The results of my analysis, while limited to the assumptions which we were able to make, show that it is possible, given current earnings (and potential earnings), to divide the assets in a way which allows for the economic growth of both parties. The Jessups have agreed to the terms of my settlement proposal in the last mediation session.

These terms provide for a reallocation of the assets which favors Judith in the very short term, allocating 55 percent of marital assets to Judith, along with five years of maintenance on a declining scale (see discussion above). We feel this level of maintenance is fair and that it is compensatory (compensating her for lost career opportunities) in nature. In addition, another adjustment to the net worths of both parties will occur when Jake must pay the principal balance on the judgment note at the end of the fifth year. The 1999 net worths for both parties, adjusted by the principal on the note, are $584,786 for Jake and $571,435 for Judith.

Jake is able to exceed Judith in net worth by the end of 1996 with the assumed wage growth rate of 4 percent, while continuing with maximum allowable retirement contributions (adjusted for inflation). The payment of the settlement note will be absorbed so that Jake's net worth will still have increased over the five-year period. In addition, due to Judith's income level (it is likely that it will never equal or exceed Jake's income) beyond the five years, Jake will once again quickly begin to increase his net worth.

VOCATIONAL REPORT

for

JUDITH JESSUP

July 11, 1994

NAME: Judith Jessup

ADDRESS: 20925 Northeast 142nd Street
              Woodinville, WA 98072

PERSONAL HISTORY

Sessions:

Education: Ms. Jessup graduated for J.F. Kennedy High School
                in Bloomington, Minnesota in 1969. During her
                senior year, she applied and was accepted at Seattle
                Univeristy. She attended Seattle University from
                1969 to 1973 and graduated with a Bachelor of Arts
                degree in Physical Education and Health. After grad-
                uation, she attended one year to complete her 5th
                year certification for teaching. In addition, she com-
                pleted her Aerobics National Test certification, ACE.

Social/Emotional: Ms. Jessup was born on April 2, 1951, and is 43
                years old. Judith and Jake Jessup were married on
                January 28, 1978 and have been married 16 years.
                Jake is Owner/President of Northwest Systems, Inc.,
                which is a distributor of forklifts and other heavy
                machinery. He has his Bachelor of Arts degree in
                Business Management from Seattle University.
                They have three children: Sam, who is 15; Jacob,
                who is 13; and Frances, who is 6. Judith has been
                experiencing some depression and anxiety resulting
                from the transition. She has sought some counseling
                and would benefit from more in-depth therapy to
                assist her with coping with her new single status.

Physical: Ms. Jessup reports being in excellent physical
                condition.

Work History: Paid:	1991 - Present	Aerobics Instructor, Bellevue Community College, Part-time, $33 an hour
	1993 - 1994	Aerobics Instructor, Seattle Athletic Club, Part-time, $25 an hour
	1986 - 1991	Owner/Instructor, J&W Aerobics
	1985 - 1991	Aerobics Instructor, King County Parks & Recreation, Part-time, $25 an hour
	1974 - 1979	Junior High Teacher and coach of three sports, Bellevue Schools, Full-time
Unpaid:	1979 - 1985	Coached volleyball for 5th and 6th graders

While attending Seattle University, Ms. Jessup built the cheer-leading squad. As a result, she decided to major in Physical Education, since she had no clear educational objective in mind. While she was involved with cheer-leading, Judith become connected with the coaches, who encouraged her to teach all the gymnastic classes. Through this effort, she earned money to pay for some of her education. She also was a vice president of her class and received payment for this office. In addition she worked at Annie Ridge Academy teaching gymnastic classes. Her industriousness led her to pay off her school loans, as well as to recognition in *Who's Who in American Colleges*. She reports that it is her tendency to overachieve and strive to "get things right." Upon graduation, she was a Physical Education instructor in the Bellevue Schools until her first child was born in 1979. In 1985, Judith decided to start teaching part-time to retain her skills and health — teaching night classes while attending to her main job of raising her family. For the last four years, Judith has worked approximately 6-12 hours a week with the intention of focusing the major portion of her time and energy on her family.

Judith professes to be a traditional woman who sees her major priority as being a wife and mother. For this reason, she feels resistant about returning to work because her children are still young and need attention. On the other hand, Judith has enjoyed working outside the home, but has difficulty in perceiving how she can handle a full time job and fulfill her family responsibilities as well. Her test results reflect this conflict.

PRESENT EARNING CAPACITY, SKILLS & FINANCIAL CONSIDERATION

Ms. Jessup encounters the following obstacles in entering the current job market:

1. Sporadic work history.
2. Concern about her ability to be able to handle both home and work responsibilities.
3. Lack of opportunity to earn an income level equivalent to her spouse's earning and potential.

At present, the job market in Seattle is competitive due to the recession. Jobs are available at the high level technical end or at entry level. Many employers only offer part-time or temporary employment while they wait for an upturn in the economy. Also, many of these position provide little or no benefits. Ms. Jessup's present employment reflects this trend.

Another consideration Ms. Jessup is confronting is her age. She realizes that her physical stamina may wane as she matures; consequently, a career change of some sort is inevitable. Teaching aerobics afforded a means to continue her skills and supplement the family income. Currently, she only earns approximately $8,500 a year. Her age would probably impede her chances for seeking a full-time position in the schools. Presently, Ms. Jessup has no desire to teach young people and has to up-to-date experience in teaching all of the sport activities required in a physical education program. For these reasons, she decided to engage in a career assessment to determine her career direction.

DISCUSSION OF VOCATIONAL ASSESSMENT RESULTS

The following inventories were administered to Ms. Jessup: the Strong Vocational Interest Inventory, the Jackson Vocational Interest Survey, the COPS Interest Inventory, the COPES Work Values Inventory and the Myers-Briggs Type Indicator.

Strong Vocational Interest Inventory

Ms. Jessup generally scored low on this inventory. A depressed or flat profile may indicate any of the following:

- Dependent upon the respondent's mood at the time of completing the SCII.
- That a person in the midst of making a career change may be indecisive or experiencing uneasiness.
- Unwillingness to make a commitment or a change.

In discussing these results, Judith indicated that she feel very conflicted about changing her role from mother to career person. This conflict may be manifested in the depressed profile.

Judith scored Moderately High on the General Occupational theme of Sales and Domestic Arts.

Judith scored Similar and Very Similar to people on the following occupational scales:

Beautician	Store Manager	Buyer
Florist	Travel Agent	Banker
Interior Decorator	Optician	

She scored 15 on the Academic Comfort indicating that she has an orientation toward practical or applied problems.

She scored 61 on the Extroversion-Introversion Scale, indicating that she probably prefers to work alone, to complete projects independently, and to work with ideas and things. These people can interact with people for a few hours, then need time to themselves to regenerate their capacity for extroverted behavior.

Jackson Vocational Interest Survey

Ms. Jessup scored above or at 80% on the following occupational scales:

(93%)   Personal Guidance — Enjoys providing services
to individuals, e.g., travel guide or cosmetician.

(87%)   Family Activity — Enjoys domestic activities, likes
to take an active part in family life and child care, in
decorating and caring for a home and garden, in
entertaining guests, and related activities.

(84%)   Finance — Interested in handling the financial needs
of the public, in solving financial problems and in
investment and trade.

(83%)   Professional Advising — Enjoys counseling and
giving expert advice.

(81%)   Law — Interested in legal matters.

(80%)   Supervision — Interested in planning, organizing
and coordinating the activities of others. Enjoys
holding a position of managerial responsibility.

She scored similar to students in the University Major Field Cluster
of Business.

She scored Similar or Very Similar to people in the following occupations:

Service Occupations
Clerical Services
Assembly Occupations — Instruments and Small Products
Occupations in Accounting, Banking and Finance
Sales Occupations
Occupations in Merchandising
Teaching and Related Occupations

COPS Interest Inventory

Ms. Jessup's profile on this inventory was flat and depressed. Her highest scores were at the 50% on the following scales.

Business Professional: Occupations include positions of high responsibility in the organization, administration and efficient functioning of businesses and governmental bureaus. Sample occupations include: Business Manager, Sales Manager, Merchandising Manager

Business Skilled: Occupations include sales, promtion, and marketing. They also include financial and organizational activities of business in regard to the promotion of businesses. Sample occupations include: Sales Representative, Buyer, Loan Officer.

COPES Work Values Inventory

Ms. Jessup scored above 90% on the following scales:

(98%) Recognition — To become well-known and famous and to know important people are major values of persons scoring high on this scale. Such persons seek the admiration of others as well as the rewards of honorary degrees.

(98%) Aesthetic — Artistic appreciation and the enjoyment of music and the arts are major values of persons scoring high on this scale. Such persons value activities in which they appreciate beauty, show artistic and emotional sensitivity and appreciate music and the arts.

(97%)   Leadership — Making decisions, directing others and speaking for the group are major values of persons scoring high on this scale. Such persons have need to be seen as important and usually take positions of leadership.

(92%)   Orderliness — Keeping things neat and in their proper place are major values of persons scoring high on this scale. Such persons value activities in which they keep things tidy and do what they are expected to do.

Myers-Briggs Type Indicator

Ms. Jessup reflects an Extroverted Intuitive with Feeling Type or Extroverted Sensing with Feeling Type. In discussing both types, Ms. Jessup indicated that she felt the Sensing Type better described her tendencies. According to the Introduction to Type description by Isabel Briggs Myers, ESFJ's tend to concentrate on the admirable qualities of other people and are loyal to respected persons, institutions, or causes, sometimes to the point of idealizing whatever they admire.

ESFJ's are at their best in jobs that deal with people and in situations where cooperation can be brought about through good will. They are found in jobs such as teaching, preaching, and selling. They are less likely to be happy in work demanding mastery of abstract ideas or impersonal analysis.

In 1986, Ms. Jessup actually started her own business, but decided to close because she was not earning enough money in relationship to the time commitment.

COMPILATION OF ASSESSMENT RESULTS

Generally, the test results reflect flat or depressed profiles indicating that Ms. Jessup is experiencing conflict about moving from marital to single status. Several patterns do emerge: Judith shows an enterprising orientation. Her interests and values correlate with people who are in management, sales, accounting, promotion, or finance. In her college and work experiences, she has taken leadership positions and seems to feel comfortable leading others. In our sessions, Judith stated that her father discouraged her from taking business courses in college, so she did not follow those inclinations.

One theme that appears very pronounced is her interest in sales occupations. Of all the occupational possibilities presented to Judith, she seems most enthused about selling some type of tangible product. Since she lacks the sales skills and business background, Judith had not pursued this possibility. To become better acquainted with this field, Ms. Jessup plans to start interviewing people in different types of sales. In addition, she wants to take business-related classes to become knowledgeable about the general aspects of business including marketing, accounting, and management. Because Judith is a person who is more interested in the application of concepts, she would perform best in a program that is more practical and applied.

It is her intent to start taking business-related classes at Bellevue Community College in preparation of completing an MBA program at City University. The MBA program is attended by adults who are working and attending school simultaneously, providing Judith with the opportunity of meeting people in a variety of occupations. This type of program offers her the chance to make contacts and may facilitate her entry into the workplace.

RECOMMENDATION

Program of Study: Preliminary courses at Bellevue Community College.

Masters in Business Administration at City University or a comparable university.

Time: Phase One: Fall, 1993 - 1994

Complete math and accounting courses at Bellevue Community College in preparation of entry into the City University MBA program.

Phase Two   Fall, 1994 - Spring, 1996

                   Complete a 46-credit MBA program
                   at City University.

                   Begin networking to develop job
                   leads.

                   Join professional and/or business
                   organizations to develop contacts.

Phase Three: Fall, 1996 - 1997

                   Start a job search, may have to work
                   part-time temporarily until she
                   secures a full-time position. The state
                   of the economy will impact the
                   length and time of this process.

Costs:

Tuition @ BCC @ $348 per quarter x 3 quarters	$ 1,044
Books @ $150 per quarter x 3 quarters	450
Tuition @ City University @ $2,210 per quarter x 6 quarters	13,260
Books @ $150 per quarter x 6 quarters	900
TOTAL	$15,654

Job Outlook: According to the Washington Occupation Information
                   Service (WOIS):

                   In Washington, this occupation is expected to grow about
                   as fast as the average for all occupations. Employment is
                   projected to increase six percent between 1992 and 1995.

                   Factors Affecting Outlook: Outllook depends on replace-
                   ment of workers who leave the oocupation, economic
                   conditions, consumer preferences and the emphasis
                   industries palce on their sales activities. Turnover is fairly

high among Sales Representatives, but competition for jobs in certain specialties is intense. The only shortage of qualified applicants is in specialties requiring technical knowledge such as computer services and engineering. Nationally, employment of Sales Representatives is expected to increase 15 percent through the year 2005.

Wages:

According to the Washington Occupation Information Service (WOIS):

Earnings vary with the product and employment setting. Beginners often receive a salary while they learn the product line. Typical earnings for trainees range from $1,000 to $1,350 per month. Some experienced sales people earn a straight commission, while others are paid a fixed salary. The majority earn a combination of salary, commission and bonus. Experienced salespeople can earn anywhere from $15,000 to $90,000 per year ($1,250 to $7,500 per month). In the Vancouver area, Sales Representatives average $1,500 to $3,090 per month, while workers in Clallam and Jefferson Counties average $1,650 to $2,680 per month. In WallaWalla, they average $1,350 to $2,400 per month, and in the Tri-Cities area, they average $1,830 to $2,520 per month. In Thurston and Mason Counties, they average $1,800 to $2,400 per month, and in the Seattle area, they average $2,400 to $3,480 per month.

In the Pacific Northwest, Field Sales Representatives with three to five years of experience average $19,215 to $40,000 per year. Senior Field Sales Representatives average $38,920 to $51,170 per year. Experienced Manufacturers' Representatives may earn $50,000 to $100,000 per year.

CONCLUSION

Ms. Jessup is a competent, energetic woman who is entering the job market at mid-age. Typical of women in her age group, she lacks consistent paid work experience. In addition, Ms. Jessup is entering the job market during a recession that does not seem to be receding. Many employers are currently hiring part-time and temporary workers to avoid paying expensive benefits and retirement. Ms. Jessup's present employment symbolizes this trend.

Since the job market is extremely competitive, Judith would benefit greatly by obtaining additional skills and knowledge to sell to an employer. If she were to teach physical education in the high school, her age would likely be a handicap. Also, Judith is concerned about her ability to cope with the physical stamina needed in this position. For this reason, Ms. Jessup is seeking an occupation more suitable to her present and future financial needs.

According to the results from the inventories, Judith shows strong inclinations toward more enterprising occupations including sales. Because she has not thoroughly researched this option, Judith intends to gather more information about this broad field and simultaneously begin to take business-related classes to gain a more theoretical basis as well.

I believe that Judith has the determination and motivation to achieve her goals. In the past, she has performed well in her educational endeavors. Once she has reached more resolution emotionally about this divorce, I think that Judith will be ready to achieve her goals of economic self-sufficiency. In the interim, she will need financial support to help her overcome both the internal and external obstacles that impede this process. I strongly encourage her to seek counseling to help facilitate her in bridging the transition from marital to single status.

I certify, under penalty of perjury, under the laws of the State of Washington, that the foregoing is true and correct.

Name: Janice E. Reha
Place: Bellevue, Washington

CHAPTER THIRTEEN

WHAT SHOULD I KNOW ABOUT BUSINESS ASPECTS OF A LONG-TERM MARRIAGE AND DIVORCE?

The events in our lives happen in a sequence in time,
But in their significance to ourselves, they find their own order ...
The continuous thread of revelation.
— Eudora Welty

LONG-TERM MARRIAGE, THE HUDSON CASE STUDY
Background Information on Gerald and Barbara Hudson

Barbara is 52 years old. She was born in 1942, graduated from high school in 1960 and from the University of Washington in 1965 with a B.A. in English. She also completed her teaching degree while at the university. She worked part-time while she was going to college as you can see from her Social Security earnings record which has been included in the case study at the end of the chapter. Barbara had completed two years of teaching experience in a private school from 1965-1967 when her first child was born.

Gerald is 57 years old. He was born in 1936, graduated from high school in 1954 and the University of California in 1959 with a degree in electrical engineering. He worked for two years in California in a small engineering firm. In 1961 Gerald moved to Seattle and started working for the Boeing Company. In 1962 he started graduate course-work in engineering at the University of Washington. After one semester, he transferred to the business department and completed an MBA in 1965. Gerald met Barbara while attending the University of Washington and they were married in 1964.

Gerald and Barbara have three children. Jason, born in 1967, is married, works at Boeing and has one child. James was born in 1968 and is a career officer/aviator in the U. S. Air Force. Jennifer was born in 1976. She is currently a senior in high school and plans to attend the University of California in one year to study electrical engineering. Barbara stayed home to raise the children and take care of the home since Jason was born.

Due to her role as caretaker, Barbara had been out of the work force for a total of 14 years. This was a choice that she and Gerald made. Her duties involved the care of the children and the home. Gerald was to be the primary wage earner for the family. When Barbara was 40 and her daughter started school, Barbara returned to work part-time and worked as a teacher's aide. In 1984, Gerald took an overseas transfer with his employer and the family lived in Brussels for three years. Other than her part-time work during college and her two years of private school teaching, Barbara had no employment work history in the United States. However, in her last year in Brussels, Barbara earned $5,000 teaching English as a foreign language part-time to Belgian business men and women.

While in Brussels, Barbara took some college credits through Boston City College Extension in order to upgrade her teaching certification. When the family returned to the U.S. in 1987, Barbara started working part-time as a teacher's aide while she finished her teaching certification requirements. A year later, Barbara started teaching in a private school. She stayed with that school through the 1992 school year (five years).

In the fall of 1992, Barbara started teaching in the public school system. Her 1994 salary was $28,000 as a full-time teacher. Her supplemental earnings over the years had been used to fund the children's college educations. Her daughter has $20,000 in a trust account saved for her college education.

Gerald is in upper management at Boeing and earned $125,000 in 1993 which included a $9,000 bonus. He has been with the Boeing Company for 33 years. At this time, Gerald plans to work at the Boeing Company until he is age 65. He is in good health and is an active outdoorsman, and he likes his work and the opportunity to travel. He is considering a transfer to an overseas office in the upcoming year.

Barbara has been distraught about the divorce and is seeing a therapist weekly. She has hired a career counselor to help her look at career and vocational options. Barbara has decided to continue in the teaching profession. However, she would like to take additional coursework which would allow her to do more teaching with adults such as her experience coaching businessmen in Brussels on English as a second language. She plans to take some coursework at a language school as well as some business courses with the hope that she will be able to expand her public and private teaching opportunities.

Barbara has enjoyed teaching in the public school system, but she is concerned about maintaining a heavy class-load of high school students as she gets older. She is a newcomer to the school system, and since her level of seniority is the lowest in her department, her classes tend to be with the more challenging students, providing her with less flexibility in what she teaches.

Barbara plans to take additional schooling during the summer and one evening a week for the next year and a half. She is in good health, although she has been treated for depression over the past year.

Gerald's work has required an extensive travel schedule the past ten years, so Barbara has been the primary family caregiver. Jennifer has been having problems with the divorce and does not visit her father regularly. The couple has agreed to start family counseling together for a three-month period to try and change the current situation.

Gerald has always handled the finances and Barbara looks forward with trepidation to getting involved with her future finances as a single person. She now is working with an attorney, a financial planner, career counselor and therapist to help her transition to a single lifestyle. It has taken time, but Barbara has begun to regain her enthusiasm for life and feels she could get excited about her enhanced career plan. She is seeking a fair property settlement from Gerald which recognizes the couple's long-term marriage.

BARBARA HUDSON'S PROFESSIONAL TEAM DURING HER DIVORCE PROCESS:
- Attorney
- Certified Financial Planner
- Career Advisor
- Actuary
- Appraisers

Gerald and Barbara each have their own attorneys. Barbara has been working with her attorney and myself since the beginning of the divorce. Thus far, I have counseled Barbara and her attorney through the financial stages of her divorce as follows:

Phase I — 3 months
1. Create the historical budget for one year prior to separation.
2. Prepare Barbara's budget to establish need for temporary support including child support until Jennifer starts college.
3. Select a career advisor (a minimum of three months is recommended for this career assessment, counseling, and completion of the written report with conclusions and recommendations). Barbara has completed her career plan with the career advisor.

Phase II — 6 months
1. Valuation of marital and separate property assets as of date of separation including the pension.
2. Assist Barbara in finding a replacement home. During this time she has been looking at townhouses and smaller homes and has decided to move into a townhouse.
3. Assist in creating Barbara's post-divorce budget.

With both parties in agreement on the above issues, the next step is to make settlement offers and to respond to those presented by Gerald's attorney. Our work continued through the following stage:

Phase III — 1-3 months
1. Create a written report and property settlement proposal.
2. Determine how Gerald and Barbara will share additional college funding costs beyond the education trust already set up for their daughter.
3. Analyze the economic impact of the divorce property settlement for Gerald and Barbara.

The following is a sample report prepared by my company which would be presented by Barbara and her attorney to Gerald and his attorney. We have attempted to cover the issues here in a way which reflects the long-term nature of their marriage. In the previous chapter, I addressed the Jessup report from a short-term perspective, with projections of five to seven years. Note the differences in the presentation and in the issues we discuss for the Hudsons. This report could have been given directly to Gerald, presented in a mediation setting, submitted in a settlement hearing, presented in court, or a combination of the above.

Throughout the report, I will give you my observations and comments which you will see in *italics*. These would not be in the written report, but have been provided as supplemental information where it seemed appropriate.

DIVORCE SETTLEMENT ANALYSIS

Prepared For:

Barbara and Gerald Hudson

Prepared By:
Kathleen Miller, MBA CFP
Miller, Bird Advisors, Inc.
1200 - 112th Ave NE Suite C178
Bellevue, WA 98004

TABLE OF CONTENTS

SUMMARY OF HUDSON FAMILY:

Husband: **Occupation/Title:** **Education:** **Age:**	Gerald Hudson Managing Engineer, Boeing BS in Electrical Engineering - 1959; Masters Degree in Business Administration - 1965 57
Wife: **Occupation/Title:** **Education:** **Age:**	Barbara Hudson Teacher - Public Schools BA in English - 1965 52
Children:	Jason, age 27 - Boeing (self-supporting) James, age 25 - Air Force (self-supporting) Jennifer, age 18 - H.S. Senior (preparing for University)
Duration of Mar.:	30 years
Husband's Sal.:	$125,000 (Including $9,000 1993 Bonus)
Wife's Salary:	$28,000
Annual Retirement Contributions:	GERALD - 401(k) - $9,240 per year; Company matching of 50% of contributions on the first 6% of salary. BARBARA - Minimum State Teacher's Retirement System contribution of 3%, or $840 per year.
Issues:	• Sale of Family Residence • Vacation Home • Pension Sharing Formula • Reallocation of Assets • Tax and Cash Flow Projections • Maintenance: Duration and amount • Social Security analysis

GERALD AND BARBARA —
CHRONOLOGICAL SUMMARY

1954	Gerald graduates from high school.
1959	Gerald graduates with an Electrical Engineering Degree.
1960	Barbara graduates from high school.
1961	Gerald moves to Seattle and starts working at Boeing. He meets Barbara at the University of Washington where he is taking night courses for his Masters in Business.
1962	Gerald and Barbara marry.
1965	Barbara graduates with an B.A. in English and Gerald completes his MBA. In the Fall, Barbara starts teaching English to high school students in a private school.
1967	Son Jason is born and Barbara resigns from her teaching position to be home raising their first child.
1968	Son James is born.
1976	Daughter Jennifer is born.
1982	Barbara does substitute teaching at her son's school.
1983	Barbara does substitute teaching part time at her daughter's school.
1984	Gerald and Barbara move to Brussels where Gerald takes a three year assignment.
1986	Barbara teaches English as a foreign language to Belgian business men and women part-time.
1987	Barbara works as a substitute teacher.
1988	Barbara teaches 3/4 time at her daughter's school and is currently employed with this school system.
1992	Barbara starts teaching full time.
1993	Gerald and Barbara separate in June. They reconcile in October for three months.
1994	Gerald moves out the first week in January. He files for divorce in February.

CURRENT STATUS OF
HUDSON DISSOLUTION NEGOTIATIONS

At the time this report was prepared, Gerald and Barbara have agreed to the following:

1. The house will to be sold and has been listed for three months. Since Barbara will need substantial cash to purchase a replacement residence, she will receive the first $205,000 and the balance of the sales proceeds will be allocated to Gerald to effectuate an agreed upon property distribution.

2. With the exception of the Boeing pension benefit, all the marital asset values have been agreed upon. The assets are listed on the analysis titled "Reallocation of Assets."

3. The amount and duration of maintenance has to be determined.

4. Gerald and Barbara have agreed to go to mediation. One week prior to the meeting, each of their attorneys will submit a written property settlement proposal to the mediator. The meeting has been scheduled for 6 hours. If an agreement cannot be reached through mediation, the attorneys will prepare for a February 1995 trial date.

Gerald and Barbara Hudson
REALLOCATION OF ASSETS

COMMUNITY ASSETS

Notes	Assets	Valuation Date	Present Position	Encum-brances	Net Equity	Gerald	Barbara
(1)	Boeing Credit Union	09/30/94	$50,300		$50,300	$20,000	$30,300
(2)	Phoenix Growth Fund	09/30/94	6,743		6,743		6,743
(3)	Sogen International Fund	09/30/94	7,826		7,826	7,826	
(4)	IDEX II Growth Fund	09/30/94	3,489		3,489	3,489	
(5)	Franklin Income Fund	09/30/94	14,368		14,368		14,368
(6)	IRA - Gerald - US Bank CD	09/30/94	6,100		6,100	6,100	
(7)	IRA - Barbara - AMCAP Fund	09/30/94	9,487		9,487		9,487
(8)	Residence	06/15/94	475,000	178,500	296,500	44,475	252,025
(9)	Boeing VIP - Gerald	09/30/94	348,620		348,620	157,906	190,714
(10)	Boeing FSP - Gerald	09/30/94	49,855		49,855	49,855	
(11)	Boeing Defined Benefit Pension		X		X	1/2	1/2
(12)	Phoenix Income Fund VII L/P	cost	5,000		5,000	2,500	2,500
(13)	Liberty Low Income Houseing L/P	cost	10,000		10,000	5,000	5,000
(14)	Cronos Leasing Inc Fund X L/P	cost	10,000		10,000	5,000	5,000
(15)	Camano Island Log Cabin	03/28/94	165,000	50,000	115,000	115,000	
(16)	86 Boston Whaler	09/30/94	12,000		12,000	12,000	
(17)	1988 Nissan Pathfinder	09/30/94	8,325		8,325	8,325	
(18)	1992 Chrysler LeBaron	09/30/94	21,000	9,832	11,168		11,168
(19)	Gun Collection	09/30/94	8,500		8,500	8,500	
(20)	Antique Doll Collection	09/30/94	5,000		5,000		5,000
(21)	Personal Property	09/30/94	35,000		35,000	10,000	25,000
	TOTALS:		**$1,251,613**	**$238,332**	**$1,013,281**	**$455,976**	**$557,305**
	Percentage Allocation:				**100.00%**	**45.00%**	**55.00%**

SEPARATE ASSETS

Notes	Assets	Valuation Date	Present Position	Encum-brances	Net Equity	Gerald	Barbara
	1/4 Interest in E. WA Farm		$80,000		$80,000		$80,000
	Seafirst CD		20,000		20,000		20,000
	Washington Mutual Fund		28,000		28,000	28,000	
	Separate Assets		**$128,000**		**$128,000**	**$28,000**	**$100,000**

Note:

Gerald agrees to pay Barbara $3,000 per month in maintenance until his retirement (projected at his age 65).

Gerald and Barbara Hudson
HOUSE SALE INCOME TAX CALCULATION

Gross Sales Price: $475,000
1st Mortgage/Debt Balance: $150,000
2nd Mortgage/Debt Balance: $0
Cost of Sale (%): 6.00% $28,500
House Tax Basis (Below): $220,985
% SaleTaxable to Wife: 45.00%
% SaleTaxable to Husband: 55.00%
% Net Cash Proceeds to Wife: 85.00%
% Net Cash Proceeds to Husband: 15.00%

INCOME TAX ALLOCATION

	Wife	Husband	Total
Cost of Replacement Home	$205,000	$0	$205,000
House Sales Price	$213,750	$261,250	$475,000
Expense of Sale	12,825	15,675	28,500
AMOUNT REALIZED	**200,925**	**245,575**	446,500
House Tax Basis	99,443	121,542	220,985
Gain on Sale	101,482	124,033	225,515
Age 55 Exemption	0	125,000	125,000
Adjusted Gain	101,482	0	101,482
Fixing Up Expenses	0	0	0
Adj Sales Price	200,925	120,575	321,500
Replacement Home	205,000	0	205,000
TAXABLE GAIN	**0**	**0**	0
Deferred Gain	101,482	0	101,482
New House Basis	103,518	0	103,518

TAX ON GAIN (28%)	$0	$0	$0

CASH FLOW ALLOCATION

House Sales Price	$403,750	$71,250	$475,000
Expense of Sale	(24,225)	(4,275)	(28,500)
Tax on Gain (28%)	0	0	0
Existing Mort/Debt Balance	(127,500)	(22,500)	(150,000)
NET SALES PROCEEDS:	**$252,025**	**$44,475**	**$296,500**

HOUSE TAX BASIS:

House tax basis from 1985 FORM 2119	$205,853
Landscaping costs	3,697
Security System	2,167
Misc Improvements	9,268
ADJUSTED TAX BASIS:	$220,985

FOOTNOTES TO "REALLOCATION OF ASSETS"

Unless otherwise stated on the "Valuation Date" column in the analysis, property values are as of 9/30/94.

Item 1: Boeing Credit Union

Since their separation, Gerald and Barbara have each withdrawn $10,000 from this account. They have agreed that they do not have to account for the withdrawn funds and that they will not be included in the allocation of assets. The account value is net of the amounts withdrawn.

Items 2, 3, 4, 5: Mutual Funds

With the help of a financial planner, Gerald has historically selected and managed the mutual fund investments. There have been no distributions or changes in mutual fund investments since separation.

Items 6 and 7: Individual Retirement Accounts

For simplicity in the property allocation, Barbara proposes that they each keep their own Individual Retirement Accounts.

Item 8: Personal Residence (Refer to House Sale Income Tax Calculation)

The primary residence is to be sold. The gross sales price is expected to be $475,000. Under the encumbrances column is listed the combination of the $150,000 mortgage balance and $28,500 estimated sales expenses. These obligations are deducted from the gross sales proceeds of the home. Since the actual sales price of the property is unknown, the ultimate distribution of the sales proceeds will be determined upon the sale of the home. Barbara proposes that when the house is sold, the first $205,000 of the proceeds will go to her, and the balance will be allocated in such a way as to effectuate the agreed upon property settlement percentages.

When an asset is sold incident to divorce, any sales costs and income taxes must be allocated and shared by the parties. In order to minimize the income taxes paid on the sale, it is proposed that the sale be disproportionately reported on the separate taxpayers income tax returns. Barbara is planning to purchase a new residence for approximately $205,000. Gerald is over 55 and is eligible to exclude up to $125,000 of gain on the sale. If the sale is allocated 45% to Barbara and 55% to Gerald, even if Gerald does not purchase a replacement residence, there will be no income taxes owed by either party.

Item 9: 40l (k) or Voluntary Investment Plan (VIP)

Since the date of separation, Gerald has continued to make contributions to the 401(k) plan. These contributions are considered his separate property and the values listed on the "reallocation of assets" is the current value, less the post-separation (February 1, 1994) contributions.

Item 10: Financial Security Plan (FSP)

Since this account value has not changed materially since separation on 2/1/94, both parties have agreed to use the account value as of 9/30/94.

Item 11: Boeing Pension

Due to the length of marriage, a present value calculation has not been prepared on the Boeing pension plan. We recommend that Gerald and Barbara share the pension income at retirement (See Pension Benefit Analysis on page 275).

Items 12, 13 and 14: Limited Partnerships

The Hudson's have invested in three limited partnerships during their marriage. With no active market to establish the actual value of the investments, it is proposed that the ownership be divided between the parties. The partnerships should be notified of the

Hudson's divorce and the ownership re-registered into separate ownership interests.

OBSERVATION: *If the partnership investment is of questionable value,
you may want to consider giving the asset to your spouse. The accounting costs of reporting the partnership activity, generally nominal cash
flow and potential income tax liability on the partnership may be
greater than the economic value of the asset.*

     *If you do split or keep the asset, be sure to obtain copies of the
initial subscription paperwork, prior year income tax returns with complete partnership K-1's and a report of "suspended passive activity
losses" relating to prior unallowed partnership losses. This information
will be needed at some point in the future, and it is surely easier to get
the information incident to divorce rather than several years down
the road.*

     *Often there is a nominal cost for this re-registration and the
actual re-registration can take months. It is best to contact the partnership to see if there are specific forms to make the name change, but
generally you will be required to send a letter of instructions to the general partners with a copy of the section of your divorce decree discussing the division of the partnership. Be sure to start early so you
will be getting the partnership information and tax reports the year the
divorce is final. We recommend that you send your re-registration
request by certified mail.*

Item 15: Camano Island Cabin

     Gerald and Barbara have jointly hired a real estate appraiser
from Camano Island and have agreed on a property value of $165,000.
The current mortgage balance is approximately $50,000. Gerald has
been living at the cabin since their separation and staying in the city in
a hotel an average of 2 nights a month. He intends to make the cabin his
personal residence after some extensive remodeling. This remodeling is
estimated to cost approximately $85,000 and will be financed through
a home equity loan.

Items 16, 17, 18, 19, 20, 21:
Gerald and Barbara have agreed on the values and allocation of these assets.

Item 22: Separate Property
Barbara and Gerald have each received inheritances during their marriage. The inherited funds have been maintained in separate accounts and each party recognized the other's separate ownership of the assets.

OBSERVATION: In a community property state such as Washington, gifts and inheritances are deemed to be the separate property of the person receiving the gift or inheritance; however, in a dissolution, the judge has the discretion to consider separate property in the allocation of assets. Since Gerald and Barbara came to mutual consent to leave the separate assets out of the settlement, only the community assets are being divided.

BOEING PENSION BENEFIT ANALYSIS

In addition to the 401(k) (Voluntary Investment Plan) and the Financial Security Plan, Boeing provides for a monthly pension income at retirement. Since this benefit is not received until death or retirement, a method of valuation or allocation must be agreed upon. The two primary methods of allocating pension income benefits include (1) preparing a present value calculation and (2) allocating the future pension benefit as either a fixed dollar amount or as a percentage of the ultimate benefit.

We feel that the present value method does not fairly address the issues regarding the allocation of pension income. Present value calculations tend to be most beneficial when spouses divorce after retirement so that the benefits are already fixed. Present Value calculations are least valuable when retirement is still several years away, especially since earlier retirement, death, disability and any other number of unforeseen factors can significantly alter the result.

METHODS OF SHARING DEFINED BENEFIT PENSION

Allocation of Future Pension Benefit:

In the allocation future pension benefits, there can be an allocation of either a fixed dollar amount, or an allocation of a percentage of the ultimate pension benefit. Traditionally, a fixed dollar amount was allocated to the non-employee spouse. There has more recently been a trend toward the participatory allocation method. (There are several names for the "participatory" allocation method, but the theories and calculations are very nearly always the same).

Fixed Dollar Amount Allocation:

Under the normal defined benefit pension plan, the final pension benefit is calculated by multiplying the average annual compensation by the average annual final salary which is multiplied by a certain percentage. If the fixed dollar amount method is used in allocating the pension, the non-employee spouse is not fully compensated for the years that the parties were married.

This method assumes that Gerald and Barbara share the retirement income from Gerald's Boeing pension when he retires at age 65 under a Qualified Domestic Relations Order (QDRO). Barbara will be 60 years old when Gerald retires at his age 65. Under this "flat" method calculation they would each receive:

- Barbara's pension . . . . . .$1,670/month starting at her age 60
- Gerald's pension . . . . $4,470/month starting at his age 65

Remember, his total estimated pension from Boeing at his age 65 is $6,140 per month from Boeing's retirement projection and based on Boeing's calculation method.

Participatory Allocation:

Under the participatory allocation method, the formula used in the calculating the allocation of benefit is as follows:

Wife's % of Retirement benefit	X	Community Yrs. of Service / Total Years of Service	X	Final Pension Benefit	=	Wife's part of Husband's Retirement benefit

OBSERVATION: *The community interest in the pension could have been based solely on the years of marriage. Instead, the courts are now beginning to recognize a community interest in the additional pension benefits obtained after the marriage. The formula shares the pension benefit based on the ratio of community years of service (years of the marriage) to the total years of service for the company paying the* *pension. This figure will decline over time, since the employee will continue to work but the community years of service remain unchanged. The wife would be allocated an agreed upon percentage of the final benefit, multiplied by this ratio. The result is that the husband begins accruing separate benefits immediately after the divorce, but there is still a community interest in the pension benefits which is shared.*

The calculation is summarized below and is based on the ratio of the number of years married (from date of marriage to date of separation) to the total number of years of service (from the date employment began to the projected employment date). Please refer to the calculation and to the graphs on the following page in reference to our results and discussion.

Barbara's Projected Pension Benefit

$$50\% \quad \times \quad \frac{30.9}{39.9} \quad \times \quad \$6,140 \quad = \quad \$2,377$$

The balance of the projected benefit, or $3,763 ($6,140 minus $2,377), will be Gerald's portion of the benefits.

Gerald & Barbara Hudson
SUMMARY OF PENSION INCOME

Year	Est Total Pension	FLAT METHOD			PARTICIPATORY METHOD		
		Community Pension	Gerald's Pension	Barbara's Pension	Community Pension	Gerald's Pension	Barbara's Pension
1993	$3,340	$3,340	$1,670	$1,670	$3,340	$1,670	$1,670
1994	3,586	3,340	1,916	1,670	3,473	1,849	1,737
1995	3,846	3,340	2,177	1,670	3,612	2,040	1,806
1996	4,122	3,340	2,452	1,670	3,757	2,244	1,878
1997	4,414	3,340	2,744	1,670	3,907	2,460	1,954
1998	4,722	3,340	3,052	1,670	4,063	2,690	2,032
1999	5,048	3,340	3,378	1,670	4,226	2,935	2,113
2000	5,392	3,340	3,722	1,670	4,395	3,194	2,197
2001	5,756	3,340	4,086	1,670	4,571	3,470	2,285
2002	6,140	3,340	4,470	1,670	4,753	3,763	2,377

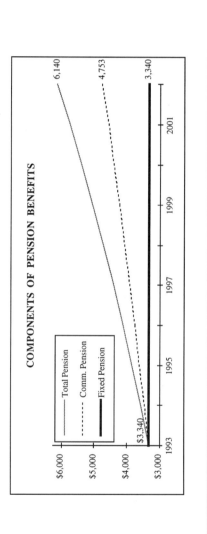

COMPONENTS OF PENSION BENEFITS

Legend:
— Total Pension
---- Comm. Pension
▬ Fixed Pension

SUMMARY OF PENSION ALLOCATION METHODS

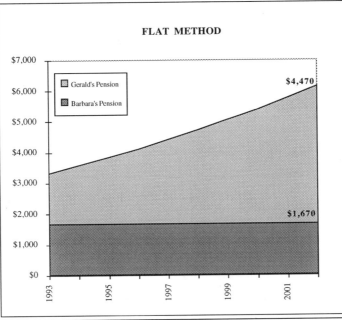

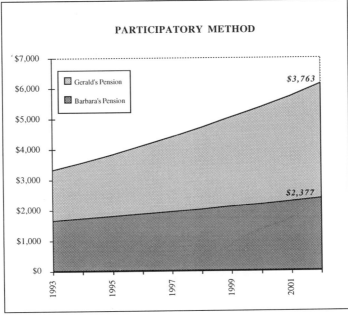

Summary of our recommendation

We believe the fair and equitable method to divide this pension is the participatory allocation method. This is because it not only recognizes Barbara's community interest in Gerald's 33 years at Boeing, but it allows her to share in the continued growth of the pension benefit to retirement based on her community interest at the date of separation. Defined benefit formulas all recognize the last few year's of the employee's earnings when calculating this retirement benefit. Barbara helped Gerald and was a partner with him in the 33 years prior to divorce and was in the marriage in the lower earning years. It is fair that she should participate in the "fruit of these labors" in his final higher earning years at Boeing.

Since we are not recommending a current present value, no dollar amount is shown on the Reallocation of Assets. There will be an allocation of the retirement income benefit that will be used in our long term cash flow analysis in the next section of the report.

A comparison of the two methods helps to clarify the significant differences in the pension to be received by each party:

	Fixed Dollar Allocation		*Participatory Allocation*	
	Monthly Inc.	Annual Inc.	Monthly Inc.	Annual Inc.
Barbara	$1,670	$20,040	*$2,377*	$28,524
Gerald	$4,470	$53,640	*$3,763*	$45,156

LONG TERM CASH FLOW ANALYSIS

INTRODUCTION

OBSERVATION: *One of the elements we have found grossly missing from the work of most attorneys is to project the future financial positions of each party after the dissolution. In a mid-term marriage, looking out five to seven years may be sufficient. In a long term marriage, it is our opinion that the future should be projected out much farther.*

As is typical in many long term marriages, and in the case of Gerald and Barbara, Gerald has a substantially greater earnings capacity than does Barbara. This is referred to as "disparity of earnings." When there is a large disparity of earnings in a long term marriage, an unequal division of assets is often awarded in addition to maintenance payments. This is because the person with the larger earnings capacity is able to replace assets in the future with the larger amount of earnings. For the Hudson's, we propose that Gerald should receive 45% of the community assets and that Barbara should receive 55% of the community assets.

Categorization of Assets Assumptions:

In this section of the report, we have attempted to illustrate the future financial position of each of the divorcing parties. To prepare a long-term cash flow analysis, it is necessary to categorize the assets into different categories. Below we have summarized these categories.

1. *Residence:* The residence is an asset, but the equity is not available to supplement living expenses.

2. *Retirement Assets:* These assets are designed for retirement, and would be fully taxable if withdrawn. Assets listed here would include 401(k), profit sharing, pension, annuities and any other tax deferred investments.

3.   *Investment Assets:* These assets would include bank accounts, mutual funds, stocks, bonds and essentially any asset not designated as one of the other asset classifications. These assets can be designated as income or growth assets.

4.   *Personal Assets:* These assets are those which produce no income. Included in this category would be personal automobiles and checking account balances.

Cash Flow Analysis:

In the retirement analysis, we have listed the assets by category. The personal residence is listed first. The residence is assumed to appreciate in value over time, but this increase in value is not readily available as a means of funding the living expenses of either person. Therefore, only after other assets have been depleted would the residence be sold to provide for living expenses.

Retirement assets are assumed to grow at the stated rate of return with additional retirement contributions added to the account value. Until the earlier of age $70^{1}/_{2}$ or the need for additional income for living expenses, the retirement assets are assumed to remain in this category. Retirement assets are used for living expenses only after all personal investment assets are depleted.

Income and growth on personal investment assets are assumed to be available for living expenses each year, and are assumed to be subject to income taxes each year. These are the first assets to be used to supplement other sources of income should the need arise. Where total income needs exceed income sources, the shortage is taken from the personal investment assets. If income sources exceed living expenses, the excess is added to the following years beginning personal investment asset balance.

Living expenses are generally composed of fixed and variable expenses. Mortgage payments are fixed in nature and will not increase with inflation. Other living expenses will increase with inflation. In the analysis, we have kept the mortgage payments constant until paid, and increased the other living expenses by the stated rate of inflation.

The income less expenses column is the difference between the total income and the gross living expenses. If this number is negative, the difference must be taken from assets. If the number is positive, the excess is added to the investment assets.

INCOME SOURCES

In allocating retirement funds, there are several factors to consider. First, after a dissolution, the accumulation of retirement funds may be inconsequential because of lower wages earned by one spouse. Retirement funds received by this individual in the dissolution may be the major retirement funds used to provide for retirement. On the other hand, when ultimately paid out, money received from a retirement account will generally be fully taxable to the recipient. If you are able to receive assets that do not have a pending income tax liability, and they are then invested and managed for future retirement, you may have a better settlement.

After meeting with a career counselor, it was determined that Barbara would need to have additional schooling to pursue her interest in teaching English as a second language. She intends to complete this schooling over the next two summers and through evening classes at a language school. After completing the necessary education, Barbara would eventually like to work in a language school and lessen her teaching commitments with the public school system. Part of Barbara's maintenance is deemed to be "compensatory."

While there may be an "equitable" distribution of the assets at the time of the dissolution, particularly in the case of a large disparity of earnings dissolution, the higher income spouse is able to set aside considerably more money for the future than the lower income spouse. This will make for a considerably more comfortable retirement for the higher earning spouse. Many ex-spouses will continue to accrue larger and larger pension benefits, as discussed in the pension section above. Social Security: Social Security is yet another area for debate. Based on the best available information, Gerald's accrued monthly Social Security benefit at age 65 will be approximately $1,251, while Barbara will be entitled to only $535 per month based on contributions to date (See the Personal Earnings and Benefits Statement below). You can see that the disparity of earnings issue does not lessen over time for women. Over the years the economic inequity only gets greater.

OBSERVATION: Part of the "Social Security - Personal Earnings and Benefits Statement" received for Barbara is presented below. We did not receive a copy of this summary for Gerald; however, his company benefits statements provided us with the estimated age 60, 62 and 65 Social Security Benefits used in our analysis. The column on the left represents the years since the social security program has been in existence up to our current year. The second column represents the maximum earnings taxed for social security and column three represents your tax earnings, or the total earnings you have had during each year. Your work history is laid out in black and white for all to see, as is your husband's. I always recommend that you order this form at the very beginning of your divorce proceedings as it can be a very effective tool in your negotiations for longer term maintenance. At the end of the earnings report, an estimate of your individual level of anticipated social security income at retirement is provided.

In addition, as wife who has stayed home to raise the children, Barbara does not have a significant earnings history with the Social Security Administration. She will be entitled to the greater of her accrued Social Security benefits, or one half of the former spouse's. While one half of the former spouse's benefit may provide the greatest income, it is still one half of the former spouse's benefit. Where we are involved in the dissolution process, we attempt to ensure that all parties are aware of the long term effects of the marriage, thereby more closely approximating a "fair share" dissolution.

EXCERPTS FROM BARBARA HUDSON'S SOCIAL SECURITY - PERSONAL EARNINGS AND BENEFITS STATEMENT

FACTS, CREDITS, AND EARNINGS

September 9, 1993

THE FACTS YOU GAVE US

Your Name	Barbara J. Hudson
Your Social Security Number	575-87-9421
Your Date of Birth	October 21, 1942
1992 Earnings	$20,622
1993 Earnings	$21,000
Your Estimated Future Average Yearly Earnings	$15,000
The Age You Plan To Retire	62
Other Social Security Numbers You've Used . .	None

We used the facts you gave us and the information in our records under your Social Security number to prepare this statement for you.

Retirement

You must have 40 Social Security credits to qualify for retirement benefits and also for Medicare at age 65. Assuming that you meet all the requirements, here are estimates of your retirement benefits based your past and any projected earnings. The estimates are in today's dollars.

If you retire at 62, your reduced monthly amount in today's dollars will be about . . . . $ 370

The earliest age at which you can get an unreduced benefit is 65 and 10 months. We call this your full retirement age. If you wait until that age to get benefits, your monthly amount in today's dollars . . . . $ 535

If you wait until you are 70 to get benefits, your monthly amount in today's dollars will be about . . . . $ 760

YOUR EARNINGS RECORD

| | SOCIAL SECURITY | | | MEDICARE | |
YEARS	Maximum Taxable Earnings	Your Taxed Earnings1	Estimated Taxes You Paid	Your Taxed Earnings2	Estimated Taxes You Paid
1937-50	$ 3,000	$ 0	$ 0		
1951	3,600	0	0		
1952	3,600	0	0		
1953	3,600	0	0		
1954	3,600	0	0		
1955	4,200	0	0		
1956	4,200	0	0		
1957	4,200	0	0		
1958	4,200	0	0		
1959	4,800	512	12		
1960	4,800	465	13		
1961	4,800	527	15		
1962	4,800	684	21		
1963	4,800	323	11		
1964	4,800	164	5		
1965	4,800	4,030	146		
1966	6,600	5,532	212	$ 5,532	$ 19
1967	6,600	1,370	53	1,370	6
1968	7,800	0	0	0	0
1969	7,800	0	0	0	0
1970	7,800	0	0	0	0
1971	7,800	0	0	0	0
1972	9,000	0	0	0	0
1973	10,800	0	0	0	0
1974	13,200	0	0	0	0
1975	14,100	0	0	0	0
1976	15,300	0	0	0	0
1977	16,500	0	0	0	0
1978	17,700	0	0	0	0
1979	22,900	0	0	0	0
1980	25,900	0	0	0	0
1981	29,700	0	0	0	0
1982	32,400	2,830	152	2,830	36
1983	35,700	2,320	125	2,320	30
1984	37,800	0	0	0	0
1985	39,600	0	0	0	0
1986	42,000	0	0	0	0
1987	43,800	6,090	347	6,090	88
1988	45,000	14,306	866	14,306	207
1989	48,000	16,989	1,029	16,989	246
1990	51,300	15,450	957	15,450	224
1991	53,400	18,706	1,159	18,708	271
1992	55,500	20,622	1,278	20,622	299
1993	57,600	Not Yet Recorded			

1 We did not estimate taxes on any railroad earnings before 1973 (See Page 6).
2 Earnings were taxes for Medicare beginning in 1966. From 1983 on, these earnings include Medicare-Qualified Government Earnings (See Page 7). In 1991, the maximum yearly earnings taxed for Medicare were $125,000. For 1992, the amount was $130,200. For 1993, the amount is $135,000.

OBSERVATION: *You do not automatically receive social security benefits but need to qualify for these benefits based on your "work credits" or those of your spouse acquired during your working years. Every three years request this earnings record to ensure that your W-2 information has been accurately reflected in your social security benefit calculation.*

College Funding:

Although the Hudson's have planned ahead for their daughter's education expenses, there are not sufficient funds available to provide for four years of college expenses. The $20,000 that is currently set aside for the daughter will be used to pay for the first two years of college. The remaining two years of college will be shared by Gerald and Barbara in proportion to their earned income.

Barbara Hudson

LONG TERM CASH FLOW ANALYSIS

Real Estate Growth Rate:	4.0%
Retirement Asset Growth Rate:	7.0%
Personal Investment Growth Rate:	6.0%
Social Security Growth Rate:	3.0%
Inflation Rate:	4.0%

Monthly Household Exps (excluding Mortgage and Inc Taxes):	$4,000
Monthly Mortgage Pmts:	$734
Monthly Combined Household and Mortgage Exps:	$4,734
Annual Combined Household and Mortgage Exps:	$56,805

Beginning of Year — Year	Age	Real Estate Equity	Retirement Assets	Personal Investment Assets	Tot. Return Personal Investments +	Social Security +	Maintenance Income +	Boeing Pension +	Teacher Pension +	Wages +	Total Return/ Income =	IRA Payout +	Living Expenses Incl. Taxes -	Income Less Exps =	TOTAL ASSETS
1995	52	$105,763	$200,201	$201,104	$ 12,066	$ -	$ 36,000	$ -	$ (840)	$ 28,000	$ 75,226	$ -	$ 73,904	$ 1,322	$507,068
1996	53	114,862	214,215	202,426	12,146	-	36,000	-	(874)	29,120	76,392	-	76,242	150	531,503
1997	54	124,363	229,210	202,575	12,155	-	36,000	-	(909)	30,285	77,531	-	78,652	(1,121)	556,149
1998	55	134,286	245,255	201,454	12,087	-	36,000	-	(945)	31,496	78,639	-	81,136	(2,497)	580,995
1999	56	144,652	262,423	198,957	11,937	-	36,000	-	(983)	32,756	79,711	-	83,695	(3,984)	606,031
2000	57	155,481	280,792	194,973	11,698	-	36,000	-	(1,022)	34,066	80,743	-	86,332	(5,590)	631,246
2001	58	166,796	300,448	189,383	11,363	-	36,000	-	(1,063)	35,429	81,729	-	89,049	(7,320)	656,627
2002	59	178,622	321,479	182,063	10,924	-	36,000	-	(1,105)	36,846	82,664	-	91,848	(9,184)	682,164
2003	60	190,983	343,983	172,879	10,373	-	-	28,524	3,600	38,320	80,817	-	93,887	(13,070)	707,845
2004	61	203,906	368,061	159,809	9,589	-	-	28,524	3,600	39,853	81,565	-	96,836	(15,271)	731,776
2005	62	217,419	393,826	144,537	8,672	14,900	-	28,524	3,600	-	55,696	-	86,761	(31,065)	755,782
2006	63	231,552	421,393	113,473	6,808	15,347	-	28,524	3,600	-	54,279	-	89,121	(34,841)	766,418
2007	64	246,336	450,891	78,631	4,718	15,808	-	28,524	3,600	-	52,649	-	91,533	(38,884)	775,858
2008	65	261,804	482,453	39,747	2,385	16,282	-	28,524	3,600	-	50,791	4,808	95,346	(39,747)	784,005
2009	66	277,992	511,081	0	0	16,770	-	28,524	3,600	-	48,894	66,227	116,270	(1,149)	789,073

Barbara Hudson
LIVING EXPENSE SUMMARY

Beginning of Year	Age	Variable Living Expenses	Fixed Housing Expenses	Other Payments	FICA	Est Income Tax	Premature Distribution Penalty	Total Living Expenses
1995	52	$ 48,000	$ 8,805	$ -	$ 2,142	$ 14,957	$ -	$ 73,904
1996	53	49,920	8,805	-	2,228	15,290	-	76,242
1997	54	51,917	8,805	-	2,317	15,613	-	78,652
1998	55	53,993	8,805	-	2,409	15,928	-	81,136
1999	56	56,153	8,805	-	2,506	16,231	-	83,695
2000	57	58,399	8,805	-	2,606	16,522	-	86,332
2001	58	60,735	8,805	-	2,710	16,798	-	89,049
2002	59	63,165	8,805	-	2,819	17,060	-	91,848
2003	60	65,691	8,805	-	2,931	16,459	-	93,887
2004	61	68,319	8,805	-	3,049	16,663	-	96,836
2005	62	71,052	8,805	-	-	6,904	-	86,761
2006	63	73,894	8,805	-	-	6,422	-	89,121
2007	64	76,850	8,805	-	-	5,879	-	91,533
2008	65	79,924	8,805	-	-	6,617	-	95,346
2009	66	83,120	8,805	-	-	24,345	-	116,270

Gerald Hudson
LONG TERM CASH FLOW ANALYSIS

Real Estate Growth Rate:	4.0%
Retirement Asset Growth Rate:	7.0%
Personal Investment Growth Rate:	6.0%
Social Security Growth Rate:	3.0%
Inflation Rate:	4.0%

Monthly Household Exps (excluding Mortgage and Inc Taxes):	$4,000
Monthly Mortgage Pmts:	$991
Monthly Combined Household and Mortgage Exps:	$4,991
Annual Combined Household and Mortgage Exps:	$59,887

Beginning of Year	Age	Real Estate Equity	Retirement Assets	Personal Investment Assets	Tot. Return Personal Investments +	Social Security +	Maintenance Payments -	Boeing Pension +	Boeing VIP +	Wages +	Total Return/ Income =	IRA Payout +	Living Expenses Incl. Taxes -	Income Less Exps =	TOTAL ASSETS
1995	57	$116,030	$213,861	$ 88,290	$ 5,297	$ -	$ (36,000)	$ -	$ (9,240)	$125,000	$ 85,057	$ -	$ 82,074	$ 2,984	$ 418,181
1996	58	127,244	241,821	91,274	5,476	-	(36,000)	-	(9,240)	130,000	90,236	-	85,573	4,664	460,339
1997	59	138,958	271,889	95,938	5,756	-	(36,000)	-	(9,240)	135,200	95,716	-	89,242	6,474	506,784
1998	60	151,197	304,217	102,412	6,145	-	(36,000)	-	(9,240)	140,608	101,513	-	93,090	8,423	557,826
1999	61	163,986	338,970	110,835	6,650	-	(36,000)	-	(9,240)	146,232	107,642	-	97,125	10,518	613,792
2000	62	177,354	376,325	121,353	7,281	-	(36,000)	-	(9,240)	152,082	114,123	-	101,355	12,768	675,032
2001	63	191,328	416,471	134,121	8,047	-	(36,000)	-	(9,240)	158,165	120,972	-	105,791	15,181	741,919
2002	64	205,939	459,608	149,302	8,958	-	(36,000)	-	(9,240)	164,491	128,210	-	110,441	17,768	814,849
2003	65	221,218	505,956	167,070	10,024	17,556	-	45,156	-	-	72,736	-	88,062	(15,326)	894,244
2004	66	237,200	541,373	151,744	9,105	18,083	-	45,156	-	-	72,343	-	90,488	(18,145)	930,317
2005	67	253,920	579,269	133,600	8,016	18,625	-	45,156	-	-	71,797	-	92,976	(21,179)	966,788
2006	68	271,415	619,818	112,421	6,745	19,184	-	45,156	-	-	71,085	-	95,526	(24,441)	1,003,653
2007	69	289,726	663,205	87,980	5,279	19,759	-	45,156	-	-	70,194	-	98,139	(27,945)	1,040,911
2008	70	308,895	709,629	60,035	3,602	20,352	-	45,156	-	-	69,110	-	100,817	(31,706)	1,078,559
2009	71	328,966	759,303	28,329	1,700	20,963	-	45,156	-	-	67,819	12,297	108,548	(28,433)	1,116,599

Gerald Hudson
LIVING EXPENSE SUMMARY

Beginning of Year	Age	Variable Living Expenses	Fixed Housing Expenses	Other Payments	FICA	Est Income Tax	Premature Distribution Penalty	Total Living Expenses
1995	57	$ 48,000	$ 11,887	$ -	$ 5,179	$ 17,007	$ -	$ 82,074
1996	58	49,920	11,887	-	5,179	18,586	-	85,573
1997	59	51,917	11,887	-	5,179	20,259	-	89,242
1998	60	53,993	11,887	-	5,179	22,030	-	93,090
1999	61	56,153	11,887	-	5,179	23,905	-	97,125
2000	62	58,399	11,887	-	5,179	25,890	-	101,355
2001	63	60,735	11,887	-	5,179	27,989	-	105,791
2002	64	63,165	11,887	-	5,179	30,210	-	110,441
2003	65	65,691	11,887	-	-	10,484	-	88,062
2004	66	68,319	11,887	-	-	10,282	-	90,488
2005	67	71,052	11,887	-	-	10,037	-	92,976
2006	68	73,894	11,887	-	-	9,745	-	95,526
2007	69	76,850	11,887	-	-	9,403	-	98,139
2008	70	79,924	11,887	-	-	9,006	-	100,817
2009	71	83,120	11,887	-	-	13,541	-	108,548

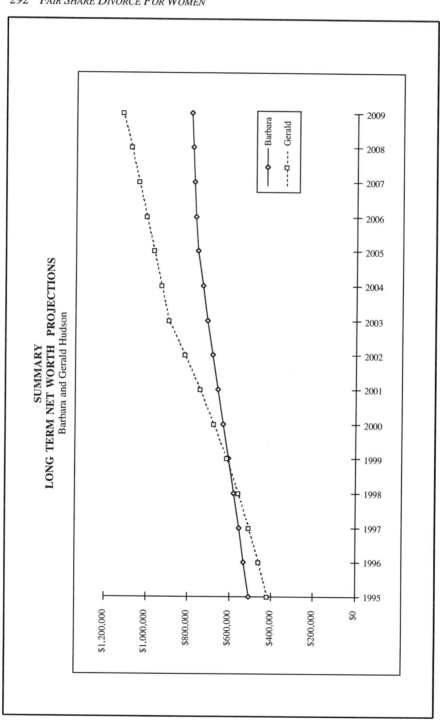

SUMMARY
LONG TERM NET WORTH PROJECTIONS
Barbara and Gerald Hudson

OBSERVATION: *The model works using several aspects of long term cash flow and income tax planning. It incorporates current tax law based on the assumptions used in our proposal and performs a pro forma (projected) calculation of the tax implications of our proposed settlement. For instance, the model will calculate not only the payment for our proposed post divorce mortgage amounts, but it will calculate the income tax deduction for home mortgage interest and incorporate the amount into the tax and cash flow projections. It also determines the point at which various assets must be utilized in maintaining the household and the applicable penalties for early distributions of IRA funds when this becomes necessary. As mentioned earlier in the report, the investment assets are depleted first and the personal residence is the last to be depleted.*

The model also uses various assumed rates for expected increases in variable living expenses, wages, real estate assets, investment assets and Social Security income. This allows us to control a rather significant number of variables in presenting our report, as well as simplifying the revision process when one or several of the assumptions are disputed. We can change each assumption and see the overall effects on each person both graphically and numerically.

Note, however, that these are projections and reality will vary depending on the economy, job markets, investment markets, inflation, etc. The individual also has a lot to do with the similarity of our projections to their actual financial picture, since they control the ultimate disposition of the assets.

CONCLUSIONS ON LONG TERM CASH FLOW ANALYSIS

Refer to the graph entitled "Long Term Net Worth Projections." Our goal was to achieve an equitable long term financial outlook for both Gerald and Barbara. Our proposal suggests a disproportionate allocation of the marital assets, leaving Barbara better off than Gerald. This may be true in the short term, but based on our analysis and Gerald's potential income, they end up approximately equal in the sixth year after their divorce, after which Gerald begins to build his net worth steadily through his retirement years. Note that both parties have an increasing net worth, even after fifteen years.

The culmination of our analysis work is that both Gerald and Barbara are able to meet their financial needs with the allocation of assets and future income presented in this report. Gerald will eventually exceed Barbara in total net worth. However, the purpose is not to achieve an exact parity, but to allow for Gerald and Barbara to maximize their post-divorce net worth and lifestyle without leaving either party financially indigent. We believe that our proposal meets this criterion.

NEED FOR LIFE INSURANCE

Gerald has agreed to maintain Barbara as 50% beneficiary on his group term life insurance coverage at Boeing until his retirement. The children are beneficiaries for the other half. He currently has $250,000 in death benefit coverage through his employment.

EXPERT WITNESS QUALIFICATIONS
OF KATHLEEN A. MILLER, CFP

ACADEMIC AND PROFESSIONAL QUALIFICATIONS

Masters in Business, City University, Seattle, WA, 1980.

Bachelor of Arts, University of Iowa, 1968, English & Creative Writing.

Memberships: Institute of Certified Financial Planners, International Association of Financial Planning, admitted to the Registry of Financial Planning Practitioners, current President of the Eastside Estate Planning Council, IBCFP, Board Member for the Women's Center at Bellevue Community College.

Expert Witness: King, Snohomish, Thurston, Whatcom, and Kitsap Counties.

Publications: *Fair Share Divorce for Women*, a book written for men and women going through the dissolution process (available in print January, 1995), Washington Family Law Deskbook and Supplements, the Journal for Financial Planning, the Washington Trial News, Bar News Bulletin, Washington Law Journal, Puget Sound Business Journal, Women's Business Owner's Newsletter, and her own newsletters — *The Miller, Bird Advisory*, a quarterly financial newsletter, and the *Market Recap*. Kathleen provided extensive sample case work illustrating the importance of financial modeling in the dissolution process for the Superior Court Judges in King County and presented in the Report of the Subcommittee on the Economic Consequences of Divorce.

Speaking: Washington Bar Association, National Association of Personal Financial Advisors, Institute of Certified Financial Planners, Bellevue Community College, Edmonds Community College, Highline and Shoreline Community Colleges, and Lake Washington Voc./Tech. She is also a frequent lecturer and guest speaker at professional seminars, corporations and civic organizations in the Northwest.

CURRENT PROFESSIONAL SERVICE

Kathleen Miller is the President of **Miller, Bird Advisors, Inc., (MBA)** in Bellevue. MBA, Inc. is a registered Investment Advisory firm with the Securities and Exchange Commission and with the Securities Division of the State of Washington. The firm offers comprehensive financial planning services which include income tax planning, pre- and post-divorce property settlement analysis, rebuttal expert witness analysis and reports, cash control management, portfolio analysis, and income tax preparation.

Miller, Bird and Associates, Inc. offers insurance and other financial services. Our securities investments are brokered through Investment Management & Research, Inc. (IM&R), a member of the National Association of Securities Dealers (NASD) and Securities Investor Protection Corporation (SIPC). All trading transactions initiated by IM&R are cleared through Raymond James & Associates, Inc., a member of the New York Stock Exchange and parent firm affiliate of IM&R. Kathleen Miller serves as a manager of her IM&R branch office.

Both companies work congruently with their affiliates to provide clients with full-service financial analysis, planning and management.

DISSOLUTION PLANNING SERVICES

During the dissolution process, Kathleen assists attorneys and their clients in these primary areas:

- Preparation of financial affidavit: historical family budget, temporary and post divorce budgets
- Financial modeling of property settlement proposals
- Income tax and cash flow analysis
- Allocation of pension and retirement benefits
- Historical wage analysis
- House sale tax & cash flow analysis, refinance, qualifying for a mortgage

Once the divorcing client's divorce is final, Kathleen provides transitional planning for the client including the following important financial and tax planning services:

- Income tax analysis
- Cash flow strategies and cash control management system
- Retirement analysis
- Implement QDRO transfers
- Reallocation of assets
- Investment implementation, monitoring and reporting
- Coordinate preparation of estate documents

GENERAL INFORMATION

Expert witness testimony provided in the past includes, but is not limited to, analysis of historical family budget, documenting the need for temporary maintenance, and the duration and amount of long term maintenance, comparison of future lifestyles, creation of decision making models comparing the income tax, cash flow and net worth with varying property settlement proposals, assistance in tracking transactions, selecting which assets are most appropriate for the client to keep from the marital assets, documentation of separate property interests, analyzing an investment portfolio, and creation of graphs and models to assist attorneys in their document presentation for mediation or litigation. A written report is provided to the client and attorney to be used in settlement conference, mediation and court testimony.

Kathleen Miller is oftentimes hired to provide a rebuttal to reports of other financial experts. Ms. Miller has been trained in mediation techniques and has worked as a co-mediator in dissolution cases.

PRIOR EXPERIENCE

Prior to forming Miller, Bird Advisors, Inc., Ms. Miller was a Senior Financial Advisor with Sheppard and Associates, a division of U.S. Bancorp. For the past fifteen years Ms. Miller has specialized in helping clients solve a diverse set of financial problems through the creation of integrated tax, retirement, and cash flow strategies. Ms. Miller has owned her own business for all but two of the past sixteen years.

REFERENCES

References provided upon request.

CHAPTER FOURTEEN

WHAT TO DO WITH MY SETTLEMENT MONEY — WOMEN AND INVESTING

Go confidently in the direction of your dreams!
Live the life you've imagined.
As you simplify your life, the laws of the universe will be simpler.
— Henry David Thoreau

WOMEN AS INVESTORS?

Did you know —

- Women make up 51 percent of the adult population?
- Women make up 40 percent of Americans with more than $500,000 in assets?
- Women earned more than $931 billion in 1990 alone, nearly 36 percent of the national income?
- The number of families headed by a female jumped 25 percent from 8.7 million in 1980 to 10.9 million in 1989 including widows, divorcees and single-parent professionals?
- Women can expect to live six years longer on average than men?
- Fifty percent of all working women do not have pensions?

Yet —

- Women's basic knowledge and investing experience remains low.
- Women have less time to devote to their personal finances.
- Women are generally more conservative investors and may place emphasis on maximum peace of mind, sacrificing total return.

Research by Oppenheimer Funds indicates that 90 percent of women and 85 percent of men no longer believe that investing is exclusively a man's job. Nearly 90 percent of women are confident they could invest $10,000 wisely and their male partners agree. We have known for years that financial decisions are discussed between partners in marriage more often than not.

Oppenheimer's survey also reveals that women recognize their lack of investment knowledge and are willing to ask for assistance. This is important because demographic trends indicate that 80 percent to 90 percent of all women will be responsible for their own finances at some point in their lives. Unfortunately for them, too many women still only face up to financial reality in the wake of a crisis in their lives.

Women do represent a major marketing segment to the financial services industry, however, most are still not prepared to take charge of their financial lives. Their cultural role models are one barrier. A second is that most women have not had financial independence until relatively recently. There is, however, strong evidence that these barriers are coming down.

The primary group servicing women today are the banks. They offer a setting in which women feel comfortable. Equally important, they have been introducing women to investment products, primarily mutual funds, in recent years, bridging the gap between bank services and investments. An estimated 90 percent of baby boomer women have savings accounts in banks and own money market accounts or CDs.

There are more than 100 million female potential investors out there and their earnings have quadrupled in the past 15 years to approximately $1 trillion annually.

This chapter is about that money in motion from a divorce and it is designed to help women make sound financial decisions with their divorce settlements.

MYTHS ABOUT MONEY

For most of us, money is never just money. It can represent love, power, happiness, security and self esteem. As a result we have intense feelings about money, feelings we often hide from, which prevent us from dealing with it productively. Divorce is about money.

Just as our feelings about money can vary, so too, can our behaviors. There are those people who hoard money while others spend it freely. Some are responsible about attending to daily financial management tasks, while others avoid these tasks and responsibilities as much as possible. Some people don't invest their money at all, others very conservatively, and still others take great financial risks.

In my initial data gathering sessions with my women clients I always try and assess their feelings about money and then how they would describe their strengths and weaknesses about dealing with money. I ask these women to do the same for their spouses. They create a list of these strengths and weaknesses on a piece of paper. I ask that they refer to this list periodically throughout their divorce process to help them understand the emotions they are feeling about their financial life. The thorough evaluation of the family spending habits presented in an earlier chapter provides a strong incentive for women to look deeply at their strengths and weaknesses and to deal honestly with what they see. Divorce does mean compromise and change and this is seen most dramatically where money is concerned.

Some typical responses to what I have just observed about women and money are:

- I never worry about money.
- I balance my checkbook regularly and have my budget on the computer and monitor it monthly and annually.
- I give to charity generously.
- I have over three months of my expenses in a savings account for emergencies.
- I like balancing my checkbook to the penny.

OR

- On occasion, I will go on a shopping binge for myself, for my children, or for my spouse or friends.
- I get a lot of overdraft notices and late charges as I have a hard time paying bills on time.
- I feel I am always in debt and must lie about how I am spending my money.
- I have a hard time spending money on myself and anyone else.

Ask yourself how you have dealt with money as a couple. What has been your role and that of your husband? What attitudes do your children have about money? How are you similar or dissimilar to the example your parents displayed about money? How would your husband rate you and your money habits (a hoarder, spendthrift, careless, disciplined)?

Olivia Mellan has written an excellent book entitled *Money Harmony: Resolving Money Conflicts in Your Life and Relationships*. The book was published in 1994 by Walker and Company and I will share some of her thoughts with you.

In her book she gives you a money personality quiz which goes way beyond the questions and exercises that I use in my planning sessions and I recommend that each of my clients take this personality quiz and share their results with me. She talks about common money myths that include:

- Money equals happiness.
- Money equals love.
- Money equals power.
- Money equals freedom.
- Money equals self-worth.
- Money equals security.

She believes, as I do, that first we need to identify those money myths which have been important in our life and our marriage and see how they are affecting us personally. Next, we must spend some time debunking the money myths one by one. Only then will we be free to use money and make decisions about our money in a way that enhances our life rather than constrains it.

Here are some practical tips to get started:
- Believe in yourself.
- Do your homework.
- Ask a lot of questions — and get the answers.
- Be enthusiastic, outgoing and visible in your research process.
- Learn the investment and financial jargon.
- Plan and prioritize your short- and long-term goals.
- Learn how to say "no."
- Conquer your feelings of inadequacy about money decisions.
- Develop a strong relationship with your financial planner.

WHY SHOULD YOU INVEST IN YOUR COMPANY'S RETIREMENT PLAN?

Investing is essentially the process of making your money grow. By participating in your employer's plan, you must make investment decisions. You have probably shared with your spouse up to this point in creating a retirement account. Now you will need to continue with an investment plan with the funds you have received under the QDRO and continue investing towards your retirement.

If you have been counting on monthly Social Security checks as the basis for your retirement income, you'll probably discover that they won't be enough. You'll need somewhere between 65 percent and 85 percent of your final annual salary to maintain your current lifestyle each year after retirement. According to the Employee Benefits Research Institute, Social Security and traditional pension plans are likely to provide only half of that amount.

The following page shows a simple example of someone who earns $30,000 per year, then she retires and receives $12,000 in Social Security. As you can see, retirement planning fills an important need.

You will probably be the decision-maker on determining how your money is invested. Here are three basic concepts about basic investing to get you started.
- What stocks and bonds are.
- How they have done over long periods of time.
- Investment risks, and how to reduce them.

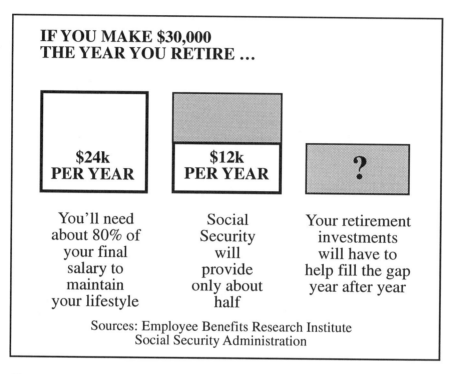

**IF YOU MAKE $30,000
THE YEAR YOU RETIRE ...**

$24k PER YEAR	**$12k PER YEAR**	**?**
You'll need about 80% of your final salary to maintain your lifestyle	Social Security will provide only about half	Your retirement investments will have to help fill the gap year after year

Sources: Employee Benefits Research Institute
Social Security Administration

BONDS AND STOCKS — TO "LOAN" OR TO "OWN?"

When you invest, you are essentially either a loaner or an owner. When you buy a bond, you are making a loan. Buy a stock and you become an owner.

Bonds:

Typically, being a loaner is a more conservative approach than being an owner. When you buy a bond, you are loaning money to the government or a corporation. A bond is basically an IOU for the money loaned. The issuer of the bond promises to return the original amount loaned (referred to as principal or capital) plus, in most cases, pay you interest. Investors who are interested in current income and preservation of capital or principal are often attracted to bonds.

Bond returns are subject to three main types of risk: *interest rate risk, credit risk and inflation risk.*

Interest rate risk occurs when interest rates fluctuate. When interest rates move higher, the prices of bonds generally move lower. And when interest rates decline, bond prices usually rise. Generally, the shorter the maturity of the bond, the less the price will fluctuate due to interest rate changes.

The *credit risk* of bonds reflects the ability of the issuer to repay the face amount of the bond as promised. Generally, the higher the quality of the issuer, the greater the likelihood that the issuer will be able to repay the face amount of the bond. The underlying risk is that if the business fails, bondholders can lose part or all of their investment. Bonds from lower quality issuers will generally pay a higher rate of interest since bondholders must be compensated for assuming additional risk.

Inflation risk is also a factor in holding bonds since the investor is locked at a fixed rate of return over the life of the bond which may be lower than the inflation rate. In this situation, the income from the bond loses purchasing power. The principal is subject to the same risk if the bond's total return does not exceed the rate of inflation.

Two other types of risk which affect all investment categories include: *Market risk* — the fluctuation up or down of the value of your investment (this is the most obvious risk of holding stock investments), and *Fundamental risk* — the effect of economic and political events on the financial markets.

Stocks:

When you buy a stock, you become a part owner in the company which has issued the stock. Stocks can pay investors in two ways. First, companies that issue stock can distribute income by paying dividends. Second, if the company prospers, the shares themselves can increase in price. Investors seeking this type of return are interested in growth of capital, sometimes referred to as "capital appreciation." If the company does poorly, of course, the shares may decrease in value.

IS IT BETTER TO BE A LOANER OR AN OWNER?

That depends on a variety of factors, including how many years will pass before you need your money and how much risk you are willing to bear in exchange for the potential rewards.

You can start to make your decision by looking at some examples from the past. History is the only experience on which investors can draw. However, it may not repeat itself. It can only serve as a guide.

Let's look at how $1,000 has grown in various investment and savings vehicles over the past 10, 20 and 30 years.

HOW $1,000 HAS GROWN

OVER THE PAST	STOCKS[1]	BONDS[1]	SAVINGS ACCOUNTS[2]
10 YEARS	$ 4,026	$ 3,713	$ 1,887
20 YEARS	11,036	6,925	4,014
30 YEARS	19,770	9,243	6,408

All figures through 12/31/93, with dividends reinvested or interest compounded.
Sources:
[1]Ibbotson Associates (Based on statistics from Standard & Poor's 500 Coomposite Index and Salomon Brothers High Grade Corporate Bond Index.

[2]Based on figures supplied by the U.S. League of Savings Institutions and the Federal Reserve Board, which reflect all kinds of savings deposits, including longer term certificates. Such deposits, if held to maturity, offer a guaranteed rate of return of principal and a fixed rate of interest, but no opportunity for capital growth. Maximum allowable interest rates were imposed by law until 1983.

As you can see, an investment in stocks would have done best in all of the time periods. The longer the period, the more dramatic the difference has been. (These figures are historical. In the future, of course, there may be periods — even long periods — when bonds or savings accounts outperform stocks.)

RISK VERSUS RETURN

As we look at the historical returns of different investment categories, an important pattern emerges. There is a fundamental relationship between risk and return. In exchange for more risk, you should expect greater returns. How much risk you can or should tolerate will depend on your personal circumstances, the amount of time you can leave your investment untouched and your personal stamina to watch the value of your savings go up and down.

MEASURING YOUR RETURN

Investment returns can be the combination of dividends, interest income and the gain or loss in the investment. It is important to note that until you actually sell the investment, changes in value (both up and down) are on paper or unrealized. The period over which you measure your return is critical.

WHAT ABOUT SELECTING BOTH STOCKS AND BONDS?

In the past five of the last 10 years, bonds had higher annual total returns than stocks. Over the past 30 calendar years, bonds beat stock 13 times. Since you cannot predict whether stocks or bonds will do better year by year, it makes sense to consider a diversified portfolio of both stocks and bonds. You can take advantage of the long-term growth potential of stocks while benefiting from the relative long-term stability which can be provided by bonds.

HOW MUCH RISK ARE YOU TAKING WHEN YOU INVEST? CAN YOU REDUCE RISK?

Risk, it is a scary word. Experienced investors know that risk and potential reward go hand-in-hand. That's why they are willing to put up with the fluctuations they experience when investing. They try to reduce risk by following two key guidelines:
1. Invest for the long-term.
2. Diversify your holdings.

The charts below illustrate the results for investors who have done both of those things. They reflect investments in a wide range of stocks as represented by Standard & Poors 500 Composite Index. Made up of 500 of the largest U.S. stocks, this index shows that the frequency of positive results increases as the time horizon increases from one to twenty years.

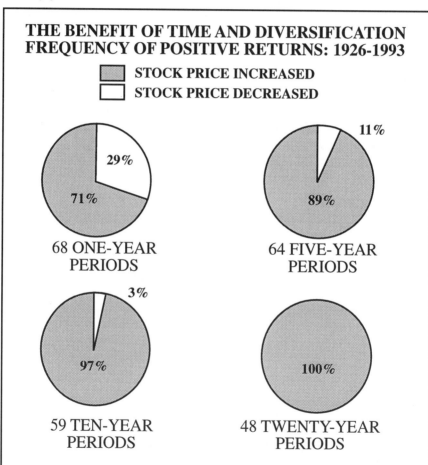

THE BENEFIT OF TIME AND DIVERSIFICATION
FREQUENCY OF POSITIVE RETURNS: 1926-1993

▨ **STOCK PRICE INCREASED**
☐ **STOCK PRICE DECREASED**

29%
71%
68 ONE-YEAR PERIODS

11%
89%
64 FIVE-YEAR PERIODS

3%
97%
59 TEN-YEAR PERIODS

100%
48 TWENTY-YEAR PERIODS

These figures reflect past results and are no indication of the future performance of any investment. Chart shows percentage of time stocks have gone up and down in the unmanaged Sandard & Poor's Composite Index during 68 calendar years ended December 31, 1993. Mutual funds investing in stocks could have done better or worse, depending on the skill of the investment advisor.

These periods span a wide range of market and economic conditions. Looking at each one year period, you can see the U.S. stock market closed higher 70 percent of the time. Over 20 years, diversified stock portfolios made money 100 percent of the time.

THE ADVANTAGES OF MUTUAL FUNDS

When people talk about using diversification as a means of reducing investment risk, what they are really saying is "don't put all your eggs in one basket." That's one reason mutual funds are included in most company retirement plans. They are the essence of diversification.

Mutual funds allow people with similar goals to pool their resources to get better professional management and greater diversification than they could as individual investors. Someone who invests $1,000 owns the same securities (stocks, bonds, money market instruments) as a person who invests $1 million.

MUTUAL FUNDS LET YOU INVEST IN MORE SECURITIES THAN YOU COULD PROBABLY PURCHASE ON YOUR OWN

If you buy just one or two stocks or bonds, you are placing all your faith in just one or two companies. It's better to spread your risk by buying stock in a wide variety of companies, but only a few individuals can afford to do that. Investing in a single share of a common stock mutual fund, however, provides partial ownership in dozens of companies — often a hundred or more. Some mutual funds even reach beyond the borders of the U.S. to include global opportunities.

MUTUAL FUNDS OFFER VARIOUS INVESTMENT OBJECTIVES

You may think your objectives are the same as everyone else's: to make money. But some people want to make it gradually and are unwilling to put up with significant bumps along the way. Others are willing to accept fluctuations in hopes of greater returns for the risk they undertake. Mutual funds invest in different types of securities to help meet many specific objectives.

MUTUAL FUNDS PROVIDE YOU WITH ACTIVE PORTFOLIO MANAGEMENT BY EXPERIENCED PROFESSIONALS

Managing investments requires a commitment of time, resources and expertise which most individuals don't have. A mutual fund's investment advisor determines which securities should be bought or sold to best serve the fund's objectives. These decisions are based on extensive, ongoing research.

RISK TOLERANCE

Your comfort level with risk is an important consideration in any investment decision. As I have discussed, increased return is almost always accompanied by additional risk. But increased knowledge about risk and an objective evaluation of your individual situation will allow you to determine how much risk is acceptable to you.

To assess your tolerance for risk, consider these questions:
- Are you comfortable with the possibility that your investment may decline in value tomorrow or a week or a year from now?
- Would you find it easy to add to your investment as it was declining in value?
- Do you feel you could insulate yourself from the emotional reactions during volatile markets that prompt so many investors to buy and sell at the wrong times?
- If six months after starting your long-term investment program your account value declined 10 percent, would you be able to retain your original, long-term perspective and hold on to the investment?

If you answered *yes* to most or all of the questions above, you are well-positioned to assume some risk in your investment program in pursuit of higher returns. If you answered *no* to most, or all of the questions, it does not mean you should not invest. Rather, you may want to choose lower risk investments (and be willing to accept the resulting lower results).

HOW MUCH MONEY WILL YOU NEED IN RETIREMENT?

Experts on retirement planning vary in their estimates of how much income will be needed at retirement. A common estimate is 70 percent of current working income. In theory, your expenses will decrease once you are no longer working. However, leisure activities, travel or the purchase of a second home can dramatically alter this assumption. In addition, it is easy to underestimate the impact inflation can have on your retirement savings. I discussed this concept in an earlier chapter.

WHEN IS IT APPROPRIATE TO CHANGE YOUR INVESTMENT OPTIONS?

Monitor your needs on an ongoing basis. If your needs change, maybe your investment strategy and asset allocation strategy should, too. Also, monitor the performance of your investments on an ongoing basis to see that it continues to meet your needs.

Investment decisions are not easy, but they need not be too difficult. Below are some investment tips for you. I believe everyone can be a successful investor. By developing a plan and sticking with it, you can build a comfortable, secure and independent retirement.

SOME GUIDELINES TO HELP SELECT AN INVESTMENT BROKER

Investments in stocks and bonds provides an opportunity for individuals to participate in the growth and development of the nation's businesses, as well as potentially earning income and building assets for the future. A professional investment broker can help you answer questions such as whether it is appropriate to participate in those markets at a particular time; whether funds might be better placed in one kind of investment over another, or some combination, or what kind of securities product, such as mutual funds, might better suit your goals. Selecting a broker requires the same careful examination, research, and comparison you would make when you select your attorney and certified financial planner.

Ready to Invest?

The money designated for investing shouldn't be money needed for everyday living expenses. Investment in the stock market could reward you with profits, but investors must be prepared to accept the financial risk of declines, even for relatively safe investments. No investment is totally protected from these risks.

One of the first steps is to determine what is wanted from an investment. This determination should be based on three elements: age, lifestyle and the amount of risk the individual is willing to absorb.

Some Things to Know as You Choose a Broker

The best source for choosing a broker has proven to be a personal reference: friends, relatives or colleagues who have experience with a particular broker or brokerage firm. You might also consult your attorney, certified financial planner, or tax professional. For example, my firm has a tax and investment division as well as the pre- and post-divorce financial planning services.

A stock broker is an employee or an independent contractor with a broker-dealer (brokerage firm) which is a member of the National Association of Securities Dealers (NASD). The firm also may be a member of one or more securities exchanges. The Securities Exchange Commission, along with the various exchanges and with the NASD function as regulators of the securities marketplaces. To qualify for a license, potential brokers much acquire knowledge of the marketplace and pass a demanding exam given by the NASD on behalf of the securities industry. The test is prepared by industry regulators.

What Questions to Ask a Potential Broker

You should interview any potential broker candidate face-to-face. If convenient, visit the firm to be sure it is what it claims to be. Legitimate securities firms work closely with federal and state regulators to rid the marketplace of unscrupulous operators. But, as with anything concerning money, judgment and caution are in order. In particular, be wary of "brokers" promising quick and large returns on risk-free investments.

During the interview, ask these questions:

- How long have you been involved in the securities business and in what capacity?
- How long have you been a broker and what qualifying exams given by the NASD have you passed? (There are many different exams brokers must take, depending upon the kinds of investments in which they are involved. For example, those involved in equities and general securities must pass the Series 7; those involved in municipal securities the Series 52; and those acting as a Branch Manager the Series 24.)
- Do you specialize in a particular product or client?
- What do you consider your firm's area of expertise?
- How are client-broker problems and disputes resolved at your firm?
- Do I need to sign an arbitration agreement?
- What additional services do you supply, such as estate planning or tax planning, and at what extra cost?
- How often (how many times a day/week/month) do you talk to your clients?
- Do you generally call your clients or do you expect them to call you?
- Are you easily accessible to answer questions?
- Is there a certain type of client you find difficult to work with?
- Who will handle my needs for information or transactions when you are away?
- What is your general approach: long-term investment or short-term gains?
- Do you have written material about your firm and the products you sell? Are these materials free (most are) and how can they be obtained so I can review them before I make a decision?
- Tell me about your firm: its history, marketplace memberships, etc.
- Where is the nearest office? Where is the firm's headquarters?
- What kind of research reports will I receive, how frequently, and at what cost (most are free)?
- What other resources and research services do you provide or are available, and at what cost?
- Can you explain your fee and charge policies, including how you are compensated on the different products you offer?

- Do you provide a personal investment portfolio report to your clients? How often do they receive this report? May I see an example of one of your reports?

At the end of the interview, ask the broker for client references and check them. Ask the questions:
- How long have you used this broker/firm?
- Why did you select this firm or broker?
- What kind of performance did you receive on your portfolio?
- If anything, what would you change about this broker?
- What makes your partnership work so well?

AFTER SELECTING A BROKER ...

Once an individual has selected a broker, schedule another meeting to define investment terms which will be used frequently in conducting transactions. It isn't enough to understand the basics of investing; the individual needs to be sure you and the broker mean the same when using industry terms. Annually, or semi-annually, you should review investment decisions and be sure your broker is doing a satisfactory job. If there is a problem, discuss it with the broker or his or her manager.

INVESTMENT TIPS FOR WOMEN

1. Get started now — the sooner you start the more you can accumulate.
2. Choose a broker carefully. Find someone you feel comfortable talking to and who answers your questions easily.
3. Get educated about financial and investment issues. It is not as difficult as you might think. You probably already know a lot more than you think.
4. Decide what your investment goals are before you spend any money. Determine what you will need for college education(s), retirement, etc.
5. Determine your financial needs, such as capital preservation, current income, tax-free income, growth of capital. Realize your

money needs will change as your life changes and as the economy changes.

6. Assess your risk tolerance. Regardless of the potential return of an investment, you want to be able to sleep at night.

7. Don't put all your money in super safe investments, such as savings accounts and certificates of deposits, since inflation will eat up your profits and growth.

8. Diversify your investments to reduce risk. Compare performance histories, risk factors and management styles. Focus on the long term.

9. Monitor your investments on an ongoing basis and if your needs change make changes in your investment plan. Ask for regular reporting.

10. Trust your own instincts.

POST DIVORCE CHECKLIST   *Date completed*

☐ Request a written document from your attorney   _____
and other experts showing the portion of
their fees which is deductible under IRS
Code Section 212. Most attorneys will provide
you with a letter similar to the one included in
Chapter Eight.

☐ If your former spouse intends to work with the   _____
prior accountant and financial planner, ask your
friends or business associates who they might
recommend.

☐ Prepare income tax estimates with your accoun-   _____
tant so that you can begin making quarterly tax
payments. Bypassing this important step could
cost you IRS fines and penalties when you file
your return.

Date completed

❒ Create your cash control system for income and
 expenses. Try to use the guidelines offered in
 Chapter Six; follow the program for at least a
 year in order to make sure that it is appropriate
 for your situation.

❒ If the settlement has not addressed the issue of
 paying the costs of divorce, you should establish
 a payment plan (included in your budget) which
 is agreeable with your creditors.

❒ Use the Status of Asset Transfers worksheet
 (near the end of Chapter Ten) to make sure your
 retirement assets are being transferred in accor-
 dance per any Qualified Domestic Relations
 Orders (QDRO's).

❒ You should also use the transfer sheet to track
 the re-registration on retirement and investment
 assets (including partnerships). You want only
 your name on the accounts as soon as possible
 after the divorce documents are signed.

❒ Redo estate planning documents, including your
 personal will, trusts, Durable Power of Attorney
 and your Directive to Physicians.

❒ Hire an investment manager to help you with
 your investment allocation, implementation and
 monitoring system. See Chapter Fourteen for
 some tips on selecting a broker.

❒ Request tax basis records on any investment or
 other asset you receive in your settlement. Contact
 either your former spouse or the appropriate
 broker for the information. This should really be
 handled before the divorce is final, but if the information is not collected very soon after the divorce,
 the tax consequences could be frustrating.

❏ You should assemble your tax returns (and the supporting documentation) and keep them in a safe place. Three years is a minimum.

Date completed

_____

❏ With your tax returns, you should be sure to have all basis information on your residence (closing statements, receipts for improvements, etc.). In addition, you should find the last IRS Form 2119 filed with your name on it since it will show any prior deferral of gain.

_____

❏ Keep good financial records on the children's expenses. Remember that child support changes over time, and you will be asked to provide this information at some point in the future.

_____

❏ Monitor your career plan, including education and/or subsequent employment, with your career advisor.

_____

CONCLUSION

*Learn to get in touch with the silence within yourself and
know that everything in this life has a purpose.*
- Elisabeth Kubler-Ross

I hope you have found the information in this book to be helpful in getting your divorce process organized and on track. No matter
where you are in this process, it is never too late to take charge and
empower yourself. I have found that your post-divorce will run more
smoothly if you follow the guidelines found in this book.

I would enjoy your sharing your divorce experience with me —
the good and the bad. Your comments about the content of this book are
appreciated. I encourage you to share this book so that we can all work
together to make our world a safer financial place for those affected by
divorce (women, men and, most important, the children). We can work
together to promote a win-win marital settlement or Fair Share Divorce.

*To contact Kathleen Miller for workshops,
seminars or consultations:*
206-451-1519
~ ~ ~

To order additional copies of
FAIR SHARE DIVORCE FOR WOMEN

For telephone ordering, call **800-468-1994.**

Please send ___ copies at $19.95 each book, plus $3.50 shipping and handling for the first book, $2.00 for each additional book in the same order.

Enclosed is my check of money order for $_____ or
[ ] Visa   [ ] MasterCard

\# _____Exp. _____/_____

Signature _____

Phone _____

Name _____

Address _____

City/St/Zip _____

(Advise if recipient and mailing address
are different from above.)

Return this order form to:
Miller, Bird Advisors, Inc.
1200 - 112th Avenue N. E., Suite C-178
Bellevue, Washington 98004
206-451-1519